Am I A Chosen One?

ALICE K JOSE

ISBN 979-8-89475-255-6

Am I a Chosen One?

The original Tamil version of this autobiography was published in July 2014 with the title *'Naan Thernthedukkappattavala?'*. Many lauded it as exceptional; attempted by an obscure woman. However, it had limited readership for obvious reasons (genre and language). Yet, when a copy was couriered to Dr A P J Abdul Kalam, our former President and the celebrated scientist, he responded with an appreciative e-mail (given in the Appendix).

The present English version, including translations of Tamil quotes, is by the author. She has judiciously edited it sans sacrificing the spirit of the original.

This translation was completed in 2018 but due to certain unforeseen circumstances, could not be printed. Then came COVID 19 and it got shelved again. Now by God's Grace, it has seen the light of the day in 2024, 10 years after the original in Tamil was published.

The author can be reached at alicekjose@rediffmail.com

Dedicated to

people of good will

"Good to meet noble souls,

Good to hear their words,

Good to enunciate their virtues,

Good to be in their company."

– AVVAIYAAR

(An Ancient Tamil Poetess)

Contents

Preface

Biographies are generally written about great achievers. Many well-known people have written autobiographies. Among them, *The Story of My Experiments with Truth* by Mahatma Gandhi has fascinated me the most. I was deeply moved on reading it and inspired to become morally courageous. Gandhiji's reason for ending his life story in 1921 is ever etched in my memory: *"My life from this point onward has been so public that there is hardly anything about it that people do not know. In fact, my pen instinctively refuses to proceed further. I set a high value on my experiments. I do not know whether I have been able to do justice to them. I can only say that I have spared no pains to give a faithful narration."* Likewise, I have also taken immense pains to present a truthful account of my life.

'What could be her achievement to write a book about herself?'-readers might question. To be frank, I have not accomplished anything great. This attempt just reveals how an ordinary woman, initially timid and diffident became brave and self-confident later. In a nutshell, my unwavering faith in God guided me through all my sufferings. The thought that sharing my experiences could be beneficial to others, goaded me into taking up this labour of love.

None on earth is without faults and foibles. Yet, many eschew temptations and lead a good life. By that yardstick, mine could be a model life. Goodness has always charmed me. I have been a good daughter, sister, friend, student, wife, daughter-in-law, mother, mother-in-law, grandmother and above all, a good teacher. I can 'see' the sarcastic smile of the reader now. *'How could one claim to be good in all one's relationships? This is nothing but self-glorification!'* When many are shamelessly and blatantly selfish and wicked, why should I hesitate to say the naked truth that I am good? To be sure, I have imperfections; nevertheless, I am a truthful woman with self-esteem.

After teaching full-time in schools and colleges for three decades in Coimbatore, Mettur, Madras (now Chennai) and Salem; part-time in Seminaries, Convents and Nursing Colleges in Bangalore for another decade, I lead a contented life now. Students from different institutions had similar ideas about me. *'You are not only a teacher who taught us the right way of living along with the subject, but also a loving mother'.* Their affection and respect expressed in English and Tamil poems are still with me as 'awards'. A few are given in the Appendices. Indeed, I take just pride in them!

After reading this autobiography, if some get inspired to lead an honest life; to live with the true coordination in their thoughts, words and deeds; to replace fear of God with LOVE OF GOD, I would feel amply rewarded for my effort.

Thanksgiving

I bow before God Almighty
With thanks countless.
Garlands of Gratitude to my
Beloved parents
For life and nurture.
Heartfelt thanks to my dear husband
Who has been with me
Through thick and thin for more than 5 decades.
Thanks are due to my three children
For their love, care and respect.
And,
To my estimable teachers
Who showed me the right path;
To loving siblings, kith and kin,
Colleagues and students
My grateful good wishes.
Also,
To all the noble souls
Who crossed my path
In life's journey
I offer the bouquet of my gratitude.

1

Significant Six

'Six' is a significant number in my life. Some important events happened when I was six; then sixteen, twenty-six, thirty-six, forty-six, and fifty-six. When I was sixty-five, I began writing the autobiography in Tamil thinking that something (perhaps, my death!) might happen in my 66th year. Due to sporadic health issues, it took two years for me to complete and it was published in July 2014. Anyway, an important event did happen when I was 66. I realized my long-cherished wish of visiting the places where the remarkable events of the life of Jesus Christ happened. My husband and I could go to the Holy Land in 2012.

There had been a rumour some years ago that the world would end in 2012. But my hope has always been to see the 'brave new world'. Since girlhood I have been feeling sad for the sufferings in the world. In my late teens I shed tears pondering over solutions for the ills of the world. Timid nature and low self-esteem had been the stumbling blocks for me to achieve anything meritorious. Yet I have never failed to pray that people should bloom in love and live in peace. It pains me to see millions still struggling in the ocean of poverty and diseases.

As a little girl I shuddered to think about death. It was due to my ignorance and in hindsight I laughed at it. The thought that I would not be able to breathe if kept in a box under the earth was indeed frightening! Later, education and sermons in churches helped me get rid of fear of death. With the sudden demise of my beloved father when I was sixteen, the dread of death disappeared. The thought that death was the sure way to meet him in heaven was consoling. I started meditating on death and philosophized that it was an integral part of this continuum called life. The added advantage was seeing God face to face! However, one thought panicked me. What about the death of my loving mother and dear siblings? Finally, a solution presented itself: my wish to pass away first.

Many years later when I lost my son in the prime of his youth, this philosophical frame of mind helped me face it with great courage and strength of spirit. Jacob, my first born, passed B.E (Hons) from BITS Pilani at the age of 20 and worked in Madras for one and a half years and in Dubai for three and a half years. Within that short period, he earned good name and much money through his sincere hard work. Four months before his 26th birthday a fatal accident took him to his Maker. Though I was heartbroken, I could also feel inexplicable peace pervading my mind. Grief gripped my heart; face and eyes became swollen with weeping yet; never did I question God's Decision even in my mind. Total surrender to God's Will alone sustained me. I could understand the depth of Omar Khayyam's lines:

The Moving Finger writes and having writ,

Moves on, nor all thy Piety nor Wit

Shall lure it back to cancel half a Line

Nor all thy Tears wash out a Word of it.

When I decided to write the story of my life, 'Significant Six' spontaneously became the first chapter. In fact, more important events have happened in my other ages also, but no other number has this sequential order.

At 6 – First Examination in School (1952)

I was born in 1946 in Coimbatore, a town in Tamil Nadu, as the second child of a Malayali couple – P. I. Ipe and Thangamma. I had basic education at home tutored by Ms. Gnanambal, a Lutheran Missionary and got admitted to second standard. According to modern 'educational style', I had not been to school for 5 classes (Play Class, Pre-KG, L.K.G, U.K.G, and 1st standard) before stepping into a primary school at the age of five years and four months! It was a Tamil medium school run by Tamil Evangelical Lutheran Church (T.E.L.C) people. Thus in 1952, when I was six, I wrote my first school examination and got promoted to 3rd standard.

My father used to distribute some snacks to the whole school (classes 1 to 5) when he admitted his children to school. Candies were distributed when my elder sister and brother went to school for the first time. On admitting my other sisters, biscuits were dealt out. Strangely, when I got admitted, he gave jackfruit bulbs and kernel pieces of coconut. I had wondered about that unusual distribution quite a few times. Later I found an inner meaning in it. Just as jackfruit and coconut can be tasted only with much effort, I struggled a great deal for 'tasting' self-realization.

At 16 – Demise of Dear Father (1962)

We called our father 'Appachan' (Daddy in Malayalam). He was the Manager of a financial concern and had good health. Most unexpectedly he passed away in 1962 before he turned 56. That bolt from the blue was the wreck of our family's hopes. Marykutty (younger sister) and I seemed to have forgotten everything we had learnt for our fast-approaching public examinations. Totally at a loss, she decided to skip the S.S.L.C (Secondary School Leaving Certificate) exam starting in 10 days' time. I made up my mind to appear for the P.U.C (Pre-University Course) exam as there were 20 days for me to study. But the very thought of writing all the subjects in English (for the first time) made me tremble. It was our good fortune that Appachan's younger sister (P. I. Ittianam) encouraged us with words of faith and hope *"Pray and write whatever you know; your success or failure is God's decision"*. The wise counsel given at the right time enabled us to successfully complete our crucial courses.

Appachan earned quite well in those days and we led a reasonably comfortable life. He also spent a fairly good portion of his income on needy relatives and for charity. He used to tell us, *"Education will be your wealth; so, study well".* And it turned out to be true. Another prophetic statement of his: *"What I give to the poor and the needy will be returned to my children later by God".* There is a Tamil proverb: *'Even a prince would become a pauper if he has five daughters'.* Neither Appachan nor his five daughters became paupers!

At 26 – Beginning of Married Life (1972)

In January 1972, I was married to K. C. Jose, a native of Kuzhupilly, a village in Ernakulam district in Kerala. At that time, he was employed in Madras Aluminium Company (MALCO) at its head office in Coimbatore. In four years, we had two children. When my daughter was six months old, I quit my Lecturer's post in a leading women's college in Coimbatore to devote more time to my kids. In 1976, it was a bold decision because I had seven years' experience and better prospects in that college. The arrival of another baby soon proved my decision to be wise. Meanwhile, I had successfully completed the Post Graduate Diploma in Education through the college I had worked.

AT 36 – Final Degree Course (1982)

'Learn while young' - so goes a Tamil saying. Learning becomes comparatively harder as we grow older. However, never does age obstruct one's learning. To the interested ones, it triumphantly marches forward till the end of their lives. I am reminded of an incident supposed to have happened in Socrates' life. The great Greek philosopher was in jail condemned to death on the charge of 'corrupting young minds' with his unconventional ideas. On the eve of that despicable day, some prisoners sang a song and Socrates liked it very much. When he expressed his wish to learn it, the jail birds burst out laughing. One queried, *"You are going to die tomorrow; what's the use of learning it now?"* The wise man's reply is truly inspiring, *"I have always longed for learning new things till my end. This offers a fine opportunity to fulfil it."*

After living nearly 33 years in my birthplace, towards the end of 1978, I had to leave Coimbatore when MALCO'S head office shifted to company's factory site at Mettur in Salem District. As Mettur had no colleges then, I started teaching in Malco Vidyalaya - the senior secondary school run by the MALCO Management. B.Ed. degree was imperative in Tamil Nadu State Board schools to handle +1 and +2 classes. Since Malco Vidyalaya was a CBSE (Central Board of Secondary Education) school then, lack of that qualification posed no problem. Nevertheless in 1982, I decided to do B.Ed. through the Distance Education Programme of Madurai Kamaraj University. At 36, my hands were full; yet, surrendering myself to God, I took the plunge. For one year I led a hectic life; with three little kids and a full-time job and completed B.Ed. with 1ˢᵗ class. Six Years later when I became the Principal of a higher secondary school in Madras, B.Ed. was indispensable.

AT 46 – Austerity in Married Life (1992)

Till Appachan's death, my time was happily spent in studying, playing, reading, listening to cine-songs on radio and gramophone. My siblings and I would fight and get punished (mildly!) by Appachan. Those were the only 'sufferings' we had faced then. Life's problems and sufferings before and after marriage made me get closer to God and at 46, I felt as if I were one with the Supreme Spirit. Close relatives viewed the transformation as a sign of insanity. But I took refuge in Jesus' words, *'Blessed are they that do hunger and thirst after righteousness for they shall be filled.'* When I realized God's presence in me (God is present in everyone; very few REALIZE it), sex became 'ex' in my life. With humble requests I reasoned Jose into the idea of family life sans sex. Of course, it was not my reasoning, but God's Will worked in the matter.

When I read about Gandhiji's brahmacharya at the age of 37, I thought, being a man he had the power to take such a vow. Could a woman achieve such a feat? God let it happen in my own life! When I compared it with our parents' lives, I found a surprising coincidence. Jose's mother and mine were married at 18 and both became widows at 38. Jose and I were husband and wife for the same 20 years and after that we have been 'friends'. There are some other similarities too.

Both are second born in our families. We are five girls and one boy and, in his family, he is the only son with four sisters. We both lost our fathers in our teenage – he, at 15 and I, at 16. There are other curious facts which will be shared later.

AT 56 – Start of Sight-Seeing Abroad (2002)

Sight-seeing trips outside India, in a way started when I was 56. As a student and as a teacher, I had visited some places in South India. In 2002, our adult children Mary and Joseph sent us to Malaysia and Singapore on a seven-day trip. It was a gift for our 30th wedding anniversary. They enthusiastically announced that they would arrange foreign tours every year as anniversary special. For the 31st anniversary we went to Sri Lanka for a week. Next, as they were planning for our pilgrimage to Jerusalem and the nearby holy places, I fell on the road and had two hair-line cracks on my right instep. The years that followed saw many a happy event:

2003 – November 16 – Mary's wedding

2004 – March 8 – Joseph's wedding

2005 – September 4 – Joseph's first baby - Aryan

2006 – October 18 – Mary's first baby - Arush

2007 – December 23 – Second baby to Joseph - Rayan

2008 – October 9 – Second baby to Mary - Adarsh

Thus, instead of our going to Holy Land, holiness came to us in the form of four grandsons! We took up the pilgrimage later in March 2012. Before that, we went to Goa in 2010. North India tour (Delhi, Agra & Jaipur) happened in October 2014. In July 2016, we had the good fortune of visiting some famous cities of 10 countries in Europe. (My blog http://alicekjose.blogspot.com has the travelogues that i had written on the trips to Holy Land and Europe). In November 2018, we went to Ahmedabad with Mary and family. My long-cherished dream of paying homage at Sabarmati Ashram, the humble and famous home of my ideal, Mahatma Gandhi, came true. Soon, in January 2019, my wish to pray at St. Mother Teresa's tomb was fulfilled when

Jose and I visited Kolkata. We could also go to Tagore's Shanti Niketan and Sri Ramakrishna Mission Ashram. My much-desired plan to visit Dr A P J Abdul Kalam's Memorial in Rameshwaram in 2020 could not be realised due to 'corona's visit'! Next to reading, I love travelling and I am destined to travel much in my old age.

In fact, our first foreign trip was in 1998 to stay with our first son, Jacob who had been working in Dubai then. Though he took us to many places in and around Dubai, we had gone there mainly to be with our son for a few days. Actually, Jacob requested me to stay with him for a month (I was not employed then), I could not fulfil his wish as Mary's final year M.C.A exams were fast approaching. How could I stay there when God had a decisive plan for my beloved son? On 29th April when we bade goodbye to him, we never knew that it was the final farewell. On 19 June, he met with a fatal road accident in Dubai. God alone could give me the strength of spirit to face the tragedy. Job's words in the Old Testament repeatedly flashed through my mind: *'The Lord gave and the Lord hath taken away; blessed be the name of the Lord.... What? Shall we receive good at the hand of God and shall we not receive the bad?'*

In those days, I had been a great source of strength to my shattered husband and heart-broken Mary and Joseph. I told them that accepting God's Will alone helps us tide over such calamitous situations. It is still fresh in my memory what a friend had said then: *"People usually lose faith in God with such terrible blows! How is that you have more faith than ever?"* My reply: *"It is possible only with unwavering faith. God wanted back one, after giving me three children. What right do I have to question God's decision? It is true no mother can face it without sorrow, but one can accept it with inexplicable feeling of peace".*

So teach us to number our days,

that we may apply our hearts unto wisdom.

– The Holy Bible

2

My Family

I was christened Elizabeth, but that name was drowned in the baptismal water! I got admitted to school as P.I. Alice – Pulakkal Ipe's daughter Alice. After marriage I am known as Alice K. Jose – Kalapparambath Jose's wife. Pulakkal and Kalapparambath are family names. Today many call me 'Teacher' because of my long (40 years) teaching career. I like to write my name as Tr. Alice as doctors prefix Dr. to their names.

Appachan was born in 1906 at Kunnamkulam in Trichur District, Kerala. He was a Syrian Jacobite – a denomination of Christianity. He lost his mother when he was 9 and his father passed away in 1946, some months after my birth. Appachan was the eighth child in the family and had seven sisters and two brothers. He left Kerala early in life to seek his fortune in Tamil Nadu. Initially, he worked as a clerk in Kerala Bank in Coimbatore. His initiative and industry enabled him later to become the manager of a concern called Coimbatore Commerce Bank where he worked till his death at the age of 55. He had always supported his family in Kerala. In 1942, he married eighteen-year-old Thangamma who was a Catholic. With six brothers and two sisters, she hailed from a family in Trichur. We called our mother 'Mummy'.

Their first baby girl was born in 1944. Though her baptismal name was Susannah, she was always known as Susheela. On a Sunday night – 27th Jan 1946 – at 9'o clock I was born. The details of my birth are what I heard from Mummy years later. I was a chubby baby with the birth weight of 9 pounds. I was quite pretty with fair complexion, thick black, curly hair and big eyes. On seeing me an elderly man from Kunnamkulam exclaimed, "*No need to be dejected because Ipe's second child is also a girl. One won't get such a baby even if one offers a country!*" Mummy's disappointment disappeared with that remark. Even today in some parts of India, when a girl is born women are sad and men are angry and many still do not know that the latter is the cause of the sex of the baby.

Appachan was an exception. After me, two boys and three girls were born. He called all of us with the same endearing expression – 'monae' (sonny in Malayalam) and brought us up without discrimination. Many admired him and to kith and kin he was a role model. Some pitied him, '*Oh, father of five girls! How is he going to marry them off?*' I am reminded of an incident which happened when I was fifteen. A middle-aged lady (Appachan's distant relative) had visited us after a long time. She was in Coimbatore to be with her daughter who was due for the first delivery. She exclaimed, "*So soon you have five daughters!*" In those days, such a comment indirectly meant that he might father more. Two days later, her daughter gave birth to triplet – all girls! Some hospital inmates eagerly came to see the three bundles of joy and the lady was said to have shouted at them. This obnoxious mind-set is sadly still prevalent.

Mummy had great faith in proverbs which are words of ancient wisdom. There is a Malayalam proverb which translates: '*The fourth boy in the family would bring prosperity to the country.*' So, she prayed for a girl when she conceived again, as the saying would be effectual only when the boy is born after three girls! The third girl, born in 1947 was named Mariam and we call her Marykutty. Next a boy was born on 17th April 1949; early morning of Easter Sunday, supposed to be the time of the Resurrection. Mummy's joy knew no bounds. She decided to call him Joy, though he was named Job in the church.

Up to Joy's birth, Mummy had her deliveries at home with the help of a mid-wife. In 1953, Jessie (baptismal name – Hannah) was born in Immaculate Conception Convent (ICC) Hospital in Coimbatore. (Years later, my sisters and I had our deliveries there.) In 1959, tragedy struck our family when the next child (boy) died at birth. It was on 8th

September, Mother Mary's birthday and Mummy was heart-broken. We were weeping at home as Appachan never let us see the dead child saying that it would increase our sorrow. The baby was given a quiet Christian burial in the ICC Hospital premises. A Tamil proverb warns, '*Name not a child before its birth*'. But we did that 'mistake'. We had decided to call him Prince, if God gave us another brother. Our little Prince went back to the King of kings without allowing us to even have a glimpse of him. Our youngest sister, Jolly was born in 1960 and she was named Esther during baptism. Mummy used to say, "*Of my seven children, Alice and the baby that died were the most beautiful at birth*". Later I felt all my sisters became more beautiful than me! My ex-colleague once said (comparing me to one of my sisters), "*She may be more beautiful, but you are prettier!*"

During General Elections of 1962, our parents went to cast votes. While waiting in the queue, Appachan experienced severe chest pain. He hid it from Mummy till they reached home after casting their votes. He was never in the habit of bothering about his illness. Even with cough and cold, he used to go to work wearing sweater and muffler. But that day, he wanted to meet our parish priest and the family doctor as soon as possible. Uncle George, Mummy's youngest brother, had been staying with us then. He rushed to bring them home. Three more doctors (two of them, Appachan's friends and the third, his employer's son) came home to examine him and their consensus was to admit him to hospital.

Two days later (on Sunday), after attending the morning service in the church, we went to the hospital. When we saw him with tubes in his nose and hands, we started crying. By then our aunt and uncles from Kunnamkulam and Trichur had come and they took turns to stay with him. The same night we were rushed to the hospital and the scene there was shocking. Appachan had removed all the tubes and was requesting the doctors to let him go home. He assured them that he was prepared to face the consequences. Fear and sorrow seized me. I felt a violent shaking of my heart for the first time and it was a terrible experience. I ran out of the room and started sobbing uncontrollably. A cousin of Mummy's consoled me and took me back to the room. I saw sadness writ large on Appachan's face.

On Monday none of us attended classes. When the doctors assured us of his improved condition, we went to school and college on Tuesday as final exams were fast approaching. The doctors asked us not to come to the hospital till he was better as the sorrow he experienced on seeing us would worsen his condition. On Thursday evening (March 1st) once again all were hastily taken to the hospital, but I was left behind with the maid as I had just then returned from college. Within minutes, they came back saying that they were bringing Appachan home. The news made me happy, but it was short-lived as only his body was brought home. He breathed his last in the presence of doctors, his sister Ittianam and Mummy's brother, Kurian. We were told that the end was painless and peaceful.

Appachan died of Coronary Thrombosis. The frightening details of the first-time-heard disease left me stunned. Coagulation of blood in a blood vessel or in the heart is the nature of this terrible illness. The blood from a wound, on contact with air, coagulates. It does so in a dead body too. However, when it happens in a live person's heart or blood vessels, it is fatal. With today's advancement in the medical field many are saved with such a condition, but few survived in 1962.

I have a vivid recollection of what had happened that day when Appachan passed away at 5.30pm. The memory is still a scar. His body was brought in on a stretcher and all were weeping. I touched his cheek and cried, "*Appacha, open your eyes and look at us*". When I repeated the words twice more, Aunt Ittianam realized that I had not grasped the reality. She sobbed out the words, "*Don't you know; my child, only for the dead do they tie a piece of cloth over their heads like this?*" Despite my age (16) and one year of college education, I knew the meaning of such a knot only then. Some present there might have thought what I said was my wishful thinking due to great sorrow. Actually, I was thoroughly misguided at that time. We had been told that he was getting better. On Thursday when they said we could see him at home, I thought it was after the cure. I attributed the use of a stretcher to his weak condition as it was used earlier to take him to hospital. In short, my knowledge about worldly ways was abysmal.

There was a large gathering for the funeral on Friday. Besides people from Kerala, there were many from Coimbatore where he had been living for more than three decades. As the procession was moving, an uncanny coincidence came to pass. A friend's family who had not met us for some time was coming to see us from Kerala. As they neared our house, they saw the procession and surmised it to be the funeral of a Malayali Syrian Christian from the black cassocks of the priests. They stopped the car and to their utter shock knew that it was none other than the person they had come to see. To their knowledge, Appachan, though lean, had been hale and hearty.

Despite Appachan being in the hospital for six days, we could neither visit nor talk to him much. Of course, the suggestion by the doctors was genuine for his better healing. But I was sad about it for quite some time. Later I felt that even if we had met him more often, he would not have shared anything with us. Mummy (38) – the mother of six – was a naïve person. Three teenaged girls were ignorant of worldly matters. The rest were a mere boy and two little girls. His piety would have enabled him to go in peace, leaving us to Divine Care. Nevertheless, on the last day of his life, Appachan entrusted his family's responsibility to Uncle Kurian. He, along with Uncle George and Mummy's widowed mother lived with us for some years. Meanwhile, the eldest three of us got jobs and started managing our family on our own.

The five girls of Ipe family had customary arranged marriages. Susheela, married to Francis, has three daughters. The eldest Preetha married to Mathews, has two sons, Ashik and Ashwin. Smitha married Charles and her daughters are Binitta and Britney. Vinitha's husband is Anil and sons are Akash and Akshit. My immediate younger sister Marykutty's husband is John. Joma, her daughter married Biju and has two sons, Nikhil and Rahul and a daughter, Sheethal. Manoj, Mary's son, helps his father in business. Next sister, Jessie married Jimmy and they have no offspring. Jolly's husband is Thomas and her daughter Merin married Agith. Her son Terrin works for an IT firm. My brother Joy enjoys single blessedness.

Even before Susheela's marriage, the eldest four in the family started working. All the earnings reached my hands as I was the most economical. My siblings used to call me *'thalaivar'* (leader in Tamil) and got the money for expenses they had to deal with. I would be very strict in doling out and record every little expense. Needless to say, it was a troublesome job consuming time and causing 'headache'. When I got married, I entrusted my earnings to my husband and made him responsible for money matters. Fortunately, he was doubly economical and carried out the job to the hilt!

Four are the attributes of a noble family;

Cheeriness, charity, graceful words, slur-free.

– Thiruvalluvar

(An ancient Tamil saint-poet)

3

Thrice at Death's Door

'When young, you knocked Death's door thrice and returned every time as the door declined to open!' Years later, Mummy said these words jokingly. When I heard the details, I was filled with wonder. Before writing about it, there needs to be a brief introduction. Born and bred in Coimbatore, we visited Kerala every summer vacation. In the 1950s, trains to Kerala were at dawn. Just a slight touch would do for us to jump out of our beds. A month's stay at our parents' homes used to be heavenly bliss. Sometimes if a friend's car was available, we would go in it and Appachan would return to Coimbatore in the car after 2 or 3 days. Later, we would come back home with one of Mummy's brothers.

Now, the first knock in Mummy's words: *"We went to Kerala for a function when Alice was six months old. We got an open car that day. By quirk of fate, we started the journey a little late. Suddenly it drizzled when we were going through a long stretch of lonely road. The driver stopped to pull the tarpaulin cover over the car. Soon, it rained heavily with thunder and lightning. The covering could not resist the fury of nature and in the downpour, we were completely drenched. That desolate region had no shelter for us and the driver drove the car as fast as he could. Appachan was praying with two-year-old Susheela on his lap. Alice was with me. Though she was well covered she was also thoroughly wet. With no movement and no sound, she looked as if she were dead. I wept and prayed for God's protection. Finally, we reached Kunnamkulam at 9pm. Appachan at once went to fetch a doctor but none was available.*

Meanwhile I rubbed the ice-cold child all over. Suddenly I cried aloud, 'Deiva puthrane rakshikka' (translates to 'Please save God's son'). Appachan and his siblings doubted about my sanity. As I remember everything even today, I'm sure I never lost my senses. Of course, I was praying for Alice's life; but why I cried with those words is still a mystery to me. After some time when she opened her eyes and cried feebly, we heaved a sigh of relief."

I knocked the 'door' a second time in a very pathetic state. Mummy narrated: *"At eight months, teething trouble started for you with a severe attack of diarrhoea. You were no more a chubby child at eighteen months. Then came another bout of dysentery which left you mere skin and bones. You passed motion 30 times a day and no medicine could control it."* I asked Mummy if the number was an exaggeration. But she said it could have been even more as sometimes it happened 2 or 3 times within an hour. She continued, *"Despite a full-time maid, I couldn't devote much time for you as I had Susheela (3 years) and Marykutty (3 months) to take care of. Fortunately, Appachan's elder sister was with us and she nursed you back to health. We thought you would die. God's Grace and Aunt Achayi's constant care saved you. You are indebted to her for your life."*

How Aunt Achayi, who lived in Kunnamkulam, happened to be in Coimbatore at that time had a sad tale behind it. When I heard her life story from Mummy, I could not control my tears. When cholera, the terribly infectious disease struck people in those days, it is said to have choked the whole village to death at times. Aunt Achayi had lost her young husband and three little children within the span of 2 months. Could there be a worse calamity in a young woman's life? She came back to live in her father's home in Kunnamkulam. No wonder, Aunt Mariam, her younger sister shunned marriage and decided to look after her younger siblings as their mother had already passed away. The youngest sister, P. I. Ittianam also renounced marital bliss and engaged herself in social service. She later became the first woman Municipal Councillor of Kunnamkulam. She adopted two orphan boys one after another and gave them good education, which helped them become successful in life.

Appachan had brought Aunt Achayi to Coimbatore for a short stay in 1947. That was the time I became seriously ill. I strongly believe that she must have earnestly prayed for my life – *Oh God, you took away all in my family. Now I pray for my brother's daughter, please save her.* When I survived, she would have felt some meaning in her otherwise drab life. Many years later when I lost my son in the prime of his youth, I could find peace and courage meditating on Aunt's life. After all, we are mere microscopic specks in the universe and the death of a person is insignificant in a way. However, in God's Master Plan, even a speck could gain great value.

Now the third knock when I was eight years old. In the 1950s, chicken pox ravaged many families in our area in Coimbatore. Mummy and all the children were down with that disease, the severest attack being mine. Despite vaccination, when such attacks happened, it was generally viewed for better resistance power in the body. When all at home recovered, my condition worsened day by day. Mummy said my survival was like a rebirth. I marvelled at my rebirth thrice! How could I die then, when I (now 78) am destined to experience many more glad and sad events in my life?!

To everything there is a season,

and a time to every purpose under the heaven.

A time to be born, and a time to die...

– The Holy Bible

4

Loving Parents

With just pride I say our parents were one of the best in the world. When Appachan died, some lamented, *"What a loving father!"* I thought whether fathers could be any different. But with education and experience I realized the truth about fathers – unloving, indifferent, abusive fathers; fathers who hide their love lest children should take advantage of them; those who deny the just wishes of their offspring in the name of saving for future, etc.

Appachan had a definite notion of bringing up children. He was a loving father and at the same time strict too. Mummy was eighteen years younger than him. That age difference combined with her naivety led him to treat her as a child. However, he specified her role as a mother: *"Look after children with patience. For that reason alone, I have engaged a full-time servant for you. If kids do any mischief, tell me when I come home and I shall punish them".* Sometimes, we 'complained' about Mummy to him, *"Today Mummy beat me on the shoulder"; "While combing my hair, Mummy shook my head"*! Anyway, that kind of arrangement was a blessing to us. *'No one can serve two masters',* says Jesus. Since Appachan was the sole master, obedience came to us naturally. Mummy was our role model as she obeyed him always. Today most of the parents behave like two masters and children get confused when parents' orders are contradictory. Opinions would differ, but they should be sorted out in the absence of children. The love and respect husband and wife show to each other, works wonders in bringing up children. Parents who do not realize this are fools despite their high education.

When we quarrelled in Appachan's absence, he never failed to verify the facts with Mummy. The importance he gave to Mummy in dealing with our problems was worthy of emulation. He meted out rather mild punishments to us. Not pain but shame of getting punished corrected us. The lesson I learnt from my parents made me consciously subject myself to my husband in the formative years of our children and our family reaped the benefit abundantly. Sons and daughters with loving and understanding parents would be an asset to families and the society at large.

In their old age, parents should be looked after with love and respect. Generally, girls after childbirth realize the worth of their mothers. The travails of motherhood mellow them quicker. Lack of it drives some sons to treat their mothers, especially widows disrespectfully. *'Be satisfied with food, clothing and shelter that I provide. Don't interfere in MY family matters'* – such words or even such an attitude would break a mother's heart. To be sure, there are exceptions. Some daughters are unkind to their mothers and there are sons who adore their mothers. *'Paradise is under the feet of your mother'* – Prophet Mohammed could not have said it better!

It is my proud privilege to enumerate the character traits of my parents. Both were pious and industrious; loving and merciful; generous and helpful. Some readers might question: *'Were your parents saints without blemish?'* None on earth can be perfect. When we see much goodness in someone the few not-so-good traits fade away. The life of my parents was a testimony to all-encompassing love and generosity.

In Christian families all the members are expected to gather for the night prayer. It is said: *'The family that prays together stays together.'* This worship in Jacobite faith is a lengthy one with Bible reading, many prayers, devotional songs and ending with silent prayer. Generally, it takes more than half an hour. Menfolk may not be present sometimes due to duties outside. Coming home late, many men would say a short prayer and making the sign of the cross would go for supper.

Appachan, as the manager of the bank had great responsibility and reached home daily only by 9 pm. Yet, after the customary ablution, he would spend half an hour in prayers omitting no part of the worship. Except on Sundays, he took supper only at 10 pm.

He was generosity personified. In the 1950s, about 8-10 beggars would come daily to the houses in our lane. Our neighbours gave food to them sometimes, but at home, Appachan's strict order was never to say 'no' to anyone seeking alms. It could be cooked rice with gravy or uncooked rice or small change. Early in life, we were trained to be merciful and respectful to the poor. We celebrated our birthdays at times sharing our special food with beggars and received blessings from them. Once on Joy's birthday, Appachan's generosity took a unique turn. He bought a big tin of coconut oil and supplied it with a ladle for the use of the untidy matted hair of beggars. To prevent the same people coming again, he never gave it in bottles or cans. Word spread like wildfire and nearly a hundred came in about ten days.

Every year, November 2nd – All Souls' Day – was an occasion for almsgiving. That evening he took us to the cemetery with small change in our pockets. Many beggars sat on either side of the road leading to the graveyard with bowls or towels spread in front of them. Appachan used to tell us to bend and put the coins gently and never throw them. Moreover, by that yearly visit, we were indirectly made to understand the importance of the final resting place. But to our innocent and ignorant minds, it was a day of joy because the whole place would be bright and beautiful at dusk with fragrant flowers and burning candles on the graves. It is significant to note that none of our relatives were buried there at that time as their graves were in Kerala.

Appachan was patriotic and had great respect for national leaders. Every 15th August, the national flag would be unfurled on top of our house and lowered in the evening. Our family photo album had fairly large pictures of Gandhiji, Nehruji and Netaji in the first few leaves. In 1994, I got those photos from my brother and today the framed leaders adorn our drawing room. Seventy-year-old black-and-white photos still have their sheen! His responsibility as a citizen was proved when Appachan voted in the General Election of 1962, unmindful of his severe chest pain, which led to his death soon after. Today many disregard their voting rights and it damages the texture of our democracy.

The 'talisman' he gave us was education. Nevertheless, we were admitted to an ordinary Tamil medium primary school very near our home. He believed in the capacity of the individual and not in the fame of the institution. He used to visit our school occasionally to know about our studies and behaviour. He was very particular that we should be obedient pupils in school giving utmost respect to teachers. At home, he never became impatient nor punished us when we committed mistakes while studying. He helped us especially with Maths which was his favourite subject. It was a blessing to have such an understanding father.

He wanted us to be familiar with household chores too. Though we had a full-time maid, my elder sister was asked to sweep the living room daily when she turned 10. After 2 years, at 10, I followed suit by cleaning one of the bedrooms. He taught us how to wash our best clothes for occasions with Lux flakes. By the way, elder sisters in our home are not called 'chechi' in Malayalam. We followed the three-language formula unknowingly with regard to relationships – 'Appachan' in Malayalam, 'Mummy' in English and 'Akkal' in Tamil!

Appachan was a staunch Jacobite. Yet he allowed us to go to Catholic Church when we visited Mummy's home in Trichur. I say this because seven decades ago people were very strict about such matters. Again, it was considered sacrilege if Christians sang songs on Hindu gods and goddesses. But Appachan was different. Our house was close to a mosque on one side and a Ganapati temple on the other. We grew up hearing the call for prayer from the mosque five times a day. We enjoyed singing devotional songs from the temple heard through loudspeakers. I can sing some songs on Ganapati and his brother Subramanya even today!

We lived in a narrow lane called Okkiliar Street in the heart of the city, near Town Hall. All the 20-odd families there, were Tamil and Kannada speaking Hindus. Ours was the only Malayali Christian family; yet none of us felt any difference. Our social interaction was such that all of us knew every member of each family by name. Today one may not know one's next-door neighbour. Appachan's broad-mindedness was one of the reasons for our harmonious living. We celebrated Deepavali with new clothes and crackers with the other children. Rarely did it happen in Christian families then. However, we never made any sweet or savoury as our house would be flooded with dishes from all our neighbours! Christmas soon followed and it would be our turn to give them items like cakes, biscuits, diamond cuts, rose cookies, fruits, etc. Preparations would start much in advance for distribution to many houses. We used to help Mummy and the maid in making rose cookies and diamond cuts as it happened to be Christmas vacation. On Christmas day we would vie with one another to take these to our friends' houses. Appachan made sure that those delicacies were given to beggars too.

Appachan gave us a timetable for our activities. After coming from school, we had an hour's time to play in our lane. Games of those days involved running, hopping and skipping – all good physical exercises. Then we had half an hour to listen to radio (the famous HMV). We were interested only in Tamil cine songs then, especially broadcast by Radio Ceylon. Next it would be time for homework. The most important 'rule' was to stop whatever we were doing and assemble for family prayer at 8 pm. Most conveniently there used to be a loud, shrill siren for more than a minute from a cotton making unit exactly at 8. As our maids were Malayali Christians from Kunnamkulam, they were also expected to join the worship. I feel proud about the way he instilled good values in us.

His love for birds and animals turned our house into a mini-Noah's ark! We had a dog, a cat, a squirrel, a pair of rabbits, a parrot, a pair of ducks, some hens and a big cock (Rhode Island variety and hens were Black Minorca and White Leghorn). Our modest backyard prevented him from buying goats and cows! Once when the cock fell ill, he carried it for injections to the veterinary hospital for four days. Though the hospital was close by, he need not have carried that heavy fowl himself. Such was his love for the dumb creatures. Moreover, every weekend we had an unusual visitor in an elephant (bank owner's).

Our house was on the way to their farm and the mahout had been instructed to bring it to our residence. We would be waiting outside with plantains to feed the calf. It was a feast to the eyes when it came majestically through our narrow lane! We were proud when the children around watched that weekly ritual with awe.

Appachan had the habit of smoking much and that could be one of the reasons for his relatively early demise. He was short-tempered too, but his anger vanished as quickly as it came. He never allowed it to poison his mind. So, the 'angry man' was loved and respected by one and all. Kith and kin called him in various manner adding respectful suffixes to his name: 'Ipettan', 'Ipeachan', 'Ipe sir', 'Manager' or 'Manager Sir'. Once, a man from our area got drunk and staggered in the narrow lane inconveniencing others. Some neighbours requested him to go home, but he shouted at them. He insisted on 'Manager sir' to tell him what he should do. Appachan allayed Mummy's fears and approached 'the hero of the scene'. He calmly asked the man to go to his weeping wife and kids at home. By God's grace he at once obeyed saying, *"Manager Sir, I'll go since you say. I won't listen to those people"*. I inherited this peace-making quality from Appachan. After self-realization at the age of 30, I had the courage for it. A later chapter gives some instances of that.

The Holy Bible had influenced him much. His words and deeds were in accordance with the following verses: *'Love your neighbour as yourself'*; *'Freely ye have received, freely give'*. Once he told us, *"Whatever we earn is not for us alone, we should help our kith and kin in their need and give a portion to the poor"*. Besides helping he lent money to the needy. The way he had absorbed the words of Jesus, *'Let not thy left hand know what thy right hand doeth'* was remarkably revealed after his death. Of their own accord some returned the money they had borrowed from him. But we could not get from some just on the strength of hearsay as Appachan had not recorded anything.

Generally, people tend to accumulate wealth for posterity. Once, an elderly relative accused Appachan after his demise, *"Did your father think about your future? He earned a lot, but his generosity has now left you in the lurch"*. Having heard similar words earlier, I was at my wits' end. I said, *"We are proud of our father's life and not worried about our future. Please don't criticize him."* The lady stared at me in disbelief as I was a timid creature then! Again, biblical verses come to my mind when I write about him: *'Take therefore no thought for the morrow; for the morrow shall take thought for the things of itself; sufficient unto the day is the evil thereof'.* Only people with true faith can live according to these verses. The Psalmist says, *'He is ever giving liberally and lending and his children became a blessing.'* Our life is in vindication of this verse.

After his sudden death, certain 'well-planned happenings' came to pass. We had been living in a fairly large house with two bedrooms for a monthly rent of Rs. 40/- (a princely rental sum in those days). When we needed two more bedrooms on the first floor, the landlord who lived at Mettur in Salem district asked Appachan to do the needful and adjust the amount in the rent. Ten months after the construction, Appachan passed away and we could live there for two more years without paying rent. Instead of expanding a rented house by spending money from his own pocket, if he had decided to shift to a bigger house (certainly for a higher rent), our loss would have been two-fold.

The other financial support was from the bank where he was the manager. The owner of the bank, a Malayali Hindu, had passed away two years earlier and that was the only time I had seen Appachan shed tears. The boss and the manager had cordial relationship and mutual regard. In appreciation of Appachan's dedicated service the family gave us half of his salary every month for two years. Over and above these, Rev. Fr. Thykkadavil, our parish priest deposited Rs.1000/- (a huge amount then) in the bank for our education. When the priest revealed the truth about the source of that money (donations from rich parishioners) we hesitated to accept it. His words of wisdom then humbled us, *"A giving hand turning to a receiving hand happens according to God's Will. Your father gave generously for the church and charity. Today, you are in need of money. You would not ask help from anyone and so I did it for you. Study well and come up in life and once again you can become cheerful givers. You'll be in my prayer. God bless you."* Fr. Thykkadavil's homilies during Sunday service used to be food for the soul.

As predicted by the wise priest, we prospered with education. We give a portion of our earnings for charity. Today we live with our grandchildren, but Appachan could not be there for the marriage of even one daughter. It showed again how his thoughts were far ahead of his times. In 1961, one year before his death, there was a good proposal for Akkal, who was 17 then. Many urged him to marry her off. But he was determined to educate us minimum to the graduation level before marriage.

In those days, it was rare to see girls without ornaments unless they were very poor. Appachan avoided getting our earlobes poked and we never wore any jewels. He foresaw the prospective thieves kidnapping his kids for the sake of gold! Later Akkal got her earlobes poked three months before her marriage and I, three months after mine! Marykutty's first baby was a girl – the mother, the daughter and my two other younger sisters had that ritual together in 1977.

Now, writing about Mummy, her naivety and generosity come to the forefront. Throughout her life she was bubbling over with joy and laughter despite many sufferings. She had diabetes for the last fourteen years of her life. Only months before her end, she became unusually silent and seemed to be in deep thought. At the age of 80, on 16th September 2004, she peacefully embraced death.

Mummy had a sympathetic heart. In those days, two Malayali women used to come home with their tales of poverty and sorrow. She always gave them food and sometimes money, getting it from Appachan who dealt with money matters. Mummy gave our usable old clothes to those ladies who had large families. (Our neighbours exchanged theirs for steel vessels.) Even after Appachan's death, she continued to be generous and we tried to curb it. Once when a beggar asked for a sari for his mother, she gave him a fairly new one. We said he must have lied and even if it were the truth, she could have given him an old sari. Her reply made us hang our heads in shame, *"He said his mother had only rags to wear. If I give an old one, how long would it last? Why should I worry when my children look after me well?"*

She spent her time and energy for her six children and ten grandchildren with love and care. Some may think, *'What's the big deal, all the mothers did the same then and many do it now, too'*. True, but how many today gratefully remember it and care for their mothers in the evening of their lives?

One of Mummy's hobbies was crocheting. She had done dozens of chemises for little girls and vests for boys in lace work. Someone suggested to her to take money from people other than relatives for thread and labour. Mummy said, *"I do it as a hobby, not for earning money and it gives me immense satisfaction. Before starting every piece, I always pray for the health and long life of the person who would be wearing it later"*.

Reading was her hobby too. Since she studied in an English-medium school up to 8th standard in the 1930s, she could speak and write English, of course with mistakes. When we tried to correct her, she said, *"It is useless to correct me now as I have been using English like this for many years. See that you learn everything correctly."* It would be amusing to listen to her reading Tamil like a child. She had learnt it on her own after marriage when she started living in Coimbatore. Once I 'wisely' suggested to her to read a short story when I saw her reading a part of a serial story in a weekly. Her ready reply, *"You read whatever you like. In order to not forget Tamil whatever I read is good enough"*. A particular mistake she did in spoken Tamil was peculiar. As a mark of respect for elders and strangers, verbs end in different ways in Tamil. Mummy could never use them properly. It was not due to disrespect for people, but she would use such verb endings faithfully for birds and animals! Today when I make some such silly mistakes in spoken Kannada, I become nostalgic.

Another passion of hers was playing '28', a card game similar to whist. Once during a train journey, Mummy and my three children in their early teens (they had already learnt the nuances of '28' by then) played the game. I was against the idea of playing cards in a public place. Mummy argued that it could be done without disturbing the co-passengers. An elderly man watching it said, "Your mother is a wonder. She enjoys the game like a child. At this age, most of the old people would be with stony faces as if all the burden were on their shoulders." After a while when she started crocheting everyone watched her curiously.

Mummy was a good cook. At times experimenting with a dish, the attempt would go awry! As children we had always enjoyed Kerala-type snacks with neighbourhood kids. On any day, if no child was present, she would go out to bring in one! Once she said, *"Love gives. If some say they love without sharing their blessings with others, they are liars".* True, but some wealthy people give not out of love; they donate for name and fame.

Mummy had her shortcomings as none can claim total goodness. However, she had been friendly with all in a consistent manner, for which I admire her much. She had said, *"If someone show indifference to me and I pay her back in her own coin, what's the difference between us? Forgiving and being friendly with them would be a better option. One should be humble to be a true Christian".*

Children begin by loving their parents;

after a time, they judge them.........

– Oscar Wilde

5

Appachan and Me

Though I have already written rather exhaustively about Appachan, this chapter is imperative to record some special moments. I realized much later that Appachan's death when I was sixteen was part of God's Master Plan. The immensity and the intensity of that great loss led me, at an early age in the path of wisdom through sufferings. In fact, it became a blessing in disguise. *'Sweet are the uses of adversity'* – there is no gainsaying the words of the Bard of Avon.

Appachan was a model for parents of those days when sons had better favours; more so among Malayali Christians. The only son in our family was not given any special treatment. Again, when there are two or three children sans much age difference, the first child's clothes would be given to the younger ones. The age difference between the first and third girls at home is three years and the second one in between is me! Appachan bought the same type of dress for the three of us in different colours. When some elders pointed out that as waste of money, his reply would be that the younger ones would feel sad in getting used clothes. At the same time, we had a rocking horse and a tricycle to share.

He used to take us to shops to buy clothes to our liking. On one occasion I realized the material I liked, was Rs.10/- per yard and I hesitated to ask for it. In the 1950s, we could get good cloth at Rs.3 or 4 per yard. But Appachan said, *"Don't bother about the price, monae, if you like it, you can have it."* Four decades later, my first-born used exactly the same words ('monae' replaced by 'mummy') in a book shop in Dubai. Was Appachan's soul sent to my son? There were many points of similarity in their character.

While at school, my favourite subject was Maths. For SSLC Examination, I scored 97% and my Maths teacher teasingly asked how I 'managed' to lose 3 marks! Appachan took my help in maintaining bank registers for adding some amounts which he would verify later. I was immensely happy to help him thus. Generally, I am praised for my neat and diligent work. It has always gladdened my heart, but I have consciously striven not to let pride take possession of my soul. Later I realized that it has always been Divine Grace that protects me from that deadly sin.

When I was in ninth class (then known as IV Form), Appachan allowed me to go on a tour from school for three days to Velankanni, famous for St. Mary's Church. Till then he had sent us only for a day's picnic. Akkal was sad and angry as she was not permitted to do so. Mummy consoled her saying that his unusual decision was because it was a pilgrim spot. Years later, I realized the truth of the matter in a different light. Parents generally hesitate to introduce something new to the first child. Their fear diminishes when it happens with the other kids. The insight dawned on me when I had my own children. The anxiety I had when Jacob started riding bicycle or scooter decreased considerably when Mary & Joseph did the same. Jacob questioned me about the leniency shown to them. I pacified him with my 'discovery', referring to the Velankanni trip.

I had been given some money for my personal expenses during the trip. Later when I counted, it was about Rs.24. In 1958, it was rather a big amount given to a little girl of a middle-class family for a school tour. After presenting the offering at the church, I bought some beautifully painted cane trays and baskets. Total expenses did not exceed Rs.14. On returning, I gave back the remainder to Appachan. Later, Mummy shared with me what Appachan had said in my absence, *"Our mon (me!) is a thrifty and selfless girl. She never bought anything for herself but did not forget to buy some things for common use."* My cup of joy was full.

Despite admiring Appachan so much, a year later, I (aged 13) had a bizarre imagination. The feeling, that he did not love me as much as he loved his other children, depressed me. I cooked up some reasons for that morbid thought. Of the five children at that time, Akkal and Jessie, as the first and last and Joy (the only son) had special love. Marykutty was very lean and cried at the drop of a hat. So during 'judgement', Appachan would at times let her go unpunished saying that she was a stubborn child. Thus, she was also special. For nearly two years, that unhealthy thought invaded my mind and made me sad. Fortunately, I was never envious of my siblings or angry with Appachan. By God's grace an incident that happened when I was 15 nipped that wretched feeling before it took deep roots.

By then the last child was born. Once, taking little Jolly, Mummy went to Kerala with Uncle Kurian. Though there was a full-time maid, Appachan had a tough time managing us. To make matters worse, I fell ill and had shivers. He covered me with a thick blanket and still my legs were shaking. He (aged 55) started rubbing my ice-cold feet with his palm. My guilty conscience made me shed tears. He became worried and enquired if there was much pain. That kindness left me sobbing uncontrollably. How could I say that it was my 'heart' that ached the most? He concluded that as a grown girl I hesitated to tell him about my predicament. His consoling words proved it, *"Don't worry, I'll ask Mummy to return at once. You'll become worse if you cry like this"*. I begged his pardon inwardly and thanked God.

Before Mummy returned from Kerala both the fever and the 'burden' bade me goodbye. I could not think it a coincidence that I had fever and shivering in Mummy's absence and that it had happened just a few months before Appachan's death. I have always believed in the saying, *'Everything happens for good'*. But when calamity strikes most unexpectedly, such high thinking would not help. How could his sudden demise be taken for our good? Even a sage would find it hard to accept the untimely death of a dear one. Yet, Appachan's death in my teens laid the foundation for the rock-like faith I gained later.

Again, it was unpardonable on my part that I had deeply hurt him once towards the end of his life. Before writing that imprudent act of mine, I must digress a little. In 1955, when Marykutty and I passed third and fifth classes respectively, Appachan decided to admit us to an English-medium school. As we were waiting to see the Headmistress, we happened to hear girls of our age talking fluently in English. We were awe-struck. In our Tamil-medium school, learning English started only from fifth class. So, I knew a little English and Marykutty knew little English! It seemed to be a real 'threat' to join that school. We pleaded with Appachan to take us back to our school. He had always been very sensitive to his children's emotions. So, he did the sensible thing of leaving the school without meeting the HM as there was no prior appointment.

In 1961, when I joined college, English became a nightmare because all the subjects had to be learnt in it. I had come off with flying colours for the SSLC Exam, standing third in our school. Since my aim was to become a doctor, I had selected science group for P.U.C. Besides English and Tamil, there were four subjects to study – Natural Science, Physical Science, Geography and Psychology. The first two were further divided into Zoology, Botany and Physics, Chemistry, all of which needed record work. I was toiling day and night; yet could score just pass marks. I thought my Tamil-medium education had crippled me terribly.

By then I had totally forgotten about the 'failed episode' of English-medium education at school level. I blamed Appachan for my poor performance in college. When he reminded me of my refusal then, I had a ready retort, *"As a little girl, how could I know what was good for me? You should have compelled me to join that school. You failed to do that and I suffer today."* How impudent I was! It would have been a rude shock to that loving soul to get such a tirade from his teenaged daughter. Very soon he passed away and I shed bitter tears.

I realized later what he did was the right thing for me. Unlike these days, English-medium schools were very few then. Many students at such schools strutted about putting on airs and looked down upon the ones who could not converse in English. Perhaps, I might have become a 'proud peacock' through such learning. Moreover, my knowledge in Tamil would have had a set-back. Today, Tamil and English are like my two eyes with proper 'vision'!

Only after Appachan's death I got to know what he had told Uncle Kurian while in hospital, "*Alice is intelligent and industrious. If possible, send her to study medicine.*" I sobbed my heart out on hearing it. Yet I am thankful to God Almighty for making me a teacher. The thought that a good number of my students must be serving the society as doctors gives me great joy.

> ***Setting one's offspring first among scholars;***
>
> ***Such is the duty and pleasure of a father.***
>
> ***– Thiruvalluvar***

6

Mummy and Me

There was a special bond between Mummy and me. Family history was dear to our hearts. We talked about old times and shared our experiences, especially after my marriage whenever she came to stay with us.

Let me begin with the marriage of my parents, the cause of my presence on this planet! Mummy said, *"My father did cloth business and earned well. His drinking habit swallowed much of that money. When I became 17, mother pleaded with him to save for dowry. Once, in a drunken stupor he challenged her, "A prince will come for Thangamma without asking for dowry!" His words were prophetic! Your Appachan came soon with a proposal – no dowry; only change of denomination from Catholic to Jacobite faith. He was also a 'prince' – tall and fair with dark, curly hair and had a good income. Due to his lean constitution, he did not look his age (36) whereas I seemed to be older than 18 years due to my plump figure. None could believe our age difference of 18 years. But everyone saw and believed our height difference – he was 6 feet tall and I, less than 5 feet! In 1942, we got married and in 1944, Susheela was born. I was terribly disappointed when I looked at my first-born. She was a thin baby with an elongated head, but within three months, she became beautiful. The lady engaged to massage her handled Susheela with such dexterity that her head became normal. Another disappointment was at your birth – a second girl! When many marvelled at your beauty, I became happy. Something about your infancy puzzled me. All of you have fair complexion; yet you alone turned deep red daily during oil bath – as if blood were oozing out of your skin. After a few weeks, that transformation stopped on its own."*

Mummy plaited our hair till our school final. That used to be quite a tiresome ritual in my case. She had to apply oil and water alternately to 'tame' my short and thick hair with corkscrew curls. Once a neighbour warned Mummy, *"Thangamma, a sparrow is coming to build its nest on Alice's head!"* After oil bath and before combing my hair, my head would look like Sathya Saibaba's! As a little girl, I used to wonder how I would manage my hair without Mummy's help.

Mummy's naivety was well-known. Much later in life, I realized about her practical wisdom. In a way, there is a coincidence in it. She and I were considered not in our right minds soon after our second deliveries. In 1976, she happened to share with me, for the first time, an incident which happened in 1946. In Mummy's words, *"After you (6 months) survived the first threat of death, Appachan left us in Kunnamkulam and went back to Coimbatore. I used to cry often thinking of some sad happenings at my parents' home in Trichur. I was not quite normal also because of my mood-swings. Appachan's siblings thought I was possessed and carried out the 'treatment', i.e., caning me. (On hearing this, I started weeping) No, no, don't cry, I did not mean that they ill-treated me. Caning was in vogue in villages to drive away evil spirits, supposed to be the cause of abnormal behavior. Moreover, they were otherwise always very kind and took care of you, Susheela and me."*

The reason for her revealing the dark side of her past after three decades was clear to me then. The previous day, Mummy had come to our house at Saibaba Colony in North Coimbatore. My mother-in-law asked her to take me home for treatment as she believed me to be insane. Mummy at once agreed to her plan and took me and six-month old Mary home with her. Nursery-class Jacob was left with his daddy and grandmother.

After reaching home, Mummy asked me not to worry about any treatment. She said, *"I could have questioned the propriety of her statement pointing to the fact that you have been doing your duty as a college lecturer. It would have been a fitting retort, but the consequences would be terrible. We may not be able to visit each other with the ensuing quarrel. That's why I brought you here without further argument. From her talk, I understood what you need now is a break from that environment. Moreover, you are in tears often and it would be irritating to Jose and his mother. There's a method to stop crying. First, pray to God. Clench your teeth and look up with wide open eyes. Tears get arrested at once."* Experience spoke, I thought!

In our motherland, a boy is 'trained' right from the beginning not to cry. *'What a shame, crying like a girl!' 'Are you a girl to cry like this?'* – such teasers are around to detract him. Boys consciously learn to stifle their sobs and suppress their emotions. No wonder, men are more prone to cardiac arrests here. This kind of lopsided advice should be avoided. Everyone has the freedom to shed tears, but it is better to be avoided in the presence of others. Crying behind closed doors would clear the eyes and purify the mind. Crocodile tears are shed to deceive others.

Mummy never hesitated to talk to strangers. While staying with us in Little Mount, she greeted an unknown lady in the most uncommon way! I was shocked to hear her asking a middle-aged Anglo-Indian lady near the gate of our apartment complex, *"Why are you so thin?"* My mind raced to save the situation. The lady could have questioned Mummy about the elegance of her question to a stranger. Fortunately, she replied in a calm manner, *"I have been suffering from asthma for quite some time now and because of that I lose weight."* From her expression, I felt that she was touched by the concern in Mummy's voice.

In India there is an unwritten rule that parents should live with their sons and not with married daughters. When Amma (aged 77) decided to stay in Kerala in the evening of her life, I thought of bringing Mummy to Bangalore for some years. I had to 'fight for my right' as my brother felt it would be a shame for him. Jose was also against the idea as it would have set tongues wagging: *'Jose has sent away his aged mother to Kerala and looks after his mother-in-law!'* Despite all that, I brought Mummy to Bangalore in 1996. She was happy to come but said she would stay only for a few months. Indian culture cannot be shaken off that easily!

The adage *'Man proposes; God disposes'* proved true within a month. Our shifting to Bangalore coincided with the coldest winter in decades as per newspaper reports. Extreme cold left Mummy unable to speak due to a mild stroke, with her mouth stretching to one side. When the doctor knew that she was my mother, his question whether she had no sons surprised me. It implied that if there was a son, a mother need not stay with her married daughter for a long time! He prescribed medicines and advised me to take her to Coimbatore once she recovered. At her age (72), he said that it was not good to introduce her to the chilly weather of Bangalore. Soon, she got well and insisted on going back to her son.

I started wearing Khadi sari at the age of 48 and two years later, I gave up ornaments. Mummy's deprecation was that I should not look like a sanyasini while living with my husband and children. I told her that I liked the simple way of living at 50 as it suited my age. Her angry retort was that I was only 50 but she, at 72, used silk saris and ornaments. Age, she said, need not be the reason for my adamant behaviour. I smilingly moved away to avoid further argument.

When Jacob passed away, Mummy consoled me saying, *"Don't cry thinking about your son. He will come back. All dead people return to earth. But we will not be able to recognize them."*

God could not be everywhere and

therefore He made mothers.

– Rudyard Kipling

7

Early Memories

People are generally immersed in thoughts of present problems or dreams of future achievements. My mind is often absorbed in reminiscing the past too. Later I realized whatever happened – good or bad – made me wiser. St. Paul says, *"All things work together for good to them that love God"*. The Psalmist sings, *"The fear of the Lord is the beginning of wisdom"*. Here, fear means dread and reverence. But as a little girl, I feared God who would punish me for my wrong doings. That fear waned as years rolled by and eventually it was replaced by love of God. I feel those who fear the Lord throughout their lives can never grow in wisdom because fear should only be a good start!

Many happenings of my early childhood are forgotten. But one scene when I was three years old is etched in my mind like a photograph. One night, I heard Mummy crying. I could not see her due to a screen in our bedroom. Our maid and a strange lady were walking to and fro with big basins. I don't remember anything after that. I did not hear the wails of a baby. Perhaps I slept as it was 3 o'clock in the morning – the time of my brother's birth at home on an Easter Sunday.

At the age of 6, when I was in class 2, there was inspection in our primary school. The School Inspector started from the highest class (5th) onwards. In our class, I gave the correct answer, but he stared at me and said, *"I saw this girl in the 4th class"*. Our teachers who came with him were upset as they realized that he had doubted their integrity.

There was a practice in vogue in those days to make bright students of higher classes to be present in the lower classes surreptitiously for the school to receive a good certificate. Suddenly a teacher understood the matter and brought Akkal from the 4th class. When the official saw us together, he smilingly nodded his head. Appachan gave me the details later. My memory about it was rather vague. My correct answer did not please the official who said something. When Akkal came to my class, everyone smiled, including the School Inspector.

All six children at home took after Appachan and sometimes the resemblance led to confusion. When, we first three girls were in High School, our teachers often mixed up our names. Here are some occasions regarding our resemblance which caused merriment. Marykutty and I (15 months apart) were of the same height and weight in our school days. When I was in class 9, a new teacher, on her first day in our school, looked at me curiously and said she had seen the same girl in class 8 during the previous period. She was English teacher for both the classes. When she questioned me about it, my classmates informed her in a chorus about my sister. Later, she shared her experience with another new teacher and during morning assembly showed my sister from a fairly long distance. She also felt we were like twins as both had curly hair. Actually, she had been looking at me and thought it was Marykutty, who unlike me had long straight hair.

The resemblance episode with Jessie (7 years younger to me) left her embarassed. Once when I introduced her to my colleague in Lutheran Theological college in Madras, he said we looked exactly alike, but wanted to know who was the elder one. I thanked him for the 'excellent' compliment. Looking at Jessie's flushed face, he mumbled an excuse and left the place quickly. Women are generally quite sensitive about their age and appearance and my sister was no exception. However, I think that every age has its own beauty and grace.

When I was compared with my youngest sister Jolly, our age difference of 15 years could be seen at the maximum – I was 25 and she was 10. It happened before my marriage. Once, I had taken

Jolly along when I went for a Tamil movie with my colleagues. They exclaimed that she was a smaller version of me. Their comment was made in Tamil to match with the title of the movie we were about to watch – '*Nootrukku Nooru*' (cent percent)!

In a college play, I had the part of a man. I wore my younger brother's pants and shirt and looked like him. A friend of mine joked, "*You look like Joy's twin brother. Since you look more handsome, I'll marry you!*" At home, the teasing continued, "*Even before you complete your graduation, a 'bride' is ready for you!*"

Coming back to early memories, once at the age of seven, I fell ill and could not attend school for a week. I had seen neighbourhood kids cry for money to buy candies from shops near the school. Having my illness as an excuse, I cried to Appachan for coins. Breaking his rule of never giving money to his children, he gave me a small purse (it is still with me!) with some change in it. Flu flew away when coins came to my *chest* (of drawers) and I started going to school.

One day I took eight annas (50 paise) from my purse and bought a large packet of burfi (a sweet made of coconut and sugar) and enjoyed sharing the pieces with my classmates. The news of my burfi distribution reached the ears of my class teacher who in turn informed Appachan when he came to the school the next day. That evening he scolded me and gave us a 'sermon'. First and foremost, eating from such petty shops was not good for health. Second, I became a bad role model for other children. They might steal from home to do the same. Finally, only when we started earning on our own could we be generous in such a way. Till then, what we got from our parents alone should be shared. It took time to know the deeper meaning of the last mentioned 'rule'. Later the purse was safe in my 'safe'; he took the coins back!

An incident that happened when I was eight proved that even the uneducated can handle dire situations expertly on account of their wisdom. Appachan had taken electricity connection for our rented house (in the early 1950s) while many families around us living in their own houses used only kerosene lamps. Aunt Achayi who had snatched me from the grip of death was with us then.

One late evening, when all of us (Appachan was at the bank) were seated in the veranda, the maid brought us the daily drink of milk and went back to the kitchen for other chores. Mummy asked Akkal to take all the empty tumblers (pure silver) inside, but she was afraid to go alone. With a 'show' of courage, I volunteered and ran inside to keep them on the dining table. While returning, power went off and it became pitch dark. I screamed and ran to the backyard where there was moonlight. By then, everyone came inside and Aunt, with great difficulty reached me all the while calling me 'monae, monae'. Then the unexpected happened. She slapped me hard on my cheek and hugged me tightly! My fear vanished and I cried loudly out of pain and confusion. Mummy explained the significance of her 'cruel' action later. It was a kind of shock treatment given in those days. Elders believed that the painful slap would drive away the frightened feeling – instant remedy for instant fear! Attention of children can be easily diverted. Moreover, children do things which they are told not to. That day, if Aunt had consoled me saying not to be afraid, my fear would have increased.

When I was nine years old, I had the taste of English for the first time in the fifth class. The newly appointed teacher for English was a North Indian and did not know a word of Tamil. She used to give us spelling test daily and warned us against copying. We had to write the words quickly as she dictated them. Once, I looked at my neighbour's notebook just to check the serial number as I had a doubt that I had missed a word. I never looked at the words – the truth that God and I alone knew. Spontaneously, I turned to the teacher who was staring at me. The next action of hers – shaking her index finger – brought tears to my eyes. While correcting my notebook, without even looking at the words, she awarded me a big zero. I burst into tears. I requested a classmate (the only girl who could speak a little English in our class) to explain the matter to the teacher who was not ready to believe it. Writing all the words correctly and getting a zero was reason enough to cry. But I wept more for being considered a dishonest girl by my new teacher. I learnt a very valuable lesson that day. It is not enough if we are honest, but consciously avoid words and deeds which might give others a wrong impression. After becoming a teacher, I shared that experience with my students and advised them to look up or look straight if they needed to think while writing their tests. It sent them into peals of laughter.

Once, Uncle George broke a long sugarcane stem by holding it at both ends and pressing it in the middle with his foot. I did the same with another stem most enthusiastically. Of course, I got two pieces of sugarcane along with a bloody face! I fell and hit my chin on the threshold. My scream in pain brought everyone there. Appachan put a temporary bandage and took me to our family doctor who quickly did an 'operation' on my chin with four sutures. Luckily the cut was not deep. I learnt never to be reckless again. One must first assess one's fitness by way of age, ability and strength before taking up a job. To be sure, I could not have thought in such a manner at that tender age of nine. Yet, my decisions later proved that God had sown the seed of that priceless lesson in my mind soon after that incident.

Again, when I was 9 years old, Soviet statesmen, Nikolai Bulganin and Nikita Khrushchev came to India (1955). The former was the Prime Minister at that time and the latter became the PM later. When they visited Coimbatore, there was a reception arranged at V.O.C Park and some students including me were selected for presenting bouquets to the Russian leaders. Both received them cheerfully from us and mine was given to Khrushchev. I was disappointed because I could not give it to the PM with a short attractive beard! ('Bulganin beard' was famously fashionable then). Before long, I had the privilege of presenting a bouquet to our beloved first Prime Minister, Pandit Jawaharlal Nehru. The same girls in the same dress (stitched for the previous occasion) lined up again at V.O.C Park. After receiving the bouquet from me, Chacha Nehru, with a sweet smile, patted my cheek twice. With that magic touch, I was floating in air for a while. How I wished for a photo of the memorable scene! Perhaps, I am there in one corner of thousands of Nehruji's snaps!

Here is a momentous event which happened when I was 12, in January 1958. It was the School Annual Day time. During lunch break, my firend and I ran home for a quick meal and returned to school for dance practice. As we neared the gate, two nuns (not teachers) came out of the school. One of them asked me to accompany them to the Primary School (branch of our High School) – a little more than a kilometer away. I asked my friend to explain to our teacher the reason for my absence for the rehearsal and followed the nuns. On reaching the school, they asked me to wait near the gate and went inside. I was perplexed. Did I come all the way just to stand outside? The answer came in the form of a fairly large wooden cross. The nuns kept it on my shoulder and instructed me to hold it tightly with both hands. They asked me to walk back to High School and followed me.

I would not say it was a heavy cross. Yet, as a lean girl, I found it quite difficult to walk with it and the sensitive age made it more so. With bowed head and tears blurring my eyes, I walked through the busy street. The thought that on the way I would be quite a sight to the students of a Boys' School (lunch break!) was burning within me. Appachan's bank was a little farther away; but he would be inside. Before I could heave a sigh of relief, I saw him standing outside talking to someone. His smile vanished when he saw me with the cross on the shoulder. On reaching the school, I handed over the cross to the nuns, wiped my 'tears of humiliation' and ran to the class. In the evening, Mummy said Appachan had been very angry about the action of the nuns. He felt that, as the brides of Christ, they should have carried the cross themselves instead of making a little girl carry it. He even thought of making a complaint to the Mother Superior. Later he desisted from it considering probable adverse reaction towards his three daughters studying there.

'Time heals all wounds', so goes the saying. The sorrow and shame of carrying the cross was forgotten after some years. But life's 'crosses' took me back to the literal carrying of a cross more than two decades earlier. Only then could I see things in the right perspective. When such an event is written in the book of my life, how could the nuns be blamed? In the first place, there was a coincidence, as the nuns had not planned to take me to the other school. They happened to meet me at the gate and I was 'called'. They avoided the sturdily-built friend of mine as she was not a Christian. Her parents could have taken offense whereas my parents might view it as a blessing! Moreover,

my friend was a notorious chatterbox and very bold too. Even while going to the other school, she would have pestered the nuns for the reason to accompany them. Since the nuns were not teachers, she might have asked them to carry it themselves! I was known for my quiet nature and obedience in school. Anyway, I came to the point of believing that I was fortunate to carry the smaller version of the big cross carried by Jesus around two thousand years ago. In 1977, with happiness and contentment I wrote a thirty-lined poem on this incident (given in the Appendix).

'Your curly hair is your identity' – many have said. When young I wanted to have long hair, but my curls would not grow beyond my shoulders! As people admired my unruly curls, later I became reconciled to it. In school, a classmate who had long straight hair once said, *"When I die, please remember to cut a lock of your hair and put it on my body. At least in my next birth, I want to have curly hair"*. How true is the saying - *One man's food is another man's poison*!

I have a passion for singing right from childhood. In my girlhood days, Radio Ceylon used to broadcast Tamil cine songs every evening. I would sing those songs differently for male and female voices. We rarely went to watch movies but bought many cine song books (each 1 anna, which was about 6 paise). My classmates in school would 'demand' for listener's choice during lunch break. I never failed them as I knew many songs; of course, humming the forgotten lines.

Later when interest in cine songs was replaced by devotional songs, I discarded all the song books retaining only one. The songs of the Tamil movie 'Devadas' (based on the Bengali novel by Saratchandra Chatterjee) were dear to my heart. As a young girl, once I sang a sad song from it in such a soulful manner that an elderly relative became teary-eyed. Even today, I remember that haunting melody of bygone days (Ellaam maayai thaana? – Is everything an illusion?).

In my school days, for Tamil-medium students, English was the second language and Hindi, as third language was optional. I gladly opted for Special Music instead, though we had General Music class compulsorily three days a week. Later, I regretted my decision of not learning Hindi. Now I have understood that whatever has to happen will happen. By the way, my *'sa ri ga ma pa da ni'* notebook of school days (1950s) is still with me!

Music helps us get closer to God. In times of sadness or depression, singing a few devotional songs behind closed doors works wonders. I have experienced peace pervading my mind after every such session. I know many songs on Jesus Christ and Mother Mary in Malayalam, Tamil and English. I encourage my children and others to sing devotional songs, not concentrating on the tunes but on their deep meanings. Only then could both the singers and listeners enter the soul of the song.

Now, a note on a childhood photograph of mine (aged 3) with Akkal (5) and Marykutty (2); Akkal with a serious face and Marykutty with a smile. I stand clutching a doll and grinning from ear to ear with my curls jutting out in all directions! Later Mummy said that she had given that doll to Akkal to hold it while posing for the photograph. She refused to take it, but I was very eager to have it. Mummy concluded, *"That's why your face is radiant with joy and Susheela has a frown"*. Of late, the snap intrigues me for the manner in which the first three Ipe children express their emotions in it.

Gentle Jesus, meek and mild

Look upon a little child

Pity my simplicity

Suffer me to come to thee.

– Charles Wesley

8

Education and Career

College education and teaching went hand-in-hand in my life – initially I taught while learning and later I learnt while teaching! During my B.A. and M.A. courses, I took tuitions at home. My last exam for final year B.A. was on 9th June 1965 and the very next day I began teaching fifth class pupils in a private primary school. I could start my career in such a dramatic fashion because of the anti-Hindi agitation raging in Tamil Nadu then. Our exams scheduled for March-April were postponed to June. Most unexpectedly, I was offered a teacher's post in May even before my exams!

It so happened that I went job-hunting for Akkal who was down with an attack of jaundice in May that year. Anyway, I was taking 'rest' due to the postponement of my exams. I went to a nearby (10-min-walk) school for my maiden attempt. 'Our Lady of Fatima Insitute' in Coimbatore was a private English-medium primary school with classes up to 5, run by the nuns of F.M.M. (Franciscan Missionaries of Mary) order. I prayed in the convent chapel and proceeded to meet the Headmistress. Vacation time silence reigned the premises.

I met a middle-aged nun and requested her to guide me to the HM's room. She wanted to know the purpose and when I said it, her seriousness gave way to smile. On knowing the reason for my proxy job-seeking, she asked me whether I needed a job too. Amused by the variety of emotions on my face, she revealed her identity as the HM. I was pleasantly surprised when she offered the post of teachers for both of us. I thanked the nun who assured me of her prayers for my sister's quick recovery and for my exams. I swam through the sea of joy to reach home. At the age of 19, I was going to be a graduate (so sure of passing even before writing the exams!) and a teacher simultaneously.

Now, let me drift back to the initial days of my college life. In 1961, when I joined PUC in Nirmala College for Women in Coimbatore, my spoken English was simply pathetic. The sudden switch from Tamil to English-medium education became an uphill task for me. With much hard work, I passed the course and joined for B.A. Economics in the same college. I started reading many English novels and short stories to improve my language skills. I have always had reading habit but till then I read only Tamil books. In college I admired our English Professor (Ms. B. S. Pillai) and wanted to become an English lecturer. For the kind of proficiency I had in English then, it could only be wishful thinking. But God's Will prevailed and I realized my dream.

I never participated in competitions or drama due to stage fright both in school and college; group singing or dancing satisfied me. While in school, I was the queen in a pantomime, for the poem 'King Solomon and the Queen of Sheba'. It was a 'great' feeling to get applauded without uttering a single word on the stage! In college, I acted in a one-word play in which the characters said just one word at a time throughout that short skit. Needless to say, it suited me well. In a man's part, I wore pants and shirt and secured my two short plaits on my head with hair pins. I covered the upright plaits with a hat and became a perfect gentleman. In a scene, I had to come out of my hiding place (under a table) and audience burst into laughter and clapped. Proof of my improved acting ability, I surmised. Later, I came to know that when I crawled out, the hat 'chose' not to be on my head and my plaits were seen as two horns!

In the final year of my degree course, my friends persuaded me to join an oratorical competition. I got on to the stage with a silent prayer and pounding heart. The speech painstakingly learnt by-heart was delivered at one go. Later, our Economics lecturer teased me, *"Alice, you were really in wonderland! Why were you so flurried? Speeches must be made slowly and boldly with a smile. You had a flushed face and frightened eyes."*

Excruciating experiences in life made me wiser and bolder and I got rid of nervousness at the age of 30. By then, I was the mother of two children. In the seventh year of my college teaching, the 'new Alice' was introduced to everyone in a meeting arranged for the topic 'Internal Assessment'. An official who spoke against the proposal presented some relevant points and concluded with a pungent remark: *"Allowing the professors to follow the scheme is like giving the key to the thief".* All laughed but I could not. I got up from the midst of the audience and said in a loud voice (no mike!), *"Excuse me, Sir, please allow me to say a few words. Your viewpoints are good, but the final comparison of teachers with thieves was in bad taste".* Those who knew me well were stunned. How could timid Alice raise her voice in criticism in a large gathering?!

Now, back to my teaching days in Fatima School. Sr. Caroline Rodricks (aka Sr. Alena Kiara), the H.M. was both kind and strict. A year later my youngest sister Jolly joined the school in I std. Thus, three sisters went to the same school – two as teachers and one as student. I wanted my little sister to be a doctor – unfulfilled dream for myself. She was quite promising initially and always stood first in class. But her interest in studies waned gradually and she refused to join college. I was sad as she has always been like a daughter to me, more so because of our age difference of 15 years.

In 1967, when Marykutty completed B.T. (now, B.Ed.) and became a teacher in our Alma Mater (Presentation Convent Girls High School, Coimbatore), I decided to quit the job and do B.T. which would enable me to handle higher classes. Actually, I should have done B.T. earlier but for the job I took up soon after B.A. Sr. Kiara and the teachers were disappointed that I was leaving the school but happy regarding my better prospects later with a teaching degree. My students vied with each other in mentioning the names of the new schools they would join as 5th standard was the highest class in that primary school. Each requested me to join their new school after B.T. and their love and enthusiasm touched me.

Prior to this, while Marykutty was still in B.T. College, one evening she came home with a piece of good news. Mrs. Sulochana Shekar, her psychology professor had suggested that I could do M.A. to further my prospects as she was aware of our family's loss. The Principal of Government Arts College (GAC), Coimbatore was her friend and she would recommend my case to him for me to get a seat for M.A. English Literature. I could not believe my ears! Yes, God's ways are mysterious. When I shared the happy news with Sr. Kiara, she gave me a testimonial mentioning my sincere service to the school.

Amused by the curiosity of my beloved students who wanted to know the name of the college where I would work later, I said, *"Let me complete my two-year M.A. course first and only then will I decide which college I would work at. Meanwhile, you must complete your schooling. Later when you join the college where I'd be working, I'll teach you again."* In the fifth year of my college teaching, a 'sweet sixteen' gladly introduced herself, *"Miss, I'm Geetha Rao – a PUC student here. You take English for our class. You had taught me in fifth std. Do you remember me?"* I was happy to see her and smilingly said, *"How can I? You are a young lady now in a different attire; not a child in school uniform!"* I am still in touch with Jacob Eapen, Geetha's classmate in school, as he is the son of our friend. He is now in Canada with his wife and two children.

Now the story of my M.A. studies unfolds thus: Mrs. Shekar had advised me to apply for B.T. as well. In case, I failed to get a seat for M.A., it would help me to continue my studies. Since I was very sure of my admission in GAC with her recommendation, I decided not to bother about B.T. I felt it was a waste to spend money on a B.T. application form! In those days, every rupee was spent after much deliberation. But I did not tell her about my decision. She took me to GAC to meet the Principal. Only then did she come to know about his transfer. However, she reminded him of her earlier request regarding my M.A. seat and introduced me to him. He went through my application form and pronounced his verdict – *"She is not eligible to do M.A. Literature"*! My heart missed a beat. His reasons – first, my graduation was not in English Literature. Second, I had only a third class in my 'chosen' subject – Economics. Third, I had come back to studies after a gap of two years and such a break would affect studies adversely. He wanted to know what I had been doing in those two years. My mouth became so dry that words failed me. Somehow, I managed to say the word – 'teaching'. He specifically wanted to know the classes I had handled. When he knew it was 5th class, he turned to Mrs. Shekar and conveyed the message in Malayalam (both were Malayalis), *"I can't do anything in this case. Hope you understand without my explanation."*

Mrs. Shekar had disappointment writ large on her face but said, *"Oh, that's alright. She has applied for B.T. also."* I almost swooned! The last date for applying for B.T. had long been over. While returning in her car, she started consoling me in Malayalam (perhaps she felt better consolation could be in mother tongue!), *"I can very well understand GAC Principal's present predicament. This is the last year of his service and he would have liked to end it here. Again, it is rather unusual to have a transfer in the last year of one's career. But the reasons he cited in your case are valid. Anyway, forget it, good that you have applied for B.T. I regret giving you high hopes in vain."* With eyes brimming with tears, I revealed the fact and begged her pardon. She seemed to be amazed as well as annoyed and looked at me in disbelief. It was certainly unpardonable on my part to have ignored her sound advice for my good.

When tears started streaming down my cheeks, she consoled me again, *"That's ok, there's no use crying over spilt milk. Continue with your job for one more year and do B.T. next year. Unfortunately, I do not know the new Principal mentioned by my friend."* I thanked her and went home with a heavy heart. Had I had the gift of the gab, I could have politely given a fitting reply to the Principal's three objections and requested for a seat. First and foremost, English Literature was not offered in our college when I had joined for degree course in 1962. Secondly, Madras University awarded first & second classes mostly for Maths and Science subjects. It was very rare to have even a second class in Arts subjects. Finally, the two-year gap was spent in teaching. He might have relented considering me to be a 'bold and brainy' girl. Those were the vain thoughts going through my mind repeatedly on that fateful day.

But God had had a marvellous plan for me. It unfolded gradually and I acted upon it confidently. Though I shuddered at the very idea of meeting a stranger in a high position alone, I decided to meet the new Principal and beg him to give me a seat for M.A. First, I went to Nirmala College, where I had done my graduation and got a testimonial from Ms. Pillai, the Head of the Department of English. She gave me a remarkable one, highlighting my interest in studies and readiness to be industrious. Armed with two testimonials (the other, by Sr. Kiara), I 'marched' to GAC. In those days, we could meet Principals without much formality. The peon outside the Principal's room took his permission and sent me in. I saw a fair-complexioned middle-aged man with a genial face and benign eyes in the Principal's seat. Just a look at him transported me to a terrain of courage. I greeted him and introduced myself and conveyed the purpose of my visit. Testimonials were handed over for his perusal.

After going through my application form, he said with a smile, *"If you are denied a seat in GAC here, will you not do M.A. course at all?"* I understood the reason for his query. Candidates had to mention in the form four different places according to their preference. Avoiding Madras, Madurai, Trichy, etc., I had written Coimbatore in all four blanks. I said that there were financial constraints due to my father's sudden untimely demise. He asked me to meet him after two days. At the precise time mentioned, I met him again and answered all his questions. Again, I had to meet him the following day when he wanted me to check the list of selected candidates. I literally ran to the notice board. '*And lo! Alice's name led all the rest*' (nothing meritorious; alphabetical order!). When I thanked the Principal with tear-filled eyes, he said, *"Actually, there are some points for your disqualification. I selected you because of your eagerness and determination. Study well; all the best!"* It was like finding a treasure when everything was lost. Later, I went to meet Mrs. Shekar, she was pleasantly surprised at the news. She appreciated my presence of mind and persistence. I thanked her for initiating the idea of M.A. course and taking the trouble for arranging a meeting with the Principal of GAC. Needless to say, without these, I would not have met the present Principal. A curious thought struck me then. If I had applied for B.T., I would have straight away joined the course when the previous Principal had denied me a seat. Everything happens with a reason which will be revealed sooner or later.

I had great respect and admiration for Dr Shabeer Hussain, GAC's new Principal. Two of his daughters were doing undergraduate courses in the same college and we became friends. Once they invited me home. Their mother was very hospitable and we chatted over coffee and snacks. The eldest girl said, *"Presenting testimonial after testimonial, you 'forced' my father (Dr Hussain was not at home) to give you a seat for M.A."* With a shy smile, I said there were only two testimonials. All had a hearty laugh. In 1972, I personally invited Dr Hussain and family for my wedding and their photos are there in my wedding album.

My student days at GAC started in a scary way. Our Head of the Department of English said that there would be no spoon-feeding there as it happened in private colleges. The professors would guide us and we should study on our own with the help of library books. We had classes for two hours in the morning and by noon we were free. After taking books from the library, we would go home to study. In my class, there were 13 students, 9 boys and 4 girls. II M.A. also had the same number of students who were the first batch for English Literature in GAC. When their final exam results were out, only 1 out of 13 had passed! It was a bombshell and for those who believed in the ill omen of '13', it was an additional 'shell'. I had no such apprehension, but wondered how many of us would clear, given the way our classes were conducted. To make matters worse, our college closed for the whole of the third term due to another anti-Hindi agitation in 1968.

Second year began with the arrival of Dr A. E. Varadarajan as our new HOD. All the professors (including him) took classes for us in both the sessions. His method of teaching and guiding sowed seeds of hope in our hearts. Once he said, *"You are all quite good at studies. Why should the result of the seniors frighten you? They were not studious and met with their deserts. If I were the Vice Chancellor of Madras University, I would appoint a Professor of Courage in every college!"* Meanwhile, one girl from our batch left for Madras to pursue her second year there.

With that, the gripping fear of '13' vanished. It would be surprising to know the total amount I spent for the 2-year M.A. course from 1967 – 1969: just Rs. 687, including Rs. 150/- for the final exam fees (source – my 1969 diary). A mere application form for a course in a private college would cost much more than that today!

Our M.A. results, announced at the end of July (1969), was far better. We three girls had passed and some boys, to boot! I applied to three women's colleges in Coimbatore. Sri Avinashilingam Home Science College for women called me for an interview. My appointment there as Lecturer in English can be said in Julius Caesar's words – *'Veni, vidi, vice'*! Classes were in full swing when I met Mrs. Sumathi Menon, the HOD of English there. She received my application when another newly appointed lady had sent in her regret letter. With the timetable prepared for her, Mrs. Menon met me on 3rd August in all urgency. After a question-answer session, she asked me to meet Dr Rajammal P. Devadas (Principal) the next morning. The Principal had already been apprised of my credentials and so Dr Devadas straightaway said, *"You should work hard for the progress of our students. Occasionally, you would be asked to come on Sundays for meetings. Do you agree to that?"* Words failed me miserably. I nodded and said I would put my heart and soul into the work. She continued, *"You are appointed as lecturer here. You can receive the order from the office."* The interview was over! I thanked her and came out heaving a huge sigh of relief.

Within seconds my relief took wings. Mrs. Menon was waiting for me in the next room (college office) and as she congratulated me, we heard the bell ring. Handing over the timetable sheet to me, she took me to the adjoining gallery class where a 'crowd' stood up and greeted the HOD. Mrs. Menon introduced me to the girls and left. My deafening heartbeats must have reached her ears too. Divine Grace alone prevented me from fainting! With a weak smile, I greeted the girls. How could a dumb soul like me, without any preparation, engage a hundred or so girls for one hour?! Desperate inward prayer was 'answered' from above. I started the class with a brief self-introduction and asked them to introduce themselves giving the name, major subject chosen, ambition in life etc. It was a combined English class for the first-year students of Maths, Physics and Chemistry. The large number of students happened to be a blessing and nearly half an hour was spent in that 'exercise'. Then I wrote a topic on the blackboard and asked them to write an essay on it for two pages in neat, legible handwriting without mistakes. I said it would help me assess their knowledge in English. It was surely enough for the other half-hour! I went the rounds with overwhelming gratitude to the Almighty. Thus after 'conducting' a class, I got my appointment order. The girls were happy to get back their corrected papers in the next English class.

In retrospect, I had wondered many a time about God's abundant blessing on that day! If Dr Devadas (a great orator) had asked me to make a speech on a topic for two minutes, she would have sent me away as unfit to be a lecturer! With the next seven years of my work there, my cup of joy was full. I value the good name I earned there more than the salary I got. At the time of becoming the senior-most member in the Department and eventually the HOD, I resigned to take care of my two little children. Though Jose did not approve of my action, I never regretted my decision. I felt that I did what a wise mother would do under the circumstances. I was jobless only for two months after I left Home Science College. I became a tuition teacher in a nearby Boys' school and taught English and Tamil for the seventh and eight standard students in the hostel. The timing suited me well – one hour before and after school hours. The long and short of it – I could earn more than half the amount of a lecturer's pay in two hours of teaching, six days a week. I found immense happiness in teaching those slow learners. It also provided more time for me to spend with my kids at home.

In mid-1978, we left Coimbatore when the Head Office of MALCO, where Jose was working, shifted to the factory site at Mettur. Since there was no college in Mettur then, I joined Malco Vidyalaya Senior Secondary School run by the MALCO management as Post Graduate Teacher (PGT) in English. Unlike the college interview, here five middle-aged men (including the Principal) interviewed me. A volley of questions followed the formal greeting. Four decades later, today I remember only one question – Who wrote the following lines:

'For men may come and men may go / But I go on forever.' With my immediate response, Alfred Lord Tennyson, in the poem, 'The Brook', the questioner seemed to be surprised and glad. Finally, they wanted me to teach a lesson imagining them to be students. Later I came to know that they were high-ranking officials in MALCO and their children were studying in Malco School. No wonder, they gave me a thorough test! I marvelled at my interviews in a college and later in a school. God knew when I could do what and 'arranged' things accordingly.

Five years later, MALCO Head Office shifted again, this time to Madras. While bidding farewell to Malco Vidyalaya, Mr. V. Balasubramanian, the Principal praised my devoted service to the school and gave me a worthy testimonial. Mr. K. Subbaiah, an officer in MALCO, in his capacity as the Secretary of the School (parent of my student) issued a finely worded testimonial. Those two were of immense use to me to procure a job in Madras. While working in Malco Vidyalaya, I completed B.Ed. degree through correspondence course in 1983.

I had to work in a school in Mettur in the absence of a college there. But in Madras, I could not get a Lecturer's post as rules had changed by then. Either M.Phil. or Ph.D. was imperative for college teaching. My first job in Madras was a temporary one in a CBSE school – Sindhi Model Senior Secondary School in Kilpauk. Our three children were admitted to the same school. Jacob, Mary & Joseph had to write entrance tests for VII, III & II classes respectively. Since they were good in studies, I was confident that they would do well. But the results shocked me as all three had failed in Hindi and Jacob scored 30% in Maths. Jacob's failure in Maths puzzled me as he had always scored above 95% in Malco School. I felt sad when the School Correspondent said that my children were not up to the standard of their school. However, Jacob proved himself by scoring 100 marks in Maths within two months in VII std. and mostly in the subsequent classes. Finally, he got centum in Maths in X std Public Examination too! I had been praying for such an achievement right from the time of his admission in Sindhi School. *'More things are wrought by prayer than this world dreams of'* - Lord Tennyson. Jacob was in Kerala when the X result was published. Jose and I went to Sindhi School and our joy knew no bounds when we saw the happy news prominently displayed there: *'Congratulations to Jacob K. Jose on getting National Rank in Mathematics in the 1987 CBSE X Examination.'* The school later gave him a copper shield with all the details – his name, school's name, class, year and with the words: *'National Rank Holder'* engraved on it. His name is still up there on the school's Roll of Honor list for the year 1986-'87.

Three years after settling in Bangalore, once again I was enamoured of pursuing studies at the age of 53! I decided to do M.A. in Gandhian Literature through the Distance Learning Programme of Madurai Kamaraj University. In 1999, I paid the full amount for the course and received all the study material. Jose even accompanied me once to Madurai to attend contact class. Despite all that, I had to give up that course mid-way. As an ardent admirer of the Mahatma, I have read a great deal about him. I have a good collection of books on him and by him. Through my teaching career and otherwise, I have consciously spread Gandhian principles among others, especially the youth. I, therefore, thought it was God's Will that I need not study about Gandhiji just to have one more feather in my cap!

Education has for its object the formation of character.

– Herbert Spencer

9

Before and after Marriage

Truth has always been dear to my heart. Even as a little girl, when circumstances forced me to lie, I would be sad and ashamed. I consoled myself considering them to be white lies. But even such lies could create problems later. Moreover, the ancient story, 'Wolf, wolf' teaches us that lies said in jest could also be dangerous. Tamil saint-poet, Thiruvalluvar says:

Lying has the nature of truth;

If it brings forth good, sans blemish.

Only saintly people could utter such 'good lies'! A classic example of a pious person lying and bringing forth good is the Bishop in Victor Hugo's world-famous novel, 'Les Misérables'. With a well-meant lie, the Bishop provided an opportunity for Jean Val Jean to repent and turn a new leaf in his life.

Even from my preteen years I had been dreaming of doing something great. The idea of invention or discovery fascinated me. To my innocent and ignorant mind then, it seemed that everything had already been found out. I thought I had nothing more to explore. But, the knowledge that by 'tapping' on the head of a 'mouse', one can go round the world makes me dizzy. The very modern way is mere 'touch'!

In my growing years, cough 'visited' me often. My continual cough used to disturb everyone's sleep at night. A brilliant idea suddenly occurred, i.e., to toll the knell for cough! I could invent a medicine to bid permanent farewell to cough. Those who take it, should never ever cough in their lives. My thoughts were in the late 1950s, but such a medicine is still not available! Years rolled by and I was painfully aware of the fact that I was neither competent nor courageous to achieve anything meritorious. Then another idea popped up. I could realize my dream through my children. Thus, I built many a castle in the air.

Reading has always been my favourite pastime. In early teenage, I read mostly love and detective stories – all in Tamil. During college days, I switched over to books of the same genre in English. Some of the books I got from my friends had too much sex in them and I read them with curiosity. On account of it, I considered myself a 'bad girl' in those days. Years later, I understood that such interest was natural at that age. Reading books of that kind went to the point of satiety and fear gripped me when I thought of marriage. What about my 'dream children' if I did not get married? I even thought how wonderful it would be if one got babies with no sex involved.

Years later, on sharing that peculiar thought with Mummy (aged 70), her immediate response shocked me, *"Oh, you wanted to have babies without sinning!"* How could Mummy, who gave birth to seven children, have such an idea? Once while reading the Bible, King David's words in Psalm 51 struck me with surprise: *"My mother conceived me in sin."*. Appachan and Mummy were in the habit of reading Malayalam Bible daily. Certainly, Mummy's words were an echo of this verse. One day, she asked me whether I knew how a baby was formed. Her idea was that a drop of blood from the heart went into the womb and developed into a baby. I almost burst into laughter; but her seriousness and sincerity checked me in time. As she had studied only up to eighth class, lack of knowledge in science could be the reason, I presumed. Another curious thought of hers: In the beginning babies came through the mouth and human race was noble-minded. When the birth mode changed, people became debased. On pondering over Mummy's ideas, the mysticism clothed in metaphorical language astonished me. Heart is the seat of love and mouth spreads wisdom and knowledge. The would-be parents, especially the mother should think, speak and do good things while copulation, conception and during pregnancy in order to get good and intelligent children. I felt Mummy's words were due to God-induced thoughts.

Before marriage, there were a few 'chances' for me to fall in love. But as a fatherless girl, I was protective about our family's honour. Love affairs and love marriages are generally shunned in our society, especially in those days. Anyway, God had not written such a chapter in my 'Life's Book'! While doing B.A., two youths travelling in the same bus used to smile at me. I was flattered but pretended not to notice it. I can never forget a daily ritual during the M.A. course at GAC in Coimbatore. As soon as I entered the college some boys standing under a tree would sing a popular Tamil cine song – '*Nooraandu kaalam vaazhga*' (May you live to be a hundred). I inwardly welcomed that 'blessing' but would walk past them with a straight face.

To reach GAC, I had to walk a little distance after alighting from the bus. A student of our college used to come on his bicycle at the same time. One day he stopped the cycle and said, "*Alice, I'd like to talk to you for a few minutes.*" Had I not been a weak-kneed person, I might have fallen in love with that handsome guy. In those days, generally, girls could not be even friends with boys. So, I told him not to follow me on the road as I had nothing to talk to him. Never once did he come after that. Even in college, on seeing me, he would turn his face and walk away. I felt sorry but could not help it.

In the first year of my working in Home Science College, a youth mostly standing near me in the bus, used to whisper my name. He must have been the brother of one of my students. At times he would offer to buy the ticket for me. I just ignored him and bought my ticket. Once I shared my experience with my colleagues. Later they started teasing me, "*Did your '10 paise' come today?*" My bus fare from home to college was 10 paise in 1969! Today when I read news items like – '*The girl committed suicide when her lover deserted her*' or '*After losing her virginity, the girl knew her lover to be a cheat*' – I feel sad and angry. Why should women be so weak and foolish? If the girls are shy or afraid when men make advances, it induces the latter to be more 'hero-like'. To be indifferent is the best way. Despite that if trouble continues, girls should look at them with fiery eyes and the glare mostly works. Courage and determination help women in such situations.

To the dismay of my family, my marriage could not be arranged even as I was nearing 26. Then all of a sudden it got fixed through a member (Mrs. Elizabeth Mathew) of our Jacobite parish. K C Jose, son of Chacko and Mary (Catholics from Cochin), had lost his father at 15. In 1962, when he joined MALCO in Coimbatore, Tamil was Greek to him! He spoke Tamil fluently by the time of our wedding in 1972. During leisure, he also worked as an LIC agent.

Before marriage, I had to change over to the Catholic faith. At that time, I did not like the attitude of most Catholics, who believed that salvation could be only through Catholicism. Fr. Thaikkadavil, the Jacobite priest who helped us when Appachan passed away, advised me: *"All Christians worship Jesus Christ whatever be their denominations. So don't worry about it. See that the family is good and the young man has no bad habits. Leave the rest to God Alimighty."*

I was sent to a nun at Alvernia Convent in Coimbatore to know more about Catholic faith and learn prayers by heart. At this juncture, I had to go to Trichy to attend an All-India English Teachers' Meet. Due to lack of time, I could not memorize the prayers. I said the prayers of Jacobite faith and begged the pardon of the Catholic priest who was to marry us. I pointed out that the ultimate aim was to know whether I knew my daily prayers. With a benign smile, the priest said, *"I understand, my child. There isn't much difference in these prayers of the two faiths. Moreover, since Jacobites venerate Mother Mary, there are also many similarities. However, you must learn everything after marriage."* With his kind and wise words, my opinion about Catholics changed for the better!

On Monday, the 10th of January, 1972 our wedding was solemnized in the Holy Trinity Church at Ramanathapuram in Coimbatore. The reception was arranged in Woodlands Hotel opposite GAC, where I did my M.A. course. Jose and I stayed in our home in Five Corner for two days and went to his home at Kuzhupilly in Ernakulam district. Akkal and her husband accompanied us to 'officially hand over the bride' to her new family. They attended the reception there and returned to Coimbatore. After four days, we both came back and reported to our duties. Prior to marriage, Jose had set up a rented house in Nanjundapuram area which was quite far away from Home Science College. Before going to office, he used to drop me at college on scooter.

My four sisters-in-law are: Ammini (elder to Jose), Celine and Baby (twins of my age) and the youngest, Ruby. Ammini and Celine were married by then. Even at the time of the proposal I had noted many similarities between our families. I made up my mind to shoulder the responsibility as the only daughter-in-law. Meanwhile, a quarter of my salary was given to Mummy every month. I could not continue that after one year as we had a baby by then. Soon came the marriages of Baby and Ruby one after the other and their deliveries followed. We had two more children during the same period. Thus, we were on a 'spending spree' for the first few years of our married life. Of course, it was only for the most important necessities of life!

My mother-in-law was an unusual type of person. Her mother once told me, "*Since she was born four years after our marriage, her father brought her up as a tomboy. She lords over everyone including me. Be patient my child, God will reward you.*" Would any mother give such a picture about her own daughter to her grandson's wife? I decided not to tell anyone about it as long as our septuagenarian Grandma was alive. God cemented that decision for twenty more years as Grandma died at the ripe old age of 95 in 1995. By then my wish to reveal the 'secret' had a natural death!

Amma had always kept her distance from me. Initially puzzled, I realized later it was due to the fear experienced by most women (especially widows) who had only one son. At times, her rude behaviour was too much to bear. My sorrow deepened as Jose was either silent or took sides with her. Shedding tears became my routine and both found fault with me for that too. My self-respect prevented me from revealing my plight to Mummy or siblings. One day, Jose complained to Uncle Kurian that there was no peace at home as I could not adjust with his mother. Only then did my folks realize the miserable life I had been leading there. Anyway, I decided to stick to my almost broken marriage for the sake of my kids. That happened to be one of the wisest decisions of my life.

Vicissitudes of life led me to take certain spiritual decisions. When I vowed to speak only truth at the age of 30, I knew I would have to go through fire and water at times. Painful experiences and my 'experiments with truth' pushed me to the level of praying for my death. Yet, the thought of committing suicide never crossed my mind. What I learnt in Sunday Bible classes when young, stood me in good stead. It is said, '*Man's extremity is God's opportunity*' and it proved to be true in my life. In Exodus, God said to Moses that he would '*harden Pharaoh's heart to multiply his signs in the land of Egypt*'. God likewise hardened Amma's heart for my good, I concluded. To tell the truth, at times she used hurtful words even to her own children. But I was hard hit as the only daughter-in-law. Once Celine said, "*Chechi, how do you adjust with our mother? My mother-in-law is very kind.*" Grandma's words echoed in me. Sometimes I felt sorry for Amma. Even if she had wished, she could not have changed.

The old house in Kuzhupilly was sold in 1974, two years after our marriage as the only son of the family had decided to stay in Tamil Nadu. Amma spent her last days in 'Maria Nivas' – a house constructed by us in North Paravoor, some years after Jacob's death in 1998. A woman was engaged to stay with Amma, as she was 80 years old then. Three of her daughters living nearby visited her often. Towards the end, Amma calmed down considerably. When I met her in 2006, she (86) did not talk to me much; but her kind tone said it all. After her departure to the heavenly abode in May that year, a relative shared with us what Amma had told him, "*Whatever happens, my daughter-in-law will not tell a lie. She is good-natured and more patient than my four daughters.*" I thanked God as my endurance was amply rewarded.

Happiness in marriage is entirely a matter of chance.

– Jane Austen

10

Blooms of Career Life

The rich and varied experiences during my four-decade-teaching career are truly edifying. Of the twenty institutions I served in five cities, the longest was as a Lecturer in English in Sri Avinashilingam Home Science College for Women in Coimbatore – seven years from 1969 – 1976. Today it is Avinashilingam University for Women.

It is for others to say how efficient my teaching was; but with sincerity, I can vouch for my being a good teacher throughout my career. I had never done any of the following which characterize certain not-fit-to-be teachers: shouting at students; using improper words; flinging their notebooks or test papers or tapping their heads with them; making an indignant walk-out when students misbehave, etc. Needless to say, about some 'rare species' who punish their wards in unthinkable ways. On the other hand, some friendly teachers are too intimate with teenage students engaging them in lengthy pleasantries. This kind of attitude is a waste of time for both the teacher and the taught and at times goes to the extent of students taking advantage of their preceptors.

I had always been kind and strict at the same time. Once a harrowing experience in Home Science College made me walk out of the classroom with bitter tears. First year degree students were taking down some important notes dictated by me after a poetry class. A girl in the last row kept whispering to her neighbour and seemed to be not writing. When asked for her notebook, she immediately brought it to me. Nothing was amiss. I felt embarrassed before the class of about 60 students. On seeing her 'victorious' smile while returning to her seat, a spark flashed within me. I commanded in a calm voice to give back her friend's book and bring her own notebook. The girl turned pale at the unexpected turn of event. I had just realized the spark and was not aware of what I was going to say. In case she had brought her own book the first time, I would have put myself to shame by my second command. Despite her defiant act, I did not shout at her. Eyes brimming with tears, I hurried out of the class and went to the staff room for the English department on the same floor. Fortunately, there was no one there. Within minutes, another lecturer (Padmasani) came in a hurry to take a book. My teary eyes and reddened face puzzled my colleague, but I was not in a position to answer her queries. By then, the class leader brought the errant student to me. When Padmasani knew what had happened, she scolded the girl for being wilfully cunning. She made her apologize to me and left the staff room. My friend's sudden appearance was indeed a godsend as I could compose myself and return to class.

Another time, after conducting a grammar class for PUC students, I elicited a pertinent sentence from them individually. An example given by a bright student who had completed her schooling in Malaysia did not make sense. She was made to repeat it but to no avail. An express prayer brought a response on wings! I asked her to write the sentence on the blackboard. I do not remember the sentence now (happened in 1971); but what confused me was clear when I looked at the first word – 'Industries'. It had been heard as 'in the streets' both the times! No wonder, the sentence did not make any sense.

The matter did not end there. Her writing on the board was illegible with letters impossibly tiny. She was given a daily exercise of copywriting. In three months, there was good improvement. After PUC, she went off to some foreign country for further studies. Three months later, I received a letter from her to the college address. Her main message in it: *"Dear Miss, I have no words to thank you. I've heard the comment – 'What a horrible handwriting' – many a time from my parents and teachers. They had also advised me to improve it. But you guided me on how to go about it. You even corrected the shape of the letters as if I were a kid. I won't forget you."* Though there was my share in the good result, I would give more credit to that student, Sakina Mukundan for her total involvement, eagerness and perseverance. The reaction of most other college girls would have been indifference, if not outright defiance. We cannot be strict with college students on such matters as we do with school children.

In my first year of college teaching, I asked Mrs. Menon, our HOD, whether it was proper on my part to visit a sick student in the hospital. The girl had requested through a classmate her wish to meet me. Mrs. Menon advised me to avoid it as it would be a compelling precedent. At home, Uncle Kurian warned me as the girl's illness could be infectious. I felt sad on knowing her family background – poverty and illiteracy. The next evening again her friend begged me on her behalf and we both went to the hospital. I touched the forehead of the frail girl and asked her not to worry as it would worsen her condition. Telling her to pray for quick recovery, I assured her of my prayers too. She thanked me with tear-filled eyes and said that my presence and words brought peace to her mind.

When I shared this experience with Mrs. Menon the next day, she quipped, *"If you have no other work, carry on with such visits!"* In a few days, the girl started coming to college regularly. One day, she confided in me her difficulty in coping with studies because of her Tamil-medium education at school. I encouraged her referring to similar plight of mine in PUC. Though she passed, she did not join the degree course due to ill-health. Some months later, her friend brought the sad news of her sudden death and it was a shock to me. However, I thanked God for giving me the wisdom to meet the hapless girl despite warnings; otherwise, I would have carried the guilt feeling to my grave.

Of the different groups of PUC in Home Science College, one had all the Tamil-medium students. They had passed the school final exam with good marks in all subjects except English. Lecturers were reluctant to teach that class as their knowledge in English was lamentable. So, the Principal gave us the responsibility in rotation. In the year of my teaching such a group, an amusing incident happened. While returning test papers, students were called individually to my seat and were told how to correct their mistakes. After a while, some students were seen standing in the class. When asked for the reason, one student said it was as per my command. I had not given any such order and wanted clarification. Another student boldly answered in Tamil (not allowed during English period) as she might have felt she could not be precise in English, *"Miss, after explaining our mistakes, you finally said 'stand' to some of us."* Totally confused, I tried to recollect some of my general comments; spelling should be improved; wrong construction of sentences; knowledge of grammar - nil, etc. All of a sudden, it struck me what the matter was. 'Nil' in Tamil (the pronunciation) is the imperative form of the verb, 'stand'! I was about to laugh but held myself back. A flash-back left me with mixed feelings of sympathy and empathy. When I shared my PUC days of somewhat similar experiences, they became saucer-eyed! The rapport, that ensued after that helped me handle the class with greater cooperation on their part.

In the first two years of my college teaching, I had admission duty for some days during summer vacation. Once a candidate accompanied by her brother had come for degree course in Tamil Literature. Handing out the application form, I sent them to the Tamil Lecturer. The next day when they came, the young man asked me whether I liked the poems of Bharathiyar – a great modern Tamil poet. I replied in the affirmative and immersed myself in the duties at hand. The next two times when he came with his sister, he talked to me for a few minutes about Bharathiyar, Jane Austen and Annadurai (former Chief Minister of Tamil Nadu – a great orator and writer). Since he behaved very decently, I did not mind his words about the great people for a few minutes. My part in the talks would be mostly monosyllabic. Once when he asked me about my family, bare minimum details were shared.

Some days later, one evening my sister said there was a visitor for me. It was a surprise to see the student's brother seated in our drawing room. On seeing me, he stood up and courteously greeted me. Reciprocating, I requested him to take his seat. He began his usual effusion on Bharathiyar, Austen and Annadurai. Talking about the same people repeatedly pointed to some kind of abnormality in him. Suddenly, I felt the genesis of fear within me. I got up and said politely, *"We shall meet in the college, if necessary"*, emphasizing the last two words. He took the cue and left immediately. I felt sad and ashamed as it amounted to insulting him. But being more hospitable would be an indirect invitation to more such visits.

After he left, 'storm' ensued. All at home blamed me for inviting a young man home. I was on the verge of tears as I had not done so. With a brief account of his eccentric nature, I said his visit was a most unexpected one. Marykutty questioned me, *"When you are aware of his strange behaviour, why did you allow him to sit and talk?"* I was at my wits' end and contrary to my nature, I shouted, *"I'm a lecturer in a reputed college. How can you expect me to behave in an impolite manner to the brother of our student? When I realized the trend of his talk, didn't I indirectly show him the door?"* All became silent; calm after the storm!

Marykutty could not be blamed for what she said. Since we were girls of marriageable age, boys, including our younger brother's friends were received only in the veranda. Young men who came with their parents alone were allowed to enter the house! Uncle Kurian was so strict about such 'rules' that we used to be irritated at times. (Later in life, I understood the value of those restrictions.) Fortunately, Uncle was not in station when the 'gale' of the queer guy blew!

The next day, the Tamil Lecturer enquired teasingly, why I 'drove away' her student's brother when he came home! Sensing my shock, she added, *"He's a thorough gentleman. When he knew you are an English Lecturer with great interest in Tamil Literature, he became enthusiastic. He is zealous about the literature of both these languages."* I explained to her the whole episode highlighting our family discipline. She then assured me that I had dealt with the situation in the right way. I felt relieved with those words from a married person much older than me.

After a few days, I received a letter from him to the college address. He had written some anecdotes about the same trinity: Bharathi, Anna & Austen! Though he had given his address, I did not reply. Yet at least twice a month, similar letters (nothing personal) kept coming. At last, his obsession was revealed through one letter. He believed me to be Jane Austen reborn! 'Literature madness' of the highest order! Where was the similarity between Austen & Alice? One, a great writer whose novels are admired world over and the other, an ordinary teacher with no writing ability. That year end (1971), I received a beautiful birthday card on December 16th with the words, *'Happy Birthday to Jane Austen'*. Austen's year of birth was known to me, but the month and date got impressed in my mind only by his greeting card. After my marriage in January 1972, his letters stopped but the birthday greetings came every December without fail for some more years. When the experience was shared with Jose, he considered him a quirk.

With self-realization years later, many thoughts of old times rushed to my mind and Jane Austen's was one among them. I re-read her life and times. During her relatively short life (1775 – 1817), contemporary England underwent many changes in social life and literature. But her critics averred that she wrote nothing about them. Her novels centred around the clashes in families due to doubts, prejudices, ideological differences, etc. Finally, all problems being solved, they had happy endings. With that, surfaced the similarity between Austen and Alice – yes, they are WORDS! Austen's fascinating written words produced world-class novels, whereas my humble spoken words help bring about peace in some quarrelling families of kith and kin. Some readers might doubt my sanity now. To be sure, everyone has a streak of eccentricity in them – whether it is positive or negative – that is the question!

Here is a note on a beautiful porcelain tea-set gifted by the PUC students for my wedding. For more than five decades now, hundreds have been offered tea in it. Still, it has not lost its gloss. Our maids never had a chance to wash those cups and saucers, lest I should not be writing about it now. The tea-set has 'travelled' a lot – 14 houses in

5 cities. Whenever tea is served in those cups, I am happy to talk about the loving gift of my students with gusto. Once during Teachers' Day celebration in the church, I was pleasantly surprised to hear Fr. Saji, our then Parish Priest mentioning the age of my teacups and asking the Catechism teachers to treasure the gifts given by their students. At the end of the function, some 'booked' for tea in those cups!

The next 'long' service was at Malco Vidyalaya in Mettur from 1978 to 1983. It was a co-educational school and the staff were both men and women. A senior lady teacher warned me about some unruly boys in class 11 when I joined there in the middle of the academic year. Mischief-makers could be made out when they stood up to greet me on the first day – tall boys with sprouting moustache and a playful gleam in their eyes. When I gave a brief self-introduction, one of 'them' wanted to know why I had come to teach in a school after being lecturer in a college. Without showing it's-none-of-your-business attitude, I gave him the reasons – first and foremost, no college in Mettur at that time, secondly, my responsibility as a mother with three little children and finally, MALCO Management requesting my service due to urgent need of a post graduate teacher for handling senior secondary section. The six-footer grinned boyishly.

Once, the same boy argued with me on a certain passage in the lesson. He seemed to be taking pleasure in disturbing the class with his pointless reasoning. I said, *"Stop quibbling, R___. Please come to the staff room in the evening and I'll clarify your doubts. Don't waste everyone's time now."* He asked me the meaning of 'quibbling' seated in a don't-care manner. He was asked to stand while talking to his teacher. He stood up at once but looked humiliated. I continued, *"I have been informed about how some of you worry the lady teachers especially. If you trouble teachers, you'll certainly regret it later"*. His immediate reaction shocked me, *"Miss, are you cursing me?"* I said in a calm voice, *"A good teacher never curses students. When you realize your mistakes, you'll be sorry for them. How can this be a curse? You are yet to grow in wisdom to understand the import of my words. Comments like, 'you'll end up achieving nothing'; 'you'll not come up in life' would amount to curses. I reiterate good parents and teachers would never curse their wards."* As I concluded my brief 'lecture', the bell rang and I left the classroom. He came after me and begged pardon. I patted him on the shoulder and thanked God Almighty!

There was a bitter experience because of a teacher in the same school. Boys used to squirm when he playfully slapped on their backs. I told the Principal to warn him about it. Two days later that teacher came to me, *"Madam, does my patting the students look like slapping to you? Alright, here is your son, a clever boy* (7-year-old Jacob was beside me). *I like him very much."* So saying, he pinched Jacob's cheeks hard with both his hands. My child cried out in pain. *"What are you crying for? How softly I held your cheeks!"* – then with a triumphant smile, he walked away. I was too shocked to utter a word. A few more complaints about that drawing teacher finally saw him out of the school. I prayed that he should take up any profession other than teaching!

In Sindhi Model Senior Secondary School in Madras, the encounter was with the School Management. In the annual examination timetable, I was surprised to see an exam marked for all classes on Good Friday. The school was mainly for the Sindhi Community. Almost all the students and most of the teachers, including the Principal, were Hindus. When the Principal was asked about it, he said it was the decision of the management. I then requested an elderly person of the Management to declare Good Friday a holiday as it was a day of solemnity. He at once pointed out that Christian schools did not declare holiday for Maha Shivaratri. I indicated, *"Sir, Hindus have many festivals like Deepavali, Ganesh Chaturthi, Ram Navami, Krishna Jayanthi, Saraswati Puja, Vijaya Dasami, Pongal, etc. and all are holidays. Christians require holidays for only three occasions of which Christmas comes during the winter vacation and Easter is always on a Sunday. It is unfortunate that you deny holiday on the death anniversary of Jesus Christ".*

My arguments convinced him to the point of condescending to allow me to take leave on that day. (Generally, leave was not granted on exam days) Regarding my children's exams on that day, he asked the Principal to assess their performance throughout the year for the particular subject for promotion. When I asked about the other

Christian staff and students, his curt comment was that I need not be their mouthpiece. The next day, the Principal congratulated me on my partial success saying that the Management never relented on such matters. Surprisingly, the next year, Good Friday was declared a holiday. (I worked there only for six months, but my children continued in the same school.) Sooner or later, our sincere efforts will bear fruits. *'Do your duty without expecting the result'* – says Bhagavad Gita.

In the next academic year (1984-85), I taught in Jain Vidyalaya at Vepery in Madras. Most of the students there belonged to the Jain community. Their parents were business people and most were not much educated. Once, in class 11, a boy put forward his 'valuable' suggestion to me, *"Miss, we are not going to be highly qualified to become doctors or engineers. After completing 12th std, we would enter our family business. What we need is just a School Leaving Certificate and some spoken English to converse with our customers. Please don't waste your time and energy teaching us English grammar!"* How concerned about his teacher was he! I said, *"You are absolutely correct. Anyway, to get the certificate, you have to pass 12th after completing 11th this year. We award cent per cent marks for correct grammar answers but you cannot expect high marks for short answers and essays. So, to enter family business at the earliest, the short-cut is to learn English grammar."* The class burst out laughing.

In the same school, a strange phenomenon occurred. A student from eighth standard would be at times possessed by the spirit of one of the Jain Gurus. She would then go round to the classes and all the students and teachers should individually bow before her to get her blessings. When the 'ritual' was done in my class, she looked at me. When I did not seek her blessing, she left for the next class. My students were aghast! *"Miss, why didn't you get Guruji's blessing? You may come to some harm"* – one boy said in all sincerity. I allayed his fears saying that I considered her only as a student who should have sought the teacher's blessing. Later when I told the Principal (a Hindu) about taking the girl to a psychiatrist, he said, *"Didn't I tell you at the time of appointment how to deal with things here? The Jain Community would not let us interfere with their belief. She does it once or twice a year and we have to adjust!"*

I was a part-time lecturer in English in Gurukul Lutheran Theological College and Research Institute in Madras for the next 3 years (1985-88). The appointment order was given with two weeks' time to join duty, as students for B.D. (Bachelor of Divinity) course had to come from different parts of India. After a week, a slight swelling was seen in my neck below the right cheek. With severe throat pain, I found it difficult to speak. (Jose had earlier suggested to me to take up office work in a good company for better salary. Being a 'born teacher', I could not imagine doing any other job.) When voice (very important for teaching) bade goodbye, I anxiously rushed to the doctor. With medicines, throat pain subsided, but there was still a disturbing factor. The small tumour gradually grew to the size of a big gooseberry. The doctor suggested a minor surgery, but my worry was about joining duty at Gurukul in three days!

Jose and I met Dr D. W. Jesudoss, Principal of Gurukul the next morning to apprise him of the surgery. He allowed me a week more to join duty and took us to meet the Lutheran Bishop residing in the campus. Bishop Dorairaj Peter led us to the chapel in the premises and prayed for the success of the surgery. They both wished me speedy recovery. Their concern and empathy moved me to tears. They could have justifiably cancelled my appointment as I had not started working in their institution.

All the B.D. students were either graduates or post-graduates and some with work experience in different fields. A few of them were older than me (I was 39). They had their degrees in vernaculars of different states and my work was to help them improve their spoken and written English. There were no textbooks for English in B.D. course. I was given the responsibility to choose the pattern for the whole programme and I was happy to take up the challenge. They had English only in the first year of the course and I taught different groups in the three years that I worked there. Gurukul had the Diamond Jubilee Celebration then and the souvenir released on the occasion had two poems of mine, one each in English and Tamil (given in the appendix).

Bimal Kujur, a Gurukul student from Bihar, who had a peculiar accent, once said, *"Madam, my English was considered the best in our village. Now, I realize my knowledge of English is rather poor."* Three years later, I received a letter from his native place where he had been teaching in a school. He mentioned in it the way he demonstrated his gratitude to me. Once a week, he would ask his students the name of his English teacher at Gurukul and they would chorus, 'Mrs. Alice K. Jose' followed by happy clapping!

Since my work in Gurukul was from 10am to 1pm, I took English class (daily one hour) for about 60 students of Diploma in Commerce course in an institute run by nuns at Pudupet in Madras. During that time, there was an opportunity for me to go to Mother Teresa University for Women in Kodaikanal for a few days. The University had requested the Superior of the convent to send two teachers for taking English and Accountancy classes for the non-teaching staff there. It was in December and that became convenient for me as Christmas vacation was for the whole month in Gurukul.

Tickets were booked for the Accountancy master and me two weeks earlier and then the unexpected happened. Three days prior to our travelling, I had an attack of flu with cough and cold. With medicines, fever was arrested in two days, but cough and cold continued unabated. Jose wanted me to cancel the trip as Kodaikanal would be very cold in December. He warned me that instead of my teaching them, their nursing me would be the result otherwise. To me, last minute cancellation was unthinkable as it might upset the University's plans. I took up the journey prayerfully. Most surprisingly, cough and cold did a vanishing act when I reached Kodaikanal! Usually the 'twins' would leave me gradually. Atheists might attribute it to medicines; but it was my firm belief that God helped me keep my word to the University. Classes went on well and Dr. Padmasani Kannan (former colleague and friend in Home Science College), the then Assistant Registrar in the University was doubly happy as she was in-charge of the programme.

Leisure in Kodaikanal was spent in sight-seeing, including boating in the lake. After the classes, when everyone left for home, only we (master & I) and the watchman were in the vast campus which was calm due to winter vacation. The beautiful scenery around was captivating. We had a stroll and returned to our rooms. After an early supper and reading for some time, I went to sleep. It was a large room with all amenities including a room heater.

Next morning the master came to my room with a pale face and asked me if I slept well. He confessed, *"Madam, I couldn't get a wink of sleep because of the eerie silence and the sudden loud noise of the howling winds. The glowing room heater looked like a spirit. Do you believe in ghosts? Weren't you frightened, Madam?"* I almost burst out laughing but checked in time. As a mother, I instilled courage in that youth (about 26 years) and wished him sound sleep in the following nights. Being 41 then, I thought that at 26, my plight could have been the same!

Due to my part-time job, I took up the work of compiling a concise English-English-Tamil dictionary during that period. When I came to know it was intended for Tamil-medium high school students, I had special interest in it. After 16 months of hard work, I completed it. Sura Publications first published it in April 1989. There were many more editions and it is still in the market. For Dr Samuel Johnson, who compiled the first dictionary in English, it would have been a back-breaking job. Likewise, the first compilers in any language would have toiled at it. Those who compiled later would have found it comparatively easier. But from personal experience, I realized that such work was difficult and time-consuming. Though I referred to three large dictionaries, I used my discretion in the selection of words and meanings both in English and Tamil to suit the need of teenagers in Tamil-medium schools. The publisher recognized and appreciated that and entrusted me with the task of compiling a larger dictionary on similar lines. Soon, I became the Principal of a matriculation higher secondary school and gave up the dictionary project in the initial stage itself.

Noble-minded or mean-minded?

One's actions, as touchstone, reveal.

– Thiruvalluvar

11

Pains of a Principled Principal

At the age of 42 (1988), I became the principal of a matriculation higher secondary school for the first time. Principalship continued for eight years but in four institutions of which in one alone, I worked for three years. In two schools, I served for 17 and 19 months. My maiden attempt as the head of a school ended after eight months.

Blue Bells Matriculation Higher Secondary School at Keelkattalai, near Madipakkam, in Madras was the school where I first served as the Principal. It was owned by an individual in his 40s and he was also the correspondent of the school. He proudly declared that he intuitively knew that I would be the principal even while interviewing me. Much to my discomfort, he flatteringly talked about me to others in my presence. Once he said, *"My Principal is a lady with principles."* But everything changed within months.

Soon after joining duty there, we shifted from Kilpauk to Madipakkam to reduce my commute time. Mary was admitted to 8th standard in the same school as Sindhi School was far away from our new residence. Jacob and Joseph had to take the electric train and bus to go to Don Bosco School in Egmore. The great distance caused Jose to go to office with much difficulty. Despite making such changes, I had to quit the school in 8 months' time.

It was rather a new school. Initially, I was kind and mild to everyone. However, when it was taken for weakness, I changed my ways. In one meeting, the teaching and non-teaching staff were exhorted to be more responsible to become good role models to students. In the meantime, the Correspondent (his residence was in one corner of the school campus) came to school almost everyday and interfered with my work. A qualified person in the post seemed to be only for the sake of rules. In short, I could not do my duty with reasonable freedom and peace of mind. Resigning at the end of the academic year presented itself as a solution. Yet, I thought it might do some good to appeal to his better sense. So, before going for Christmas vacation, I handed him a letter wherein mentioning that if staff and students considered me as a mere rubber-stamp, I could not work in the school with self-respect. He was requested to visit the school once a week and discuss the points on which his attention was needed. In between, he could also contact me over the phone, as it might be necessary because of my lack of previous experience as principal.

The school reopened on January 2nd (1989) but the correspondent said nothing about my letter. My personal diary has just four words for Jan 3rd: '*A Day of uncertainty*'. On 4th morning when I reached school, the Correspondent told me outright to quit the institution after handing over everything to a senior teacher. He was ready to give me one month's salary in lieu of the notice period. I was not surprised by his reaction but felt it was unwise of him to send me away in the final term of the academic year. When I offered to complete the year, his retort was, "*I know how to run my school without a principal.*" 'Glad' to say that the school vehicle was provided for me to go home!

Later, parents of some students came home to express their disappointment as they felt my leaving the school was a loss for their children. They said I was the sixth principal there, in two years' time, after the school got approval for +1 & +2 classes. The earlier ones were men, four of whom resigned after serving some months each and the fifth one left within two days. They congratulated me on my 'long service' in the school. It was clear then why he selected me. A woman with no previous experience as principal could be 'easily' made a puppet!

The abrupt way he 'got rid' of me from the school did hurt me initially. But it turned out to be a blessing in disguise. It gave me enough time to search for a suitable school in Madipakkam before the end of the academic year. Secondly, it was a beneficial break from the two-decade-long teaching career with hectic schedule. I valued the third blessing the most. Studying in 8th standard in Blue Bells School, Mary used to score the highest marks in all subjects most of the time. Sarcastic comments by a few reached me indirectly, *'The daughter getting the highest marks is no wonder. Her mother is the principal who receives the manuscripts of all question papers in advance.'* (For my earlier nature, I would have shed copious tears on hearing such an allegation.) But even after my leaving the school, Mary scored the highest marks; once 100% in Physics. Thus, when favour follows unkind allegations, I harbour no ill-feelings towards the ones who are the cause of my sufferings. My faith in the adage, *'Everything happens for good'*, deepens.

In May 1989, I became the Principal of St. Thomas Matriculation Higher Secondary School in the same area. It was run by the members of the Orthodox Syrian Church. In my first year (1989-90), we achieved cent per cent result in the Board Exam. In that year, the then Tamil Nadu Education Minister, Mr. K. Anbazhagan awarded certificates to all the schools which produced cent per cent results mentioning therein the names of the principals. The management, parents, teachers and students of St. Thomas School were extremely happy as they had not had such a good result till then. For the next two years that I served there, the school produced cent per cent result.

My bitter experiences in the previous school taught me to be strict with everyone right from the beginning in St. Thomas School. The advice given by an elderly priest Rev. Fr. Kurian was of great help for that: *"First, surrender your humility totally to the Almighty. When you are in a responsible position, wield your power judiciously and with authority. Otherwise, you won't be able to do justice to your duty. Seek wisdom from above and handle people differently according to their nature. May God bless you!"*

Frankly speaking, at the time of my joining there, St. Thomas School was in a messy state. I prepared some guidelines for teachers after finding out the reasons for the disorder. The fact that the success of a school depends on teamwork was emphasised in its introduction. They were requested to be aware of the nobility of their profession. Students were entrusted to their care seemingly by parents but actually by God. That realization would help them do a better job. In a short time, there was discipline in school and my approach was appreciated.

Apart from my duty as Principal, I taught English grammar and Value Education for classes 10, 11 and 12. Besides that, I took Moral Science for classes 3, 4 and 5. Generally, Principals do not handle primary classes; but my idea was to *'catch them young'* (Gandhiji's exhortation). Once in 4th class, while dealing with the topic of cleanliness, the students were asked how to keep ourselves clean. All the students enthusiastically chorused, *'by bathing everyday'.* When asked about the cleanliness of mind, they gave me a vacant stare. Quoting the Mahatma, *"As water cleanses our body, prayer purifies our mind",* I told them to not ask God for clothes, ornaments, house, car, etc., which can be bought. They should pray for good character, intelligence, memory power, wisdom, courage and sound health. Some might think that it is too idealistic. Could 4th class students understand such high ideals and put them into practice? In my opinion only young children would try to follow them. Teenagers in higher classes would have 'judged' me, *'This madam is not worldly-wise!'* In Value Education classes, those adolescents were made to debate on social evils oppressing India.

Next, they were asked to mention something which would keep them clean besides bathing. A boy stood up to say, *'cutting the nails'.* Amidst laughter, I congratulated him and told them the importance of clipping their nails periodically. A girl said, *'brushing the teeth'* and my question – *'when?'* – resulted in another hearty laughter. To clear my 'doubt', one said, *'in the morning'.* I said, *"You are absolutely correct; but how many of you do it only after getting reminders from your parents?"* When asked about brushing at night, no one answered. I continued, *"More importantly, you must not forget to brush your teeth before going to bed. Massaging your gums well after brushing teeth both the times helps you have good oral health."*

I became the beneficiary of my own teaching in 1990! Till then, I was rather irregular in brushing teeth at night! But, from that night onwards, I did it without fail. Naturally, visiting a dentist happened once in a blue moon! Good teachers practise what they preach and preach what can be practised. At times, a thought pops up: how many of those little ones follow my advice to this day!

Apart from confronting some irresponsible teachers, I had the cooperation of most of the staff in St. Thomas School. Mention must be made of three teachers in particular. Mrs. Bhavani Swaminathan, in her capacity as Headmistress of the school, had been there right from its inception, 20 years earlier. I also had 20 years' experience by then, but in nine institutions in three cities! Bhavani worked with utmost devotion and extended her full support to me.

Mr. Xavier Absalom, the '77-year young man' was the Physical Education teacher. He was indeed a phenomenon! An ex-military man, he had shared with me his traumatic experiences during the II World War when he and the other soldiers were in Burma (now Myanmar). The war had 'presented' him a twisted right wrist after which he learnt to write quite legibly with his left hand. The freedom lover that he was, he lived alone after his wife's death despite having a son and 4 daughters. A dog and a rifle were his companions.

He used to come to school (usually the first one to arrive) riding a bicycle from home, 15 kilometres away. One day when Mr. Absalom came late to school with a bandaged head, his explanation was classic – *"On my way to school this morning, a youngster dashed his cycle against mine and rode away. Perhaps he was in a hurry. I fell on the road and had a small cut on my head. I went to a nearby nursing home for an injection after which they sent me with the bandage."* Not a word against the person who caused him injury, nor did he take a day's leave! Another time he was badly hurt in the boxing ring. When I visited the heavily bandaged old man, he said cheerfully, *"Oh, it's nothing, Madam. I'll be coming to school in two days."* Yes, to a soldier, such injuries were nothing!

Soft-spoken Vasuki was a dedicated young teacher, always willing to take up extra work cheerfully. Her obedience was something rare for a teacher. She was respectful to everyone and her 'specially noticeable respect' for me made her the butt of jokes by some teachers. While talking to me, she would shield her mouth with her fingers. After much persuasion, she revealed the reason – to prevent her spittle falling on me by any mischance! I was reminded of another obedient Vasuki, the wife of Thiruvalluvar, the Tamil saint-poet who lived more than 2000 years ago. Perhaps, that Vasuki's spirit was sent to this Vasuki (name-induced thought!).

At the end of my second year there (1991), Mr. Thomas, the School Manager, completed his term and another person took over the responsibility. In the farewell meeting, Mr. Thomas said, "*Our Principal has sincerity of purpose. If all of you (the staff) cooperate with her, our school will progress well.*" It was a pleasant surprise to me because he was quite reserved and his impatient words earlier had hurt me a few times. I had taken it positively as he was much older than me. Bhavani later shared her opinion about it: "*Thomas sir is not easily satisfied with our work. What he said about you is something very rare.*" The joy one feels when one's sincere work is appreciated is inexplicable. Yet, I had to leave the school after serving there for 3 years due to some personal problems.

Let me bid goodbye to St. Thomas School on a lighter note. Before joining duty there (1989), I had bobbed my hair. One evening, after classes were over, a second standard boy dragged his younger brother to my room and boomed out, "*Madam, Madam, my brother says you are a 'motta thale'* (Tamil for completely shaven head)." I suppressed my laughter. Valid complaint should not be belittled! Touching the LKG boy's hair, I asked him what it was. In a feeble voice he replied, '*hair*'. To my question, "*When I also have hair, how can I be a motta thale?*", he quickly admitted in a frightened voice that I was not. Patting him on the back, I advised him to not comment on elders in such a way. The older boy seemed to be a little disappointed with the way the matter fizzled out.

Soon, I became the Principal of Sree Narayana Mission Senior Secondary School at West Mambalam in Madras. The school was run by the followers of Sree Narayana Guru (1855 – 1928), a great soul of Kerala. He brought about reformation in the society of his times through revolutionary ideas and actions. His clarion call was: *'One caste, one religion, one God for man'.* Another famous saying of his: *'Whatever be the religion, man must be good.'* Ironically, religion played a part when they suddenly dismissed me from the school after 17 months.

Started in 1967, Sree Narayana Mission School was co-educational. With a strength of about 1000 students, it had only lady teachers. Lack of discipline was the main issue there, said the Secretary of the School. Residents of the apartment complexes near the school complained about the noise made by the students throughout the day. On the very first day, I appealed to the good sense of the staff and students during the morning assembly. It was pointed out that the disrepute could be changed to a better image of the school, if they cooperated to maintain discipline. When the 'miracle of silence' happened, the Secretary lauded me flatteringly. My bitter experience in Blue Bells School warned me that it could be transient.

Towards the end of the third term, we received a message from the Education Department regarding School Inspection in the beginning of the next academic year. As the dates were not specified, we quickly made preparations for it. In the meantime, nearing the age of 48, I had menopause problems, coupled with prolapsing uterus and the presence of fibroids which necessitated hysterectomy at the earliest. So, after making thorough arrangements with the cooperation of two vice-principals for the smooth conduct of the Inspection, I spoke to the Secretary about my predicament. Leave application for two months with medical certificate was also submitted. He seemed perplexed that my surgery would be in Coimbatore and not in Madras where there were many good hospitals. I explained that my aged mother-in-law would be in difficulty if it was in Madras. Since my mother and sister were in Coimbatore, it would be of great help to me during and after the surgery. When I could sense his doubt still, I happened to mention that being a Gandhian, I spoke truth always. (Later, in a committee meeting regarding this matter, the Secretary used the word 'Christian', instead of 'Gandhian'.)

Two months after surgery, I joined duty in October. When news came that Jose's younger sister's husband was battling for life in the advanced stage of cancer, we decided to see him at the earliest. Meanwhile, the wedding of my elder sister's daughter was fixed for October 24th. I was compelled to apply for 4 days leave again to go to Kerala. Since we had a good certificate from the School Inspector, I thought the Management would have realized my hard work behind it and sincerely believed that they would comply with my reasonable request. But the Secretary chose to be silent about my leave application and my trip to Kerala was cancelled.

While my niece's wedding was being solemnized at Arthat Church in Kunnamkulam on a Sunday, I was in the school busy with new admissions of tiny tots as Oct 24 1993 happened to be Vijaya Dasami day. The very next day I received my termination order with a month's salary in lieu of the notice period. Earlier experience helped me accept it with a smile. When the news spread, teachers rushed to the Principal's room to express their shock and unhappiness. One wondered, *"If the Principal is treated in this manner, what would be the plight of teachers?"* I assured them not to worry as it was a 'special treatment' accorded to me. Wishing them success in their career, I asked them to inspire their students with high ideals.

Later, it was shocking to know from one of the members of the Managing Committee what had transpired during my medical leave. The Secretary had said in the Committee Meeting, *"Madam Principal's dereliction of duty at the crucial time of our School's Inspection is improper and unwarranted. Under the pretext of surgery, she had gone to Coimbatore to attend some interviews (his assumption). She also said, being a Christian, she would not tell a lie. In my opinion, a person of such arrogance need not continue here."* I had attended committee meetings earlier and the members had been very cordial and appreciative of my work. All of them were Hindus and the Secretary's use of the word 'Christian' had the desired effect of alienating me from them. The same Secretary had praised me many a time during the one year that I had served there before surgery. Why should he be so resolute in dismissing me unceremoniously? My inference was that sooner or later; a truthful person could be problematic as the head of their institution.

Soon I realized how blessed I was to be 'sent out' of school at that particular phase. During that time, very wide and deep pits had been dug for the construction of a subway near the school. All the nine days that I attended school after medical leave, Jose had to hold my hand to cover that dangerous path. Heavy rains had made it slushy with the risk of us slipping into those pits. Losing the job was far better than losing life or limb! Again, my inner voice warned, '*Those who had been praising you would hereafter be looking for chances to disparage you.*' Above all, I felt the rest I had taken after an abdominal hysterectomy was insufficient to recover in toto. When such thoughts dominated my mind, I became peaceful. I wrote a letter to the Secretary thanking him for the opportunity to serve in their institution. '*My experiments with Gandhian ideals*' were written in a brief manner in it. Eventually, I changed my mind and did not send it to him. There are a few other letters written when I had been highly emotional and later never posted. They served as outlets for my bruised heart and agitated mind in such trying times.

The first thing we did after 'my freedom from job' was to visit our ailing brother-in-law. It was unbearable to see the suffering of that kind-hearted man who was emaciated by cancer. His relief came through death very soon. After my return from Kerala, some teachers from Narayana Mission School came home to enquire after my health. They felt that the Management had treated me in a ruthless manner when I was weak after the surgery. They were informed about a letter I had received to my Coimbatore address from a parent of the school wishing me speedy recovery and long service in Narayana Mission School. The irony was that instead of long service, I received a short notice to quit at once!

During that time, there was a news item in The Hindu (Nov 28, 1993) which was shocking. Gopal Godse, brother of Nathuram Godse (assassin of Gandhiji) had heaped humiliations upon the Father of the Nation. Late Shri. V. R. Krishna Iyer, former Supreme Court Judge condemned Gopal Godse for his audacity and impudence. He had also criticized the authorities for not taking stern action against Godse. My eyes welled up when I read the last line of his write-up, 'Gandhiji, thou art dead, shot dead with none to shed a tear – none, none.' At once I wrote an article on Gandhiji as a response to Iyer's expression of grief. I sent it to The Hindu, but it was not published. My article and his write-up were published in the school magazine of the next institution where I became the Principal.

Till then I was content practising the greatest of Gandhian ideals – truthfulness. It was unknown to many as I felt it was a personal matter. But from January 1994, at the age of 48, I started wearing only khadi – the outward sign of Gandhism. I bought three khadi saris and decided to wear only those three for all occasions till they could not be used. I had already stopped buying new saris some years earlier and so there were not many. Three of those saris were given to my daughter and the rest were donated to a home for destitute women.

Soon after leaving Narayana Mission School, I had the misfortune of seeing the sufferings of the roadside dwellers in front of our apartment complex. Though I had seen them since the time we moved in there, only my 'forced leisure' gave me a clear picture of their miserable life. The sky was their common roof. Sudden heavy rain would spoil their cooking with three stones serving as a stove. They would run to the nearby church and school, leaving everything as such. Their meagre possessions would have been covered with a tarpaulin, yet they would be wet. Aluminium plates and tumblers would be floating in the waterlogged road. When the sun shone, they would dry out everything. With the next rain, the whole process would be repeated. My loss of job seemed nothing in comparison.

In the primary class, when I learnt about basic necessities of life as food, clothing and shelter, I could not understand why the last mentioned should be included in that list. My idea was that beggars who came to our houses went back to their shelters with the food collected. Later, I knew they slept by roadsides, in bus and railway stations or wherever a little space available to stretch themselves. There are many ways for the rich to become richer. They are a minority and some of them are rich enough to 'buy' the world. The gap between the haves and have-nots is getting wider day by day. Gandhiji's dream was *to wipe every tear from every eye*. When will that happen? I have been writing about the evils in the society and about the unity of religions. They are in my blog (created by my daughter): http://alicekjose.blogspot.com Some of them have been published in dailies and weeklies.

After taking rest for three more months, I began applying for principal's post in February 1994. Surprisingly and most unusually, there had never been a call for interview till the end of March! Suddenly a thought flashed – does God want me (now khadi-clad) to leave Madras and work elsewhere? Many women leave their families to work in foreign countries for better salary. But I wanted to work somewhere in India for the sake of my principles. Predictably, Jose was against the idea.

My sister Marykutty had been told earlier about my interest in leaving home to work in some other city. In April, she phoned me to say that she had arranged with the management of a higher secondary school in Salem for me to work as its Principal. She also requested me to stay with her when I take up the post. I suggested that she could work there as she had the necessary qualifications and was also a gold medallist for M.A. She pleaded her inability on account of constraints at home. She insisted that it was most suitable for me as Dr C. Balakrishnan, the Founder-Correspondent of Holy Flower Matriculation Higher Secondary School in Salem was a Gandhian! Since he was known to us, Jose finally agreed that I could work in Salem. Thus, for the first time in my life, I was going to stay away from home at the age of 48.

The new post was taken up in May 1994 and I preferred the school hostel to Marykutty's house, which was rather far away. The hostel was a large double-storied building near the school and I stayed there in a room on the ground floor. It had 30 students, mostly children of primary classes. There were three women and an elderly man as caretakers. Using the three khadi saris for the next 19 months, I served as Principal of Holy Flower School. I washed and ironed the saris myself for daily use. Sitting down on a mat, I took meals along with the children. The cot and the bed offered by the Management were not used and I slept on a mat on the floor. Thus, a simple life was led there, and my childhood wish of living in a single room was partially fulfilled!

By then, I had discarded the few ornaments that I had been wearing. So, in the simple khadi sari, I looked like a nun. Hence, Mr. Hrudhayaraj, the Vice-Principal who was a Tamil Catholic referred to me as 'Mother Superior' at times! Once a funny incident took place because of my attire. A young girl (maid) complained to me that she was not allowed to enter the school during lunch break to feed a KG student. When asked who prevented her, the innocent girl promptly replied, "*Madam, it is the ayah (school maid) who is wearing the same kind of sari as yours!*" Suppressing a smile, I told her to follow the school rules. On that day, mine was a blue khadi sari (the colour of ayah's uniform). The poor girl tried to help me identify the ayah easily by her precise comparison!

That destiny took me there when Holy Flower School celebrated Gandhiji's 125th Birth Anniversary was proved by two factors. First, my search for a job in Madras for two months had been a fiasco. Secondly, the Principal who had been serving Holy Flower school Salem for more than a decade had resigned in 1994. We published a souvenir to commemorate Bapu's Birth Anniversary and to honour the 8th World Tamil Meet in January 1995 at Thanjavoor. It was in this souvenir that my article on the Mahatma and Justice Krishna Iyer's write-up were published.

I introduced C.C. classes (counselling cum coaching) to help the slow learners in the school. Accordingly, each teacher had 10 to 12 pupils under his/her care for half an hour every evening after school. During such a class, one day I found some teachers bargaining for saris with a salesman who was using the school premises for the sale of his ware. Coming to know that it was a periodical affair, I objected to making the temple of learning a marketplace. In the next staff meeting, the teachers were reminded of the nobility of the teaching profession and were instructed not to engage in activities that would lower its sanctity.

Once, parents of an eighth standard boy lamented that their son's grades steadily went down, despite all the facilities provided for him – separate room to study, car for commuting, etc. The boy was questioned in their presence and to their utter shock; he burst out, *"Madam, they ill-treat me at home. I study well, but they are always after me asking whether I studied this or that. They don't give me the freedom to study on my own. They also keep comparing me with my younger sister."* He started sobbing like a little child. I patted him and said, *"Your parents are eager to see you shine better in studies. I'll talk to them later. Now, you must apologize to them for your harsh words. They are the ones who gave you life and continue to give everything you need."* The boy silently turned his face away. My next sentence had the desired effect, *"If you don't say sorry to them, it would mean you disobey your principal."*

After he left, I told the pale-faced parents how the facilities they had made available to him were nullified by their over-anxiety and impatience. Also, their negative comparison with his sister would make him dislike her. Children, especially teenagers should be brought up with understanding and love shown openly. As a parting message, they were asked not to rake up the issue in the evening when he came home. This incident was a fine example to be quoted anonymously in the PTA meeting later.

Every year during Gandhi Jayanti, the Founder of the School took Pada Yatra (journey on foot) to the hamlets in and around Salem to propagate Gandhian ideals. Most of the teachers and some higher-class students also joined it. The year I joined the school (1994), the three-day Pada Yatra was in connection with the Mahatma's 125th Birth Anniversary. We published a booklet in Tamil to be distributed among the villagers. It contained eulogies about Bapu by famous Americans taken from the book, 'Profiles of Gandhi – America Remembers a World Leader'. The translation to Tamil was done by me but it was not mentioned in the booklet.

The Pada Yatra started on 30th September – Friday – the day of my full fasting. When Dr Balakrishnan knew it, he asked me to travel by the school bus which carried the necessities for the journey. He was apprehensive about my stamina to walk in the hot sun of Salem on an empty stomach as it was my maiden venture (aged 48). Placing my trust in God, I walked (about 15 km) the whole day drinking only water and with constant inward prayer.

On the third day (Oct 2nd) we reached Mettur, taking a round-about route (about 40kms in 3 days) to enable us to distribute booklets to more people. We had an inter-religious prayer at Malco Vidyalaya where I had worked earlier for 5 years. While returning to Salem by bus, certain thoughts flashed through my mind. On the first day, if I had fainted due to hunger and fatigue, I would have heaped humiliation upon myself and inconvenienced others. I felt Divine Grace had been with me throughout and thanked God Almighty countless times. As my humble offering for the Mahatma's 125th Birth Anniversary, I bought 100 copies of Gandhiji's autobiography and distributed them among the teaching and non-teaching staff.

Due to certain unexpected events in my family life, I had to resign in December 1995, before the end of the academic year. As a parting gift, I gave copies of 'Thiru Kural' to all the staff. It is a well-known Tamil book of wise sayings comprising of 1330 couplets by the ancient Tamil saint-poet, Thiruvalluvar. Thus, my long teaching career which started in 1965 came to an end in a way in December 1995 when I was one month short of my 50th birthday. In between, even while doing M.A. (1967-69), I used to take tuition for school children!

The staff of Holy Flower School presented me four wonderful books at the farewell. Having taken a vow earlier not to accept any gift from anyone, I thankfully received and donated them to the school library. The Vice-Principal looked disappointed and said, "*Madam, you need not do anything against your principles. Please take them home to read and return. Just inform me after reading, I shall come and collect them for the school library.*" It was indeed a valuable suggestion and I thanked him. Later I came to know that he had initiated the idea of presenting me with books. The leisure that ensued was happily spent in reading those books. Here are they:

1.   The Spirit of Religion – Dr S. Radhakrishnan

2.   O Jerusalem! – Larry Collins and Dominique Lapierre

3.   We, the Nation – Nani A. Palkhivala

4.   Think Like a Winner – Dr Walter Doyle Staples

Being a bibliophile, it was rather hard for me to part with those marvellous books. But the thought that they would be widely used in school library made me happy. After writing many interesting passages from them in a notebook, I sent them back to Holy Flower School. Making notes has always been my practice, when the books are not mine.

I entered the portals of the teaching profession as a teacher for the 5th class in 1965 and came out as the principal of a Higher Secondary School in 1995. At the age of 30, Jesus was given 12 disciples by God. The same Dispenser of Destiny sent me to 12 educational institutions in 30 years. It is curious that I worked with different communities – three Catholic, one Jacobite, one Lutheran, one Ramakrishna Mission, one Narayana Mission, one Sindhi, one Jain, two Hindu (individual & management), one Gandhian. I met with selfless and selfish people; broad-minded and narrow-minded ones in all those places. Needless to say, all religions show the right path, though rituals vary. Many think their own religion to be the greatest because of pride and ignorance. Actually, with such thoughts, they belittle themselves.

After those 30 years of service in the educational field, I became a proudly contented person. The feeling that I could give my mite for the betterment of the society through my teaching career was exhilarating! Countless thanks to God almighty.

Always avoid deeds that bring not

Blessings as well as lasting glory.

– Thiruvalluvar

12

Three Priceless Pearls

As a teenager I dreamt of married life with four children (2 boys and 2 girls!). When married at 26, my idea changed with the times and decided to have only two. However, my wish that my children should work for the amelioration of the world remained the same. Soon, I conceived and my colleagues teased me, *"Why do you want a baby now? Enjoy life without that 'burden' for a while."* I said, *"I won't consider children burdensome. Don't you know the saying, 'Marry early, or else you'd be toiling for your offspring in your old age'? I'll be almost 27 by the time my baby......"* Before I could finish, they chorused, *"Teacher, please stop preaching!"*

Generally, pregnancy causes nausea. It was rather severe for me in the first trimester. With gnawing hunger and tear-filled eyes, I'd be staring at breakfast. Jose would be impatient, *"Quick, I must go to office on time after dropping you at college".* When it happened day after day, my question to God was: *'Where is justice? Why should women have all the pains?'* My sad and angry feelings were because I used to have unbearable stomach-ache during the first day of my periods since the time of puberty at thirteen. For the birth of a baby, man's part is only minutes of pleasure, but a woman's ordeal is endless. Right from carrying the 'sweet burden', being in labour, giving birth, feeding the baby, attending to all its needs, spending sleepless nights, etc. etc. Of course, I was thrilled to become a mother and had done everything for my kids with love and care. My argument with God was for *womankind*!

After two months, a lady doctor examined me and said mine was a tumour and not a foetus. That thunderbolt left me heart broken. We went for a second opinion and when that doctor confirmed my pregnancy, I felt as if I had a rebirth before giving birth! She advised me to avoid cooked food to counter nausea. I started taking milk with Horlicks, fruits and raw vegetables to college for lunch. My friends predicted an 'apple boy' for me. A colleague felt sure that I would have twins because of my huge belly! Climbing to the third floor in the college to take classes would leave me panting. Later, due to knee weakness and varicose veins when I climbed stairs slowly like a little child, I remembered those painfully sweet days. These days I totally avoid even that.

On October 26th (1972), I was in labour and was admitted to Immaculate Conception Convent (ICC) Hospital near my maternal home in Coimbatore. By night it proved to be false pains. Contractions began next evening and went on for hours. At last, after midnight at 1:20 (Oct 28th), I delivered a cute boy of 6½ pounds. We christened him Jacob (paternal grandfather's name) and called him Jaimon at home. Sister-in-law Ammini and her husband, Devassy became his godparents.

I experienced severe pain while suckling the baby. Despite trying to control myself, my face was streaming with tears. When Jaimon was eight months old, for want of a trustworthy maid, he was left with Mummy. I had to stop feeding my baby as we could go to Mummy's place only during weekends. Expelling milk happened to be another distressing job. A woman has to climb many a step to attain motherhood and I was made to undergo physical agonies at all those steps.

Many years later, when I pondered over the sufferings of women and the hapless children born through rapes and because of the reckless passion of husbands, a peculiar idea struck me forcefully. Men and women, who love children and are capable of bringing them up well, should get babies individually through some other mode of birth. When I shared this thought with Akkal, she was aghast at the seriousness of my tone. She said, *"Don't babble like a baby. Without consummation, how can there be a baby?"* I asked her whose idea the present mode of birth was, in the beginning of human race. Without hesitation she replied, *"Of course, God's idea!"* I told her with conviction that the same God could change it any time. She must have doubted my sanity!

My second child – a girl of 8½ pounds was born in the same hospital at 6:30 am on October 9th, 1975 – the International Women's Year. She was very pretty with thick black hair. Her chubby cheeks were like two tiny apples. Uncle George exclaimed, *"It's for the first time I see a just-born so beautiful. Most of the new-borns don't look good."* (I wondered about somewhat similar words uttered by an elderly man at my birth.) We named her Mary after her paternal grandmother and called her Maimol. My sister, Marykutty and her husband John became her godparents.

In 1976, on December 23rd, another boy (7½ pounds) was born at 12:20 pm. That year's Christmas for us and for Mummy, was in ICC Hospital. The nuns and nurses decorated the chapel and the hospital; sang carols and distributed cakes for all. The nativity play, enacted by the nurses was directed by a nun. The rooms where mothers and to-be mothers stayed became the 'inns' visited by Joseph and Mary. We were asked to shut the door when they came seeking shelter. In the end, they would go to the 'cowshed' put up at the end of the veranda. When all others faithfully followed the instruction, I said, *"Please come in, there's room here."* All burst into laughter. The 'director' chided me playfully, *"Alice, how can you change the great event of the birth of Jesus?"* I said politely, *"Sorry Sister, I was transported to that period for a moment."*

The third child was named after my father – Joseph – though Appachan had always been known as 'Ipe'. Joseph is Babu at home and Joe to friends. Celine, my sister-in-law and her husband, Johnson were godparents. Thus, my children, Jacob, Mary & Joseph became 'JMJ' to me. Its actual expansion – Jesus Mary Joseph – is well known. This was possible only because of their grandparents' names. Yet, if they were born in a different order, they would not have been 'JMJ'!

It looked as though my children should be just 'JMJ' because when I conceived for the fourth time, I begged for God's mercy and got it aborted. Despite taking much care, when it happened, I felt troubled. To tell the truth, I was too ashamed to ask for maternity leave for the fourth child soon after joining Malco Vidyalaya. Jose also had similar views, and in a way, we were compelled to commit that grave sin. After self-realization, I firmly believed it to be a leaf in the 'Book of My Life'. Anyway, I feel light-hearted after making this open confession in my autobiography.

When Maimol was four months old, Jaimon who was just over 3 years old, had measles in its severest form. With homeopathic treatment, there was no improvement in his condition for more than a week. Since I was breast-feeding Maimol, Jose and Amma did not allow me to go near my son. They and Baby (sister-in-law) had been looking after him. All were also busy with the arrangements for Baby's impending marriage. Tempers flared and tension mounted. On the whole, the house was in turmoil. The impatient shouts of Jose and Amma hurt me so much that I feared for my sanity. To top it all, one night, by mistake Amma gave one glass full of homeopathic medicine (water-like) to Jaimon. She thought it was tender coconut water. Surely, my son's Guardian Angel intervened. The way she poured it in the dim light of the bedroom lamp, the medicine fell over his chin and chest, instead of going into his mouth. On knowing about that terrible incident, I fainted. When I regained consciousness, there was deafening silence at home. The medicine was supposed to have been given just a spoonful at regular intervals. I shuddered at the thought of what might have happened. I wept and thanked God for the great blessing.

This incident became the proverbial last straw. I took a decision and accordingly went to nearby Avila Convent straight from college one evening. I requested the Mother Superior (meeting her for the first time) for a room in the convent for me and my two little children. I was ready to pay for the board and lodging and for the care of my kids when I went to work. In my confused state, it never occurred to me that it would be against the rules of the convent. But the elderly nun smiled and said, *"We are hard-pressed for rooms here. How can I accommodate you and kids?"* Tears flowed freely down my cheeks. I implored her, *"If you have 'room' in your heart, Mother, there will be a corner for us here."* After knowing the reasons for the unusual request from a strange woman, Mother Mary Leo asked me to wait for a week. Meanwhile, I had to pray for a better solution and she assured me of her prayers too. After a week, if I went there with the same request, she would certainly consider it. I was overjoyed and thanked her profusely. Before sending me away, she talked about the sanctity of marriage and motherhood. She averred that the love and care of both the parents was of utmost importance in bringing up children.

Within a week, wonder of wonders happened – I did not need accommodation in the convent! When I went there to inform her about it with reasons, Mother Leo tenderly looked at me and said, *"I knew for certain God won't let you break your marriage vows. Convents are not to cater to such needs. I did not tell you so then, as your highly disturbed mind would not have accepted it. Bear everything patiently. You'll have a bright future."* After that momentous second meeting, I visited her more often, taking her as my spiritual guide. Wherever she was transferred, I was in touch with her through letters. When I met her for the last time at their convent in Trichur, she was in a wheelchair; yet immersed in writing work. The infirmity in her old age moved my heart and holding her hands, I shed grateful tears. Her happiness in seeing us together with our three teenaged children was quite evident in her beatific smile.

After my initial meeting with Mother Leo, I was building castles in the air. I dreamt of a secluded life with my kids in the safety of the convent. It never occurred to me then whether their father would let me take them away that easily. When the choice was between career and married life, I preferred the former. A respectable job with a good pay seemed far better than struggles and sufferings of family life. Seven years of service in that college had made me next-in-line to become the head of the department. I concluded, leaving home would be the knell for all my woes. None except Mother Leo knew about my plans. But the sudden spurt of happiness in me puzzled my close friends in college. To their shock, they came to know my intended separation from Jose. I thought what if my bosom friends knew something which would be known to all in a week's time. It became the starting point for a new course of events.

Two days later, Mrs. Nalina Devi of the Child Development Department of our college enquired whether the latest 'news' about me was true. When I confirmed it, she quoted Jesus – *'What God put together, let no man put asunder'* – and questioned me about the propriety of my decision. I felt ashamed of myself when a Hindu (an ardent devotee of Jesus) pointed out that biblical verse to me, a Christian by birth and nurture. Prayers and advice of two sincere souls (Mother Leo and Ms. Nalina) resulted in my resigning the job instead of leaving home. It was a decision that needed immense courage for a young woman with good prospects as I had consulted none but God. I kept silent about the resignation for a few days for fear of Jose asking me to repeal it.

There was a whirlwind at home when the truth was revealed eventually. A volley of questions bombarded me: *How dare you resign a well-paid job without consulting me? Who instigated you to do this foolish deed? Why did you hide it from me for a week?* Amma was also shocked, but as had been her wont, she casually pronounced her judgement, "*All because of improper upbringing.*" That indirect and unjust accusation of my parents brought tears to my eyes. I replied, "*I made the decision after consulting God alone. If I had requested, you would not have allowed me to resign. It would have been worse, if I had disobeyed you and resigned. To tell you frankly, however hard I tried I could not do justice to my responsible college job these days.*" Though I argued logically, I could understand how justifiable his anger was. With increased expenses after the arrival of the second child, the loss of a substantial amount every month would go hard with us. Later, I told Jose about my interactions with Mother Leo and Mrs. Nalina (whom he already knew as my colleague) and how I had valued my position and earnings more than my family life. My belief, *'God shuts a door to open another'* proved right. Soon, I became a reasonably well-paid tuition teacher in a nearby school run by CMI congregation. I taught English and Tamil for some slow learners in their hostel, 1 hour before and 1 hour after school hours. Though the remuneration was much less than a lecturer's pay, the job for 2 hours per day suited me well to devote more time to the needs of my little ones.

After some days, Mrs. Nalina gifted me a copy of the Holy Bible in Tamil, with the words, '*With love and prayers To Dear Alice from Nalina*'. She had written five verses from the Bible in its first blank page and the first verse attracted my attention: '*Be truthful unto death, and I will give you the crown of life.*' – Revelation 2:10. I found a coincidence in it as I took the vow of truthfulness on 27th January of the same year (1976), my 30th birthday, after fasting the whole day with solemn prayers.

The greatest good accrued from that vow is the unshakeable faith my children have always placed in me. I had not conceived Babu then and the other two were too young to understand such high ideals. But, in their growing years, they discerned my truthful nature. On the same birthday, talcum powder, the only cosmetic that I had been using, was abandoned. After a few years, when I renounced silk saris and ornaments step by step, I reached the peak of freedom! Maimol was also not interested in cosmetics even as a teenager and Jose blamed me for that – '*Like mother; like daughter*'.

Most often, parenting became an issue for argument between Jose and me. It was due to the different ways we were brought up. My parents disciplined us with much freedom and minimum punishments. In his home, they were punished much and had very little freedom. No doubt, parents have good intentions, but their methods of nurturing vary. The adage, '*Spare the rod and spoil the child*' is indeed true. At the same time there is another proverb, '*Too much of anything is good for nothing*'. I was hurt and felt helpless when children were punished, sometimes severely, by Jose and Amma for silly mistakes. The attitude seemed to be that it was their right and responsibility. I never intervened for the sake of peace at home, but would shed tears going away from the scene of punishment. When children came to me crying, I would pacify them, "*They punish you only to make you better.*"

In the absence of 'JMJ', I would request Amma and Jose (individually) to be more considerate to the children. Once I told Amma if she beat them often, they might dislike her and it would affect their attitude to others later. She retorted, *"If your children become bad because of me, so be it".* In a good mood, she would proudly say, 'my grandchildren'; if angry, it would turn to your/her children. In retrospect, I am amazed at the way I managed years and years of daily struggles. Nothing but God's Grace and thanking God became my second nature.

I never had breathing space, especially when 'JMJ' were young. My correction work would start when all went to bed and I slept mostly well past midnight. I would wake up at dawn, prepare breakfast and lunch, get kids and myself ready for school. I used to always prioritize my duties. A part-time maid who did dishes, swept and washed clothes was of great help in those days (early 1980s). But I could not have that luxury always. Amma's short temper and accusing nature made sure that maids didn't last for long. The five years that we lived in Mettur, I lost count of the maids who worked for us. Since we lived in the staff quarters, Amma would bring another maid and proudly declare, *"If servants 'run away' because of me, it is I who find the next one!"* Needless to say, till then, I had to manage every bit of work at home, apart from my school work. I earnestly prayed for strength of body and mind and received it abundantly.

Much later in life, I realized that all those struggles were a blessing in disguise. It is said, *'Man's extremity is God's opportunity'.* True, I was chased and caught by the *'Hound of Heaven'.* Mother Leo's words of wisdom helped me get extraordinary patience, *"If you were brought up the way your mother-in-law was, you would behave as she does. Be thankful to God for the way you were nurtured and for your good education. Never have the idea that you are always right and others are wrong. You'll also be disappointed if you expect others to change to suit your thinking. Their change would happen at the God-appointed time. Be patient and make your life a model for others. The Bible says, 'The meek shall inherit the earth'. You and your family are in my daily prayers."* In those days, Gandhiji's life used to be a source of great inspiration. Compared to his untold sufferings for our country's freedom and unity, mine, for my own family, paled to nothing.

Generally, parents pray for the health and intelligence of their offspring. Very few, like me, pray for wisdom for themselves to bring up their children well. I opine that parenting should be part of the curriculum both in higher secondary classes and in graduation course. Some may counter my opinion saying even illiterate parents brought up children well in the past. But times are-a-changing and influences bombard youngsters from different angles. With the best of intentions, parents go wrong in dealing with their progeny's problems. Even educated parents are often at their wits' end. However, educated or uneducated, those who raise their children with love and patience will succeed in making them good and capable. Moreover, it is said, *'Contentment is more than a kingdom'* – when parents imbibe the deep meaning of this maxim and live accordingly, their wards would become good human beings without greed and jealousy. I have practised whatever I say and can vouch for abundant recompense. Proper education and wisdom from above are most important for raising families.

When they were young, 'JMJ' were never allowed to be fussy. If they refused to eat any food item, I would tell them about starving millions who would be ready to eat anything offered. Also, I made them understand that I did not have time to cook to their fancy. In case the complaint came up again, before I said anything, they would teasingly chorus, *"Thinking of the starving kids in the world, we eat this now!"* Years later, when Jaimon was in Calcutta for six months of Practice School in the final semester of B.E., he acknowledged the 'training' I had given him in eating habits. *"Not being fussy about food helps me survive here!"* - he wrote in a letter.

Once, while sharing about my girlhood days, I happened to tell 'JMJ' that we (siblings and I) quarrelled when young but made up then and there. One day, when I scolded my 'priceless pearls' for fighting in Karate style, they reminded me, *"Didn't you say it is alright to fight when small so that we would not quarrel when we grow big?"*

I have always been a bookworm and my children also developed the reading habit early in life. Reading habit helped them also to be good in studies. Stage-fright was my weakness; so, I consciously worked towards making them get rid of it. They participated in various competitions like recitation, speech-making, essay writing, etc. and won prizes and certificates. For fancy dress competitions, I dressed 'JMJ' as great people. While in 4th standard, Jaimon in saffron robe boomed out Swami Vivekananda's inspiring words, *"Be brave my boys, starry vault will come under your feet"* and got first prize. In the same year (1981), when Maimol was in UKG, she dressed up as Mother Teresa and got third prize. We took them to a studio to have a photo taken in those attires. I sent a copy of it to Mother Teresa along with a letter, requesting her autograph on the reverse of the photo. The address was *'Mother Teresa, Calcutta, West Bengal'*! I had also included a self-addressed envelope for reply. Almost a month passed and I wondered whether it was lost. Then it came back with a reply. On the reverse side of the photo, Mother had signed with the words, *'Love others as God loves you. God bless you.'* The short letter of blessing is given here:

13th March 1981

Dear Mrs. Jose,

Thank you for your letter of 24th February 1981. As desired by you, the photograph of your two lovely children has been signed by Mother and we are enclosing it herewith.

Assuring you of our prayers,

Yours sincerely in Christ,

/signed/

Though the letter had been dated 13th March I received it after ten days. The laminated photograph is kept in our showcase and the letter is treasured in our album.

When Maimol was in II standard, we had shaven her head and her milk teeth had fallen then. By birth, she had 'Gandhi ears' and with dhoti, rounded specs, a staff in hand, the switch over to the Mahatma was complete! Jaimon in sixth standard won the second prize dressing up like Bharathiyar, reciting the poet's famous lines:

Achamillai, achamillai, acham enbadhillaye;

Uchimeedhu vaanidinthu veezhugindra podhilum,

Achamillai, achamillai, acham enbadhillaye!

(No fear, no fear, no fear at all;

Even if the sky falls on our heads,

No fear, no fear, no fear at all!)

In writing about Maimol, I start with her sweet smile and dimpled cheeks. As a baby, she was not troublesome. In fact, 'JMJ' were not cry-babies and I have always thanked God for it. In those days of endless work and perennial problems, it would have been enervating if kids had been colicky (however, in their preteen years, they had quarrelled much and driven me to despair at times!) When Maimol was 16 months old, three-week-old Babu and my sister-in-law's daughter were like 'twins', born 3 days apart. If one baby cried, Maimol would toddle into that room and sing 'la la la' patting on the bed. Meanwhile, if the other baby cried in the other room, she would almost run there with her lullaby. A baby herself, she had such motherly feelings. They say siblings with very little age difference would be hard to manage. The elder one sometimes beats, pinches or pushes the younger one. But Maimol had been a 'foster mother' to Babu in those days.

She started her schooling in Malco Vidyalaya, Mettur. While she was in 3rd std., we shifted to Madras. She was then admitted, along with her brothers to Sindhi Model Senior Secondary School, where she studied till 7th std. Then 8th in Blue Bells Matriculation Higher Secondary School; 9th and 10th in St. Dominic's Anglo-Indian Higher Secondary School; +1 in St. Thomas Matriculation Higher Secondary School and +2 in Holy Angels' Anglo-Indian Higher Secondary School! She was sad and angry for being always on the hop with regard to schools. I understood her justifiable feelings but advised her to look at the positive side of it – new teachers, new friends, new surroundings, etc. Apart from some valid reasons for changes, especially shifting, God's Will worked in everything.

Another embarrassment for her was her height – always very tall for her age. While in 8ᵗʰ std, she was selected to play the part of Motilal Nehru in a skit. The girl selected for Jawaharlal's part was rather short and plump. It was a play to be telecast on Doordarshan and the man who came from DD for directing it, changed Maimol's part to Jawaharlal's, because of her height. I feel that was a turning point and later when many started complimenting her on her height (5'9"), she gradually got rid of that complex.

Maimol took her favourite subject Physics for graduation at Stella Maris College in Madras. She got I class for B.Sc. and the Best Outgoing Student Award of the Physics Department in 1996 (Jessie, my younger sister had been given such an award from the Economics Department of Nirmala College, Coimbatore in 1973). In college, Maimol was in NCC (National Cadet Corps) and had the opportunity to go to Delhi to participate in the Basic Leadership Camp in October 1994. Later, in the Madras City Colleges' meet, she was awarded II prize in rifle-shooting and got I prize for guitar recital (Jaimon was her instructor!) She did MCA through Distance Education Programme of Bharathidasan University. She also joined NIIT and received Honours Diploma in Network-Centred Computing. She stood first in her batch and got a job through their placement.

When she was almost 22, she took up her first job as Software Engineer in Churchill Software Services India Pvt. Ltd., Bangalore and carried on with work and studies (MCA) together. She was fortunate to join duty in 1997 on a blessed day – September 8ᵗʰ – Mother Mary's birthday. Maimol worked in Churchill Software for 21 months. When she completed her MCA in 1999, she got an offer from Oracle Software India Pvt. Ltd. as Member, Technical Staff. While working there, she went twice to the UK, twice to the USA (California) and once to Indonesia on official trips. During that time, she could visit countries like Scotland and Singapore. After her marriage in 2003, she got a transfer to Mumbai as a Senior Consultant for Support Services of Oracle. She received the Best Performer Award in 2006.

My daughter was also interested in Fine Arts. She learnt Bharathanatyam as a little girl for some months in Mettur and had to quit when we shifted to Madras. Much later, she again had a chance to pursue it in Bangalore. She had to abandon it again due to lack of time when she started her career while studying for MCA. She dabbled in music with Carnatic on violin and Hindustani on flute for some time. With regard to these partial learnings, it may be said of her, '*Jack of all trades; master of none*'!

Kuriakose, son of Cherian and Cecelia, is Maimol's husband. He was born and brought up in Thane, near Mumbai. Their native place is Irinjalakuda in Kerala. Kuriakose (called Babu at home), B.E., MMM (Master in Marketing Management) was Consultant at i-flex Solutions Ltd. at the time of their marriage. Later, the company was taken over by Oracle and it is known as Oracle Financial Services Software Ltd. Though Maimol had a flourishing career, she resigned after the birth of her first baby, Arush in 2006. With the arrival of the second child, Adarsh in 2008, she decided to put her career on the backburner. Nowadays, she volunteers with an NGO, eVidyaloka for online teaching of English and AI to Tamil-medium government school students in rural Tamil Nadu. Also, she is involved in church activities.

Coming to my youngest child, Babu was an extraordinarily quiet baby. What I noticed in him and in my sister-in-law's baby girl, who was born 3 days after his birth, was surprising. The wails of the girl would be pitiable but not a drop of tear came out. Babu's eyes would shed copious tears as he started whimpering! Amma, in her characteristic style remarked, "*What's the wonder? He has inherited his mother's tears!*"

In Kerala, soon after a delivery, there is the custom of oil massaging and bathing the mother and the baby for 28 days by experienced women. I went to Mummy's place for my first two deliveries and everything was done according to norm. When Babu was born, I did not go there because my sister-in-law also had her first delivery at that time. So, we engaged an elderly woman for that purpose. Once, pointing to Babu, she remarked, "*This boy will grow up to be somebody. He is just 3 weeks old but see how intently he observes everything!*" When

I gladly shared this with Jose, he said, *"She certainly knows how to butter up."* But I felt her remark was genuine. I have faith in old people's words coming to pass. Today, when I see Babu in a high position with good name and much earning, I am reminded of her words. In his responsible job, he has to travel often within India and abroad. He has already covered 34 countries across 6 continents! Kith and kin call him *'Ulagam sutrum vaaliban'* (globe-trotting youth)! The old lady's words are partially vindicated.

When 'JMJ' were young I told them, *"When you grow up, let Jaimon become an engineer, Maimol, a doctor and Babu, a lawyer".* Four-year old Babu's immediate question amazed me, *"What is the advantage of becoming a lawyer?"* – he asked in Malayalam. Of course, he could not have known the advantage of the other two professions at that age; but was at least familiar with the words. What surprised me most was his use of the Malayalam word 'prayojanam' in the contextually correct manner! As a boy, he used to stutter occasionally. Amma tried to correct him by scolding and teasing. Requesting her to not do so would have made matters worse. I earnestly prayed and did some acts of self-denial. Today, he can speak in five languages sans stammer. He was a lecturer in a college for two years. He was also called to give guest lectures in a few other colleges. The present job demands discourses and he does them well.

When Babu was born, I was not a career woman and so suckled him till he was 18 months old. That was the period when I had turned vegetarian. I became thin and weak resulting in the prolapsing of uterus. A lady doctor of repute in Coimbatore suggested hysterectomy. I knew about health issues after that surgery when it is done at a relatively young age and I was only 33 then. We took a second opinion from a not-so-busy doctor who asked me some questions regarding my health over the years. She taught me some exercises to arrest prolapsing. Next, she advised me to stop feeding the baby since he was nearing two. When she knew of my new-fangled idea of vegetarianism, she asked me to take some non-veg food saying that the sudden loss of some essential nutrients might add to the problem. She also clarified that vegetarians by birth may not be so affected.

I did the exercises and stopped breast-feeding Babu by leaving him at Mummy's home for a few days. But my refusal to eat non-veg items triggered arguments at home. Jose accused me of purposely spoiling my health in the name of principles. I turned to Mother Mary Leo for a solution. She advised me, *"At your age, it is a kind of sacrifice when you don't eat fish and meat. Make it a different kind of sacrifice by eating that which you don't relish much. Don't be the cause of quarrels at home again."* I started taking fish. Eventually, hysterectomy was done at the age of 48 due to problems of menopause. Some busy doctors come to hasty conclusions at times. Beware of such doctors! Taking a second opinion is always a good option in serious health issues.

Babu completed his primary classes in Malco Vidyalaya and Sindhi Model School. From 6th onwards, he studied in Don Bosco Matriculation Higher Secondary School at Egmore, Madras, taking French as second language. After +2, he did Diploma in Hotel Management and Catering Technology (DHMCT) in Shevaroys Institute of Catering and Hotel Management at Yercaud, Salem. He was awarded first rank in F&B (Food and Beverages) and got second place for Outstanding Performance in that three-year course (1994-97). During the same three-year period, he got BBA degree in first class through Distance Learning Programme of Madras University.

At the age of 21, Babu took up his first job as Demi Chef-de-partie at Park Sheraton Hotel in Chennai. A year later, when Jaimon passed away, he resigned and came to Bangalore. For the next two years, he was a lecturer in Oxford College of Tourism and Hotel Management in J. P. Nagar. In the meantime, he had completed MTM (Master of Tourism Management) in first class through the Distance Education Programme of Madurai Kamaraj University. Since then, he had taken up tourism-related jobs. He served as Executive Leisure Sales for 3 years in Cox and Kings India Ltd. Next, he was with Tourism Malaysia as Marketing Manager for 4 years. In the succeeding years, he served in various capacities as Chief Operating Officer (COO), CEO, Vice President in a few more leading travel companies like Travel Tours Pvt Ltd, via.com, pathfndr.io, etc. Currently he is with Udaan India Pvt Ltd as Senior Vice President for Strategy.

While studying in Shevaroys, Babu fell in love with his classmate, Sridevi, a Tamil Hindu girl. She is the daughter of Gopalan and Pragatha from Thanjavoor. Though initially both the families were against the marriage, Babu and Devi could marry in 2004 with everyone's blessings. Devi had learnt Japanese and worked in Nihongobashi Software Pvt. Ltd. as Operation Executive. Later, she was promoted as Operation Manager. Meanwhile, she had completed her MTM through correspondence course. After working for seven years, she resigned and now is a homemaker. Since Babu used to travel often, her presence at home became imperative to take care of their two sons – Aryan, born in 2005 and Rayan, in 2007.

A later chapter is devoted to write about Jaimon – our first-born – who was taken back by God four months before his 26th birthday. Maimol and Babu keep their Chettan's memory alive through their actions. They visit Jaimon's grave soon after every milestone in their lives – their marriages, birth of their children, taking up new jobs, buying a flat or vehicle, etc. They share a lot about him with their children who consider their uncle a great hero. I am forever thankful to God Almighty for my three 'priceless pearls'.

Children endowed with sound intellect

Are the best blessing of married life.

– Thiruvalluvar

13

Fascination of Friendship

From girlhood I have been fascinated by friendship. In student days, I made friends with many in school and in our neighbourhood. There is an advantage in being a friend to everyone. Rarely did unsavoury news about others reached my ears. Moreover, even close friends were not allowed to keep their arms over my shoulders. They would tease me asking whether I was a block of ice to melt at their touch. I preferred nearness of mind and spirit.

In 1951, when I was admitted to second standard, Parvathy became my best friend. We completed schooling together. Soon she married and settled in North India. After some years I lost touch with her. Decades later, I got her phone number by chance, and we renewed our friendship over phone. In 2014, during our tour of North India, we visited her home in New Delhi and had a warm get-together reviving old memories over a sumptuous dinner. Now, Parvathy and her husband are settled in Coimbatore.

Parameswari and I studied together from 5th std to PUC. She became a doctor and our friendship continues till date. Since she had her practice in Coimbatore, we used to meet when I went to Mummy's place during summer vacation. By quirk of fate, I missed inviting her to my wedding in 1972. Later when I apologized, she was magnanimous enough to understand the circumstances which led to such a lapse. For some, such a happening would be enough to put an end to friendship. I am happy to say that she came from Coimbatore to Bangalore in 2003 to attend my daughter's wedding. We have been friends since 1954!

In high school, my close friends were Jagatheswari, Suseela, Vijaya and Savithri. During my college days, I lost touch with them except Jagatheswari. She also came from Coimbatore with her husband for Maimol's wedding. Sad to say she is no more today. Suseela was good at singing, drawing and her writing was like clear print. Vijaya was King Solomon and I was Queen of Sheba in a pantomime when we were in 9th std. Savithri was a Malayali but could not speak her mother tongue. It was because her parents did not mind their children always speaking in Tamil even at home. Only then did I understand the implication of Appachan's strict order that we should speak only Malayalam at home. Our spoken Malayalam is really strong, unlike some of our cousins who mix many Tamil words while speaking Malayalam. Since we did not know to read and write our mother-tongue, when we went to Kerala, our relatives would tease us: *'Our Tamil cousins have come!'*

Today, I read Malayalam fairly well but cannot write. Aunt Ittianam (Appachan's younger sister) found a short-cut to make Akkal and me read it in our school days when we were in Kunnamkulam for summer vacation. During prayer, she would ask us to say the prayers (already memorized) looking at the prayer book. Since we were good at spoken Malayalam, we could easily correlate the written words with what we prayed. We read the Bible in the same way. I know the 1st and 23rd psalms by heart in Malayalam even now. Actually, vacation time would be spent in my learning to write Malayalam. When school reopened there would be no time to devote for that exercise. The language had many complicated combined letters in those days and I stopped learning to write it.

A digression crept in because of my friend Savithri. While studying in PUC, initially close friendship with anyone eluded me as I plunged into a 'battle' with English. Yet there was a quiet girl by name Sheila Francis who inspired me by her deep faith in Jesus. At that young age she had to struggle with rheumatism but bore it with great fortitude. She could play many hymns on the piano at her home.

During graduation, Viji (Vijayalakshmi) and Subla (Subbulakshmi) became my bosom friends. By the end of the three-year course, we became well known in college by some sobriquets – 'Three Angels', 'Three Graces', 'Three Witches', 'Three Musketeers', etc. Viji had studied in an English-medium school in Pondicherrry. Subla had been a Tamil-medium student like me. If we made mistakes in conversation, Viji would subtly correct us by repeating the sentences correctly and we used to take the cue. My spoken English improved in those days mainly because of Viji.

It has already been mentioned in a previous chapter how 'horns' sprouted on my head in a one-word play. We three were the main characters in it. Subla being somewhat short and stout became the wife and Viji with medium height and weight was her husband. The role of lover was given to me as I was tall and lean. Subla looked smart in a frilled frock and all admired her. Jovial comments were showered upon me: *'So handsome'*; *'so nice'*; *'I'll marry you'*; etc. Viji was totally ignored by our classmates. She looked sad and told me later, *"I think this role did not suit me"*. I said, *"Viji, I'm tall and thin with short hair and looked good in a man's attire. You are so lady-like with long hair and so a man's role did not suit you much. But think of many other performances to your credit. The saving grace for me is that it was a one-word play!"* Viji's bright smile made me happy.

Having studied in Pondicherry, Viji knew French. She taught Subla and me a French farewell song. In 1964, we three sang that song for the farewell party to our seniors. Here are its first four lines:

Faut-il nous quitter sans espoir

Sans espoir de retour?

Faut-il nous quitter sans espoir

De nous revoir un jour?

This is a tribute to Viji who is no more today. The way I knew it still makes me disbelieve it.

In 1965, after graduation, I became a teacher in a private primary school. Subla completed her B.T. next year and worked in a high school. Viji left for Madurai to do post-graduation in English Literature. Two years later, she came back to Coimbatore and got appointed as a lecturer in Nirmala College, our Alma Mater. Subla's wedding took place first and we both attended it. Next, for Viji's marriage, Subla could not come due to her first delivery at that time. Soon, Viji went off to North India saying that she would write to us with her new address. Neither of us received her letter. Perhaps the postal department was to be blamed. Anyway, there was no contact after that.

More than two decades later, during a train journey in 1997, I happened to converse with a co-passenger of my age. When the conversation turned to our college days, I was thrilled to know that she was Viji's cousin. When asked about Viji's whereabouts, her reply was a bolt from the blue. Viji had passed away some years earlier. Every detail I gave to confirm Viji's identity was corroborated by her cousin. Unfortunately, she did not remember the family's address. Before I could clearly understand the cause of my friend's untimely death, the lady's destination arrived.

Viji used to write short poems in English and Tamil. Subla and I enjoyed reading them. During breaks, Viji's imagination would take wings and a poem would emerge. One such poem confirmed how much she valued my friendship:

To expect great respect

Is possible through pure love

Only through pure love of no sect

That is what Alice, the white dove

Said to Viji, her dearmost friend.

This friend was attracted by

Those words and she did sigh

She expected no respect but love

Alice, the pure dove was ready to give.

With Subla, I have a long and continuous friendship for more than six decades. Our interest in writing regular letters worked the miracle. Her younger sisters – Seetha, Girija and Geetha – also became my good friends. Subla moved to Bangalore as her husband, Balasubramanian had been working in HAL. When we settled in Bangalore in 1996, letters stopped and contacts were in person and over the phone. Her son Kumar and daughter Priya became friends of my children. Her son-in-law, Aravind is an avid reader of my writings on religious and social issues. His positive comments for each piece gladdened my heart.

Of my M.A. classmates, my friendship today continues only with Susan. Soon after she got married, she went to Baroda where her husband, Charles Mathew worked in Central Warehousing Corporation. They are now settled in Coimbatore leading a happy retired life. Four colleagues of mine from Home Science College – Padmasani, Hilda Sarojini, Jean Anandam and Vijayalakshmi – continued to be in touch with me occasionally. Two of them passed away recently: Jean Anandam in 2021 and Padmasini in 2022.

During summer vacation in 1971, Hilda invited me to her brother's house in Naduvattom near Ooty. I was happy to go as it was the famous Flower Show time in Ooty but could not go with her, due to prior engagements. My trip to Ooty was alone (for the first time) after a few days and needless to say, it was with mixed feelings of excitement and anxiety. Hilda had promised to meet me at Naduvattom bus stop. Enjoying the scenic beauty of the hill region with many hairpin bends, initially I did not notice the enveloping darkness. Suddenly, when it became pitch dark, I was perturbed for a valid reason. At each stop, passengers coolly stepped into the darkness – would they walk on the road or fall into the steep slope? Perhaps they had torches but I did not have one. What if Naduvattom was such a place with my friend not in sight! The very thought made me tremble.

To top it all, the conductor asked me whether I would alight at Upper or Down Naduvattom. Hilda's thorough instructions did not have any 'up & down' in it. I confessed my ignorance about the area and requested the conductor to stop the bus for a few minutes more at the 'first' Naduvattom. I was prepared to go to the 'next' one in case I found no one to receive me. I made some quick decisions then. If I did not find Hilda at both the stops, I would go to the terminus and take the return bus to Ooty. My speedy thoughts got arrested when I realized my journey upto Ooty would do me no good. There would be two more buses to catch before I would reach home (if at all I reached!), well past midnight. A 'babe in the bus' (just a score and four years!), I prayed tearfully, *'Oh God, hereafter I would not venture out anywhere alone; please let me meet my friend.'* Then with a start, I heard the announcement: 'Upper Naduvattom'. A well-lighted place first gave me the much-needed relief. Next, I saw my friend's beaming face. Thanking God countless times and the conductor once, I got down from the bus. We had a good time for a few days seeing places in and around Ooty including the flower show.

My friendship with Mary Stanley who worked with me in Malco Vidyalaya, Mettur in the early 1980s still continues. There she had taught Jaimon in 6th and 7th std. After the death of her husband, she has been living with her only daughter, Sowmya's family in Bangalore. Since she lives rather close by, we meet occasionally.

Mr. Xavier Absalom from St. Thomas School had been in touch with me till his death at the age of 98. We used to write letters and every letter of his started with the salutation, 'Dear & Respected Madam'. Even after my principal's position ceased, he used to refer to me as 'My Principal'. When Jaimon passed away in 1998, Mr. Absalom (86) was in Madras with his son's family. He came to Bangalore later to be with his daughter, Hemala, who is also my good friend. Soon, he visited us with two bags full of cakes, biscuits and a variety of fruit. Christmas was just round the corner and he knew we would not be in a celebratory mood. His love and thoughtfulness made all of us shed tears. He stayed with us for a day and expressed his happiness in joining us for the family prayer at night. His consoling words of faith and hope brought peace to our mind.

In 2004, he visited us again for the last time in 'Jacob Sadhan'. Even at 92, it was amazing that he was able to travel alone. After reaching Arakere, he had trouble in finding our house. When he phoned from a public booth, Jose went and brought him home. Mr. Absalom handed over a big shopping bag to me. My eyes welled up on seeing a variety of fruits and vegetables this loving soul troubled himself to get for us, even at that old age. I had always seen him as a father-figure.

I met him in Madras for the last time in May 2010, when he was 6 months short of 98. We were surprised to see him come slowly to the drawing room to welcome us! My mind raced back to the time when he rode the cycle to reach school in his late 70s. He was immensely happy to see us – Jose, Maimol and her 2 sons were with me. His words were incomprehensible, yet I could make out his sadness in not being able to attend Holy Mass at church. The fact that he lived very near the famous Santhome Cathedral in Mylapore made him sadder still. On October 21st, the same year, he passed away peacefully. My short poem given in the Appendix is my humble tribute to this remarkable man.

Many friends of 'JMJ' are mine too; just three from the 'battalion' are given here. Ram Balasubramanian (Ramki) studied with Jaimon both in Sindhi School and in BITS. He has been settled in the USA for more than two decades now. Whenever he visits India – alone or with wife and two sons – he would come home. He has also donated to Jacob Foundation a few times. Every year, on Oct 28th and Jun 19th, Ramki never fails to send emails sharing his thoughts about Jacob.

Maimol's Oracle colleague and friend, Lakshmi lived close to our residence and we became family friends. Her parents, very friendly souls, are no more today. Her brother Vinod, sister Vidya and niece Nikita all stay together in their new residence rather far from our place. Now the contact is mostly over phone but now and then they make thoughtful visits. Lakshmi calls me aunty, but at times, it would be 'friend'!

While studying at Yercaud, Babu had many friends of whom I shall mention Chackochan here. He used to call me 'Mummy' in those days. He is settled in Kerala with wife and two children. They visit us when they come to Bangalore.

As we shifted houses many times, we had the friendship of many more in different places. The next chapter on residences details some of them.

The only reward of virtue is virtue,

The only way to have a friend is to be one.

– R. W. Emerson

14

Residences Eighteen

After my marriage, we had been shifting houses for various reasons and today we live in the fifteenth house (one of which happened to be for me in a hostel in Salem)! Prior to these, I had lived with my parents in three houses. Appachan had his ancestral house in Kunnamkulam and Mummy in Trichur, but all their children were born in Coimbatore. My parents shifted to the third house when I was two and I lived there till the time of my wedding at 26. Twenty-four years in that house witnessed many happy events of my childhood and adolescent years and also the great tragedy of Appachan's untimely death.

'House' reminds me of a short story read long ago. Pursuing their own ambitions, two friends became a sage and a businessman. Years later when they met, the businessman was shocked to see his friend living in a shack. Their conversation went thus:

"Why do you live in poverty when you have many followers? I live in a magnificent mansion with all facilities. Please tell me what you want; I'm ready to help you."

"Thank you, but I don't need anything. I'm contented with what I have. Your mansion seems to be far from here. Where do you stay here?"

"Oh, I stay here in a rented room. That's only for a short while. After my work is over, I'll go back home."

"My dear friend, I have a mansion too....."

"Oh good! Where is it? Why didn't you say so earlier?"

"I'm 'here' only for 'a while'. Once my 'work' is over, I'll go to the 'Mansion' kept ready for me."

I am tempted to compare it with what I read some years later in the humour column of a weekly. A man said to his multi-millionaire politician friend:

"You look troubled. Haven't you amassed enough wealth for four generations to live lavishly?"

"Don't I know that? My present worry is about my fifth generation!"

Coming back to my story, once, with the curiosity of an eight-year-old, I took a peep into a one-room tenement near our house. The room was very neat with the bare necessities neatly arranged. Innocence coupled with ignorance made me think, *"How nice to have just one room! Easy to keep it clean and tidy."* I have always been obsessed with the ideas of keeping the house neat. Cooking was not my forte because of the mess it made in the kitchen! Anyway, the naive wish of a child to live in a single room was fulfilled twice by God many years later in the most unexpected ways. I shall write about it presently. Moreover, I was also interested in changing the positions of the furniture occasionally to ward off monotony. Mummy and siblings called it madness. But God took that 'madness' into account and made me live in a variety of houses.

In the first house at Nanjundapuram in Coimbatore, Jose and I lived only for four months. One Sunday, I fainted while attending the morning Mass. When a nun knew about my pregnancy, she advised us to shift to a house near the college where I taught. Till then, I used to ride pillion with Jose for 8km to reach college in North Coimbatore. With the shift, the rent doubled and we were pinched for money. We had learned to be thrifty when we lost our fathers early in life – he, at 15 and I, at 16. To be economical together came easily to us! As is my wont, I kept the house spick and span. A friend once teased, *"There is no merit in neatness and order now. Let me see the house after the arrival of the little one."* But, 'JMJ' were given training right from childhood to keep things in order. My 'slogan' for it was, *"Everything has a place and everything in its place."* My 'command' helped me in another way; changing the place of a thing to a prominent spot would act as a reminder later to do a task on time!

In the second house, when the landlord needed the side portion which was occupied by us, we shifted to the third house. We celebrated Jaimon's first birthday there. As a child, Jaimon was very active and observant and would joyfully shout, *'plane, plane'* and run out to look at the blinking lights even at night. Later, he (aged 18 months) started crying and running to me even during daytime at the sound of a passing plane. We came to know from a neighbour that the full-time maid we had engaged to take care of him, used to threaten the child in our absence, *"Here comes a genie to take you up".* We sent her away and left Jaimon at Mummy's place. Her house was far from my college and we went there only for weekends.

In 1975, when Amma and Baby left Kerala to live with us in Coimbatore, we shifted to a more spacious house in the same area. By then, Ruby had a job in Thrissur where she stayed in a hostel. This fourth house was on the first floor and the owner, V. K. Krishnan and family lived downstairs. In the same compound, his close friend Rajan had a similar house and had rented out upstairs. Since Malayalis lived in all the four houses, Jaimon never picked up Tamil till he went to school. We lived there for four years and Krishnan - Rajan families were friendly and very helpful. Some important events of my life took place there – birth of Maimol & Babu; Jaimon starting school; marriages of two sisters-in-law; my turning to vegetarianism; thoughts of separation and timely abandoning of the idea; resignation of lecturer's post and Mother Mary Leo becoming my spiritual guide.

Mid-1978, we left Coimbatore for good. So, the fifth house was in Mettur – Staff Quarters of MALCO. Of many families who were good friends there, we had contact with only one family for a long time – Jasper & Wilsy and their daughters, Scynthia and Sylvia. Scynthia was Jaimon's classmate in Malco Vidyalaya. Mr. V. D. Sundaram, an elderly person, who was living with his son's family in the next house was a retired teacher. He also became my good friend there. Once he said that peace pervaded his mind while talking to me and I was in my early 30s then. In fact, his kind words used to be a balm to my bruised heart due to Amma's abrasive tongue. Mr. Sundaram's parting words (details in the next chapter) at the time of our shifting to Madras proved prophetic!

Towards the end of 1983, we shifted to Madras. We lived there in 6 houses in a span of 12 years. The first one (the sixth house) was at Secretariat Colony in Kilpauk. It was the side-portion of a big house where the owners lived in the larger portion. It was a matter of great happiness that Jaimon achieved National Rank by getting 100% in Maths in std 10 of the CBSE examination, studying with the minimum facilities available in that dwelling. Our next-door neighbour there, was an Anglo-Indian family who were very friendly. They visited us some months after Jaimon's death. In their opinion, we should not have sent him to Dubai to work. Theirs were sorrow-induced words. My sorrow, by then, had drowned in the sea of serenity. The terrible truth about death is that none knows when, where and how it would claim a person.

While living in Kilpauk house, Jose and 'JMJ' were down with chicken pox, one after the other. Fortunately, I was spared then as I had had it in my childhood. It was one of the most difficult periods to tide over. Some months later, I had to undergo a minor surgery in my neck. After a four-year-stint in that house, when the landlord needed the side portion for their own use, we had to shift to the seventh house opposite ESI Hospital in the same area. The owners, the Dhanaraj family became our good friends. We are in touch with them even today.

Next year (1988), I became the Principal of a higher secondary school in Keelkattalai, far from Kilpauk. So, we shifted again to reduce my commute time. The eighth house was a spacious one with a garden and a well in Madipakkam, an underdeveloped area at that time. Jaimon passed +2 with high first class while we were there and got admission on merit in the man-making institution – BITS, Pilani in Rajasthan.

Once I happened to be alone in that house for four days as JMJ had gone to Kerala with their daddy. Jose had requested Latha, a friendly neighbour, to be with me during nights and I was in the dark about it. On the first night when she came and let the cat out of the bag, I asked her to return home as she had left her little daughter with her mother. Latha pleaded with me saying that Uncle Jose would feel let down. I convinced her that it was needless as I had no problem in staying alone. Moreover, I had fever on that day and I warned her about contagion. Finally, she went back reluctantly.

On the third night of my 'home alone', there was a knock on the gate. A piercing voice thundered in the silence of the night, *"Sir, telegram"*! It was close to midnight and I knew it would be bad news coming at that unearthly hour. But my immediate problem was the risk of going to the gate to sign and receive it. My doubt was that it could be an imposter who had known my staying alone at home. The neighbourhood was silent; people there generally went to bed early. I decided to call out to a neighbour for help. But it was embarrassing to shout out at midnight! (In the 1980s, most of us didn't even have landline. We had to apply and wait for years to get the connection!) Again, the voice came louder, *"Sir, telegram"* and the words that followed became the soothing balm for my agitated mind: *"It is for you, Mr. Ramanathan"*. At once I switched on the light (till then the racing thoughts were in darkness!) and through the window, informed him it was not for us. Heaving a huge sigh of relief, I turned off the light. When I shared the dreadful experience with the neighbours the next day, they assured me of their willing ears to my 'call' for the remaining one night! The present generation, with its mobile, SMS, WhatsApp and whatnot may not know the significance of a telegram which had its knell recently.

The landlord of the Madipakkam house had been staying in a rented house to be near his work place. With another change he decided to return to his own house. So, after two years, we shifted to a house very near St. Thomas School where I was the Principal then. Coincidentally, this owner was going to a rented house to be near his office. This ninth house had a lovely name – *'Shobana'*. One would stop awhile when passing by it, to admire its beautiful garden. There was a bed of Korean grass in the façade and the house was surrounded by a variety of plants and trees. The house was also quite big. It had a spacious L-shaped drawing cum dining room, two bedrooms and a fairly large kitchen. The monthly rent was Rs.650/-, because it was in the outskirts of the city and the year was 1990. Our kith and kin felt we were lucky to get such an attractive abode. A remark by a distant relative was rather derisive, *"After all, it is a rented house. You both have been working for years and still haven't built one!"* I knew owning a house would only be possible after 'JMJ' completed their education. Jose said he would not even dream of own house as long as I hopped from job to job! True, without a steady income it would be unwise to commit ourselves. Since Maimol and Babu (Jaimon was at BITS) were not 'troubled' by such thoughts, they competed with each other to water the plants with the hose left by the landlord.

The mention of 'own house' made me muse over certain incidents. At a house-warming function, I unwittingly heard the conversation of two ladies. One said, *"We should keep the place we live neat and tidy and we need not do it for somebody's house. So, we have started building our own house and it is almost complete"*. Amused, I thought whether one should think to such an extent to clean the place where one resides. Once an over-smart maid in Madipakkam said, *"Why should you bother about the moss in the garden? After all, it is only a rented house, not your own."* Her face darkened when I said, *"Every house is mine as long as I live there. The idea of cleaning must come from within; own or rented should not be the criterion."*

Once in my absence, Babu's friend and his mother visited *'Shobana'* house. The lady knew that I was the principal of a higher secondary school and she wondered about who maintained the house in such order. Babu gave the credit to me. When I knew it later, I told him all in the family had a share in it. But what he spontaneously said had an element of truth in it. I realized it four years later, when I returned from Coimbatore after a two-month stay there, due to hysterectomy. It was shocking to see the mess in our Little Mount apartment. Amma, Jose, 'JMJ' and a part-time maid were busy with their own duties. None had the time or mind to see to the overall order of the house. It became quite evident that one should be responsible for that.

Today, I am a happy and proud mother. Maimol and Babu (their spouses, too) keep their houses in order. What we teach our children in the impressionable age and practising what we preach will never be in vain. When Jose and I went to Dubai, I was glad at the neatness reigning in our bachelor son's beautiful flat. I appreciated it and Jaimon smiled, *"Mummy, I took extra care to keep it very neat since you were coming."* However, I knew such order could not be achieved in a day or two. After his death, when his friends met me, they averred that he took care to do everything neatly. Earlier when Jaimon was studying in BITS, a relative once said, *"You must have done many a good turn to get such a son."*

During that time, we befriended the nuns of Holy Family Convent from Kerala. They had come to Madras with the intention of starting a Matriculation school in Keelkattalai near Madippakam. As I was the principal of St. Thomas Matriculation Higher Secondary School in the nearby area, they came to me for some clarifications and that was how the friendship started. I would like to gratefully mention here the names of three nuns – Sr. Bianca, Sr. Candida and Sr. Joshua. Their prayers and advice helped us during the times of crises.

Before joining duty as Principal in St. Thomas School I got my hair bobbed in May 1989 mainly for the sake of convenience and as a time-saving measure. Jose did not like it but 'JMJ' certified that it was 'passable'. There was another remark from an unexpected quarter. My maid said that one of her friends asked her whether she was working in 'that Indira Gandhi madam's house'. A bob-induced comparison!

So far, I have visited beauty parlours only five times in the past 35 years! Initial visit was to have my hair bobbed in Coimbatore and the next three in Madras. Spending precious time and much money in such parlours became a 'burden' to my head. I decided to trim my hair periodically sitting in front of a mirror – hardly ten minutes' job with a pair of scissors and a comb. What a sense of freedom! My tamed curly hair (once unruly!) after my self-hair-cut gave the look as if I had just visited a parlour. The fifth time was in 2006 in Bangalore. Reason? Maimol, pregnant with her first baby, had a 'craving' to see my hair in a different style!

The shift to the 10th house happened when I became the principal of Sree Narayana Mission Senior Secondary School at Mambalam. The house was in Little Mount near the well-known Church of Our Lady of Health. On completion of six months, the landlady demanded a higher rent without rhyme or reason. Fortunately, we could fix a flat (11th house) for the same rent in Viswashanthi Apartment complex opposite the church. That proximity helped me to go to church most evenings to pray and meditate in the serene atmosphere. The biblical verse – '*I have engraved you in my palm*' – made me feel God's hand enveloping me. Many doubts of mine were cleared in that place where Doubting Thomas had lived for some time 2000 years ago. It was my good fortune that I had self-realisation in such a holy place.

In that church, I used to take up Bible readings regularly both in English and Tamil for Holy Mass. On such days I went to church a little early and read the day's passage once and if necessary, twice to grasp the inner meaning. Only then did I read it during the celebration of the Mass. Once a middle-aged lady said, "*Madam, when you read the Bible, I am able to understand the meaning of the verses better.*" I thanked her and offered greater gratitude to God Almighty.

In 1994, Mother Teresa visited her organization '*Karunai Illam*' (Home for mentally-challenged men) near our apartment. It was run by her Order's Brothers of Charity. I went there with Maimol taking my children's photo autographed by Mother more than a decade earlier. I thought we would have a chance to meet her because it was not a public place. Yet there was a large crowd which was cordoned off by the police. When she came nearer, I stretched my hand through the crowd to touch her. I could succeed in touching only the hem of her iconic blue-bordered white sari. Even that gave me a thrill of joy and peace. The frail nun aged 84 had a compassionate countenance which glowed in beauty despite many wrinkles. Her face revealed the truth of Gandhiji's words: '*The real beauty is the beauty of the soul*'. I was reminded of what I had read in a magazine: '*Every wrinkle is a witness to a thousand deeds of Mother's selfless service*'.

Later when I shared my experience with a cousin of mine, he teased me, "*Chechi, with that touch you are sure to go to heaven*". I did not like the way he trivialised my admiration for a living saint. I retorted, *"I'd go to heaven even otherwise. Tell me what you think about the craze people have for buying the used dresses of cine stars and cricketers!"* He immediately apologized to me.

Mary Teresa Bojaxhiu (Mother Teresa) was born on 26th August 1910 at Skopje in Albania. When 12 she felt the desire to become a nun. She went to Ireland at the age of 18 to learn English and landed in India on 6th January 1929. After becoming a nun at Loreto Convent in Darjeeling she came to Calcutta and worked as a teacher in St. Mary's High School at Entally, a suburb in Calcutta. Though she became later the principal of the school she wished to serve the poorest of the poor and stepped out of the Loreto Convent. She founded a new order of Catholic community – Missionaries of Charity – which spread to many countries. Needless to say, she became mother of countless giving birth to none. How befitting it was that the inspiring mother-cum-teacher passed away on 5th September (1997), our Nation's Teachers' Day! Nobel Prize was ennobled by being awarded to such a noble nun.

Earlier we had a chance to be on the dais (to stand in a corner!) where Mother Teresa was being honoured for the award of Nobel Prize by the then Chief Minister of Tamil Nadu, Mr. M. G. Ramachandran (MGR). It was a grand function arranged at Valluvar Kottam in Madras. Only after reaching the venue, did we know that people with pass alone would be allowed inside. Seeing the sea of humanity outside the Kottam, Jose suggested that we return home. I prayed for a way to see her and got one instantly. Accordingly, I started inching towards the gate and Jose with 'JMJ' followed me. I showed my children's photograph with Mother's autograph and requested the Police Officer to allow us inside to get Mother's blessings. I was prepared to get a shouting in 'Madras Tamil' but he silently took the photo and intently looked at 'Mother Teresa' (Maimol!) and also checked Mother's signature on the reverse and allowed us inside. With a sigh of relief, I marched forward with my 'battalion'. Whenever anyone asked for the pass, I showed the photo and before I began my 'refrain', they nodded as if they knew!

Suddenly a thought struck me. We would be able to see Mother only as a speck if we went to the last row of the audience as the place was packed. So, I moved towards the back of the dais and the rest followed me as kids behind the mother goat! Finally, the persevering and perspiring five climbed on the back stage. If anybody looked askance at us, I showed the magic snap and they smiled. Thus we 'shared' the dais with the V.V.I.P.s and saw Mother at close quarters, mostly her back. Whenever she turned to talk to the Chief Minister, we could see her glowing profile. Because of the 'adventure', we saw MGR, the erstwhile famous cine star and well-known philanthropist.

Of the many friends in Little Mount, I would like to make special mention about Mr. Edwards an elderly man who once said, *"Even though Gandhiji was a staunch Hindu he followed the Sermon on the Mount better than many Christians. Who can say that he was not baptized? The heartless deed of Godse gave Gandhiji blood baptism!"* Uncle Edwards is no more today but I have contacts with Jessie, his daughter-in-law. Another family with whom camaraderie continues till date is Himachal's. Actually, it started as friendship between Babu and Himachal who lived in the nearby colony. Since Himachal was the only child of his parents, he looked upon 'JMJ' as his siblings and called Jaimon, 'Chetta'. His father passed away some years ago. With mother, wife and two children, he lives in Chennai. They never fail to visit us when they come to Bangalore.

In the Little Mount flat, we lived for 2 years and 6 months. Nevertheless, after 18 months I moved to Salem to take up the post of Principal in Holy Flower Matriculation Higher Secondary School. I stayed in the school hostel and so the 12th 'house' happened to be for me alone. My girlhood wish to stay in a 'single room' was partially fulfilled. After the completion of one year in the hostel, I was in for another shift. Jose had been working in MALCO for 33 years and decided to quit when the head office was shifted to Mettur again. Meanwhile Holy Flower School's sister institution, Informatics Computer Institute, was in need of a Director and the post was offered to Jose. Thus, we had to leave for Salem bidding goodbye to Madras.

Usually searching and fixing a house would be done by both of us together. Since I was in Salem, the job was done by me alone. I found one near Holy Flower School in the first floor of a building where the owners lived in the ground floor. It had spacious rooms and was well ventilated but the disadvantage was that there was only one bedroom. When I noticed a locked door on the other side of the staircase just four steps away from the portion I had seen, I requested the landlord to rent out that too. Though initially he hesitated, the house was finally fixed for a slightly higher rent. I was happy to see that large room with two windows facing each other as it could be used by Jacob (in Dubai) and Joseph (in Yercaud) as their bedroom when they came for holidays. There were also many shelves where our books could be arranged.

Thus, for the first time (May, 1995) we resided in a house where 'one room' was separate from the main portion, yet very close by. Even after shifting to that 13th house, the single room was mostly locked. Sometimes I did my school work there and kept the key always in my handbag. After the one-year gap (hostel life) my routine – cooking and other chores – started again. Amma's 'routine' also began i.e., finding fault with me and the maid. As his wont, Jose sided with her. I had learned to live with that habitual sorrow. My only worry was that if people around came to know the way I was treated at home, it would be shameful. I was, by then, known in that area as a Principal with Gandhian principles.

On 22nd July 1995 – one of the most unforgettable days in my life – when I came from school, Amma wanted to know about something that she had kept under her cot. (Later I knew it to be some trinket). When I said the maid might have shifted it while sweeping, she shouted why others should meddle with her things. I requested her to talk softly as some heads popped out from the first floor of the opposite house. My 'instruction' irritated her and with a childish stubbornness, she stood at the threshold to rail at me and the maid. I was aghast and almost in tears. I opened the single room and shut myself inside.

After becoming morally courageous I never shed tears but that day I cried my heart out. Amma went on for some time and stopped.

I waited for Jose to return from office to tell him that peace of mind was imperative in my responsible position. (Amma had been mostly in Kerala during the time I had been principal in Madras.) Only when I became thirsty did I realise that I did not even have a cup of coffee after coming from school. Everything happened so quickly on my entering the house. In the single room there was only plenty of 'food' for thought.

The sound of scooter was heard when my 'fasting and meditation' went on for an hour and a half. To my sadness and shock, it took Jose another hour and a half to knock at the door at 8 pm. When I opened the door, he just said, *"Come and get the supper ready"*. I felt the floor under my feet giving way! Never caring to know what I had to say about the incident when he wanted me to prepare supper, I became a different 'avatar'. Showing him a seat, I closed the door and started walking up and down like a caged animal. Narrating some earlier events which had hurt me deeply, I came to the day's happening. My tears dried up when I spoke for justice. At the end of the 'long lecture' I informed him about my decision (taken just then) to live alone in that room thereafter and calmly requested him to leave the room.

After he went, I looked at the watch – 9 pm! It was incredible that in the one hour I spoke he never uttered a word. Perhaps he was stunned to silence by my unusually non-stop tirade. Deep disappointments and righteous anger had made me powerfully vocal. At 9.30 pm I went to 'their house' to make use of the washroom. After brushing the teeth (no supper), I came back to 'my room' with a bottle of drinking water. I took my clothes – 3 khadi saris (including the one I was wearing), some home wear, a mat and a pillow. The mother-son duo pretended not to watch me. Thus my 'one-room' life in the true sense and in full measure was from 23rd July – another unforgettable date on which Jaimon had left for Pilani in 1989, which was the first time we experienced separation in our family.

The next morning Marykutty came to meet me and I guessed that Jose must have phoned her. With no explanation I just said there was no change in my decision. She implored, *"You need not tell me anything. I have full faith in you. But your hasty decision will land you in trouble in your responsible position."* I assured her of my confidence in doing my duties properly as Principal. She tearfully pleaded with me, *"Though I pointed out your job, actually I'm more worried about your children. Whose side can they take? They need both of you."* As I had already planned for my future the previous night I said, *"I have done a lot for my children's physical, mental, intellectual and spiritual development. Let them be with their daddy and grandmother. At the end of this academic year, I'd resign and go somewhere for social service."* That was a bombshell to my sister and she went to the main portion to apprise Jose about it.

My specific request to Jose and Marykutty was not to reveal my plan immediately to 'JMJ'. But message was sent to Mummy and other siblings who called me from Coimbatore and persuaded me to change my mind. Maimol and Babu knew it only when they came for the vacation. My daughter wept, *"Mummy, Ammachi is in the habit of scolding you often. Why should you take offence now and decide to leave us?"* I told her that there was a limit for everything. Their daddy's latest indifference to my sorrow became the proverbial last straw. Jaimon called from Dubai and asked me not to rush up things. He wanted me to go with him and continue my career in Dubai. My emphatic reply was 'no' to everyone's request.

My 'room-alone' life went on for eight months including five months as Principal. Generally, such 'juicy' news would spread like wild fire through the gossip of neighbours and servants. But nothing reached my ears; being a Principal was the saving grace. Had I been a teacher at that time, there would have been crucifying questions from many. I resigned with one month's notice and got relieved of my duties at the end of December 1995.

Now, a quick look at my lonely life. Getting up at dawn, after prayers I would go to the main house for the ablutions and washing my clothes. I returned to the room with drinking water and a small bucket of water for washing fruits and vegetables like carrot, cucumber, etc. which could be eaten uncooked. Day time would be spent in school. In the evening, I went to the main portion for a wash and came back with water and the dried clothes. My last visit of the day was for using the washroom. After doing any pending work I would read, pray and go to bed.

A note on my meals in those eight months. That was the time I observed full fasting every Friday. For the other six days I did not need crockery nor did I cook. Bakery items, banana chips, peanuts, murukku, etc. were kept in cans. Variety of fruits and vegetables were in a basket. Whenever hungry I ate whatever I liked from the things mentioned above. Regular meals thrice a day became a thing of past. At school, since I had a cubicle, without attracting attention I had my 'daily bread' (literally!) for lunch. Besides these I had a special item to consume. The Host – the bread that turns to Christ's body during the Holy Mass is usually prepared by nuns. In a convent in Salem, the round wafers were sent to churches and the remaining shapeless pieces were sold in bulk for a meagre amount. I regularly bought and had them as 'manna'! Once a month, I went to a hotel alone (never before and never after in my life!) to have lunch – not out of craving but for the 'show of freedom'. Again, Marykutty and I met at times in the church for the evening mass and later had masala dosa in a nearby eatery. Despite eating in such a fashion for months together, I was fit as a fiddle.

In the third month of my lonely life, Marykutty brought to my room two nuns to counsel me. They advised me in right earnest for a fairly long time and while taking leave one said, *"Birth of the Son of God is fast approaching. Please celebrate the joy and peace of the season with your family."* The words 'Son of God' caught my imagination. I said, *"If Jesus is the Son of God, I'm the daughter of God…………"* The shocked nuns asked me how I could say it so irreverently. I continued, *"Sisters, you both and my sister, are also God's daughters."* One of them said in an impatient tone, *"Who doesn't know we are all God's children?"* I clarified, *"True sister, except atheists, all believe in that. But only very few 'realise' it and I'm one among them. That's why I behave differently."* Mission failed and they left with my disappointed sister.

My thought that I could stay in an orphanage and do social service was a fiasco. No institution was willing to accommodate me when they knew me to be the mother of three children and my idea of leaving them and their father. They agreed to my visiting them for some hours and help in their work. As I could not expect salary for service, board and lodging became the problem. Anyway, I went on sending letters to different parts of India to get a 'corner' somewhere.

Six months later, on my 50th birthday (27th January 1996), Jose and Babu came to my room with a greeting card and cake to 'invite me home'. (Jaimon was in Dubai and Maimol, in Madras). They requested me to forget the past and join the family. But I was firm on my stand. I made them understand that though initially I was sad and disappointed, later I had accepted the change happily and whole heartedly. Marykutty and her children came with the birthday cake to greet me. There were calls from Coimbatore and Dubai for conveying birthday wishes. Above all, what I valued most was Maimol's greeting card pregnant with meaning and a soul-stirring letter from Madras. She had mentioned in it, what I had done for her in her growing years and also my character traits as she had perceived. I never showed that beautiful expression of love and gratitude to anyone for nearly two decades. Finally, I added it in the appendix of my autobiography (Tamil version published in 2014). Girls and boys of her age (She wrote it at 20) can take a lesson or two from it to be loving and grateful to their mothers.

In February, Mummy, Joy and my sisters from Coimbatore came for Marykutty's house-warming ceremony. They put forth another suggestion that I could go for social service when 'JMJ' settled in life. My determined negative response made them 'conspire' with Jose and they carried out their plan soon. As a result, I was reunited with family the details of which are given in another chapter. When the cloud showed the silver lining, Jose accused me of fixing a house with a separate room on a pre-meditated plan. To be sure, everything pointed to such a plan. It was also true that it was very well-planned but the ultimate truth was that it was God's plan!

When I sincerely believed that I would go for social service, I changed my attire for the sake of safety in my lonely life. As a little girl I wore frocks; then full-length skirt and blouse and later added Tamil-style daavani (half sari). From the age of 19, I used only saris till I turned 50. But when I stopped my 'full-time' teaching career at 50 and decided to be a 'lonely traveller', I switched over to khadi kurta-pyjama to look like a man. Bobbed hair had already made me 'half-man' and with the new attire I became picture perfect! A decade later, when I turned 60, I used a dupatta to have a more dignified look! Adarsh, my grandson, when 3 would have a towel around his neck and say, "*I'm Ammachi*". Here are some comments I had heard in Salem in the initial stage of my changed apparel:

'*Hello Mister, move back. You are standing very close to that girl.*' (in a queue).

'*This is ladies' side. Gents should stand at the rear*'. (in a bus).

When I turned smilingly to face the persons who made such comments from behind, they would apologise, "*Sorry madam, seeing from here we thought………*". I completed their sentences with, "*That's okay*" or "*No problem*".

Since I had the wish to go for social service after some years, I decided not to change over to sari again though Jose insisted on it. But Jaimon's passing away within two years turned everything topsy-turvy. When things happened in quick succession, I realised that '*there is a Divine Cause behind every physical calamity.*' (Gandhiji). Had I left home as planned, soon after losing me alive, my family would have lost Jaimon. The spiritual strength I had gained over the years was of immense value at that moment of our greatest grief. It became clear then everything happened in such order so that I would be in the family and lead a more detached life. Needless to say, this was a greater challenge. As if to prove my line of thought, something happened later. Maimol went to Mumbai after marriage and Babu and Devi were with us in Jacob Sadhan. I was meditating on my next move when Babu came home one day with the news of his transfer to Madras.

The 14th house we moved in 1996 was a flat (Jeevan Griha) at J P Nagar in Bangalore when Jose took up a new job there. Jaimon, who was well employed in Dubai, asked me to put a period to my thirty-year-long teaching career and suggested to spend time in reading ("*Reading is your passion, Mummy!*"). He encouraged me to write something with my vast experience both in personal and career life. However, I decided not to try for the post of a principal for a different reason. It was because of my ignorance of Kannada, the local language. In Tamil Nadu, the knowledge of Tamil helped me function at all levels with ease and confidence. So, in order to be physically active (aged 51) I did all the household chores without engaging a domestic help. Maimol was of immense help to me at that time.

On the 50th death anniversary of Mahatma Gandhi in 1998, I started weekly free moral science classes for the little children of the flats in the apartment complex. It was my humble tribute to the Mahatma's memory. Gandhiji's exhortation had always inspired me: '*Catch them young.*' Every Sunday from 11 am to 12 noon these classes were conducted. Parents and children alike were happy as it involved no expenses, no books and no tests! Children began with a prayer repeating after me for the peace and happiness of the world. Then they spent time singing devotional songs taught by me and narrating moral stories. I gave talks on topics like good manners, obedience to elders, to be of help to others, etc. Children were also made to narrate a moral story in rotation. The classes ended with simple yoga exercises and the kids were sent home with some eatables like toffees / biscuits / chips / peanut balls, etc.

Till we left Jeevan Griha at the end of 1999, those classes continued for almost two years. I stopped the classes for 40 days at the time of Jaimon's death. In those days of deep sorrow, teaching morals to the kids gave me immense peace of mind. When the parents shared the happiness regarding their children's better behaviour, I thanked God. Easy-to-learn devotional songs were repeated many times till the children committed them to memory. I could teach them more than 30 songs and here are the first lines of some of them:

♦ Allah, Paramapitha, Harihara Brahmam, Arul Buddhane Saranam

♦ Krishna Krishna Mukunda Janardhana

♦ Narayana Jaya (3) Namo Namo

- Saranam (4) Preethi Swaroopane Saranam

- O Devane Jagadeeshane, Sweekara Maadu Ee Prarthane

- God's love is so wonderful

- Glory to God (2) Glory to the Father

- In the name of Jesus (2) we have the victory

- We shall overcome (3) someday

- Be careful little eyes what you see (2) there's God in you

During that period, 'The Hindu' had been publishing the final momentous events of Gandhiji's life under the title *'The Last 200 Days of the Mahatma'* (15th July 1947 – 30th January 1948). I clipped and stuck them in an old record book of Babu's. In every page in the space left out, I wrote quotations on and by the Mahatma. The 'album' has the pride of place in our library.

My part-time teaching in 1999 started when I took English classes for the novices in Maria Bhavan, the seminary of Montfort community near Dairy Circle in Bangalore. It was one hour class in the afternoon and when it was completed two more seminaries and a convent in the same area requested me to teach English for their novices too. They could not pay me much. In fact, I was happy to work there more in the spirit of service. Maimol and Babu, by then were well employed. I left home at 1.30 pm and taking class in three close-by institutions (2 – 5.30 pm) returned home by 6 pm commuting by bus. Once, a friend 'pitied' me for working so hard in the old age for a meagre salary. With a smile I replied, *"Though I'm 53, I feel quite young and am in good health. To you it may seem hard work; but I enjoy teaching. Above all, earning money is not my motive now."*

In Holy Family Convent, I taught only for a few months. But in the two seminaries run by Somascans and OMI (Oblates of Mary Immaculate) communities, my work had been for four years each. After + 2 course those youngsters joined the seminary for a decade-long study to become Catholic priests. They had English only in the first year. Now and then I talked to them about the unity of religions. I quoted Gandhiji's famous utterance, '*I am a True Hindu, True Christian, True Muslim*' and told them if everyone stood rooted in one's own religion and respected all other religions, there would be peace and happiness in the world. The youth showed great interest in such ideas.

Once, an OMI student raised a question, "*It is said Jesus died for the sins of all the people. How could he die earlier for the sins of the people who lived after him?*" I could give an immediate reply and thanked God for it. "*Those who meditate on the glorious teachings and the undeserved death of Jesus at the youthful age of 33 will desist from committing sins. Therefore, the selfless life and the triumphant death of Jesus Christ is for all times and for all peoples.*"

When I taught in the Somascan community at Yuva Vikas, Fr. Alberto Monis, an Italian priest was its superior. He was in his early 30s and had a good working knowledge of English. His sermons at Christu Prabhalaya Church in Jayanagar used to be short and impressive. Yet he attended my classes for the novitiates to further improve his English. His humility touched my heart. One evening after the classes when I was waiting for bus, Fr. Alberto happened to come that way by motor bike. He offered to take me home but I politely declined it. When he insisted, I went home that day riding pillion. Since he had a prior engagement, he could not come in though I invited him home. The next day he was at the gate with his bike to take me home and I refused firmly. His request then made my eyes moist: "*Teacher, please let me do it for you because you are a mother*". I was 54 then. That day he spent some time with Jose and me over tea and snacks. Maimol and Babu had not returned from work. Jose shared the details of Jaimon's tragic death and Fr. Alberto's consoling words comforted us. Till his transfer he brought me home every evening. Occasionally, when engaged otherwise, he would thoughtfully send word through a student.

Mention about Fr. Alberto's short sermons made me think of the lengthy sermons by some priests. There was a snippet in a book by name 'Church Humour'. A priest and a bus driver died at the same time and arrived at the Pearly Gate. The driver was taken to Paradise at once but the priest's name was added to the waiting list. To the shocked priest St. Peter justified his action: *'Your long winding sermons made the congregation sleep in the church. But the minute that man started to drive, all in the bus earnestly prayed to God. Now tell me, who succeeded in making people pray!'*

In 1999, the 15th house became our own at last. To avoid carrying our precious books (more than a 1000 then) from house to house it was better to own one. Earlier when I had mentioned it, Jaimon jokingly asked whether a house was for people or books! With his death in 1998, my wish to build a house also died. I started searching for a house or a flat through newspaper ads. Months elapsed without success. It would be either too expensive or not suitable for us. One day to my great surprise an ad flashed, *'A spacious house at Arakere in 40x60 site'* for a price which we could afford.

Jose was not willing to buy a house in that village far away from the city. He refused to take me there saying that the relatively low price was due to its location. But I insisted and what we saw was a three-in-one dwelling! Without mentioning that there were three houses (2 on the 1st floor), the owner had given the built-up area of all three together and I was 'tricked' in a splendid way. Jose and I, each worked for 40 years and ended up with no pension because all were in private concerns and institutions with break of service. Today the rent from the two houses is our 'pension'.

Mr. Mariappa, a Kannada Catholic built that house in 1997. At our first visit in 1999, we saw a fairly large statue of Mother Mary in their prayer room and I felt the blessing of Our Lady at once. Mariappa expressed his happiness that a Catholic family bought his house. Jaimon as a Civil Engineer had a dream house in his mind. If it had come into being, my wish was to name it 'JMJ' cottage. Now we named our house *'Jacob Sadhan'* as we bought it one year after Jaimon's passing away.

Generally, transaction of a house is done in full vacant possession but, we bought it with one tenant! Balaji and Pratima with their two children continued to reside there for eight more years and vacated only after building their own house. The other vacated house was kept by us for multi-purpose use. For some years, I conducted Spoken English Course for a nominal fee. My students were mostly homemakers. Neighbourhood children (including our tenant's children, Wagilya and Raghunandan) came for free moral science classes on Sundays. We could arrange our vast collection of books in steel book cases which we bought after shifting. Moreover, two bedrooms upstairs had been quite convenient when guests arrived. Only after the marriages of Maimol and Babu, we started renting it out from 2005.

The three years we lived in Jeevan Griha, we were parishioners of Christu Prabhalaya Church in Jayanagar. During Holy Mass, I had taken up Bible readings many times in Tamil and English in that church. Now we are parishioners of Santhome Parish Church in Hulimavu. Since the Mass is celebrated only in Malayalam, I hesitate to take up Bible reading because of my average reading ability in my mother tongue! In both these churches, we have befriended many families. After more than two decades of our living in Arakere, we have many friends here. It is a long list and so I avoid mentioning their names. But a close friend lives far away. Our friendship, in fact, started over the phone. She is Nagalakshmi (aka Lakshmi) mother of Balakumar who was Maimol's Oracle colleague. After reading my autobiography in Tamil, she sent me a wonderfully worded letter of appreciation which made me happy and grateful.

When kith and kin knew about my writing, many asked whether they would make an appearance in my life-story. Some were genuine in their eagerness. However, some might have made fun of me for my venture. It was revealed by a comment by one friend on the sly (heard from a reliable source), *"Even autobiographies by great people are ignored these days. Who would read hers? At this old age (I was 65 then), she need not have taken the trouble!"* When I heard it, I was halfway through the Tamil version. Well, if people do not read mine, I would take it as God's will. But the fact remains that I have written it with good intention. Readers can discern it when they read about my trying experiences and how I survived the vicissitudes of life through my unwavering faith in God. Anyway, the spiritual satisfaction I attained after writing it is inexplicable.

Finally, searching for houses has stopped in my life. What is left for me is to go to my *'Magnificent Mansion'* once 'my work here' is completed.

'Mid pleasures and palaces though we may roam;

Be it ever so humble, there's no place like home.

– J. H. Payne

15

Memorable Maids

'*We live by admiration, hope and love*' – William Wordsworth. Years ago, coming across the great poet's words, I wondered whether admiring others has such importance in life. On becoming wiser, I understood its full implication. Some disparagers do not admire even noble souls like Mahatma Gandhi and Mother Teresa, who are held in high esteem world over. Cynics are indifferent to the 98 percent goodness in great people and harp on their 2 percent shortcomings. Many make a show of admiration for the rich and the powerful with selfish motives. Lack of sincere admiration for others leads to the obnoxious tendency of self-admiration. Only with true love and humility can one admire others.

Admiration for not-so-great people should include those who serve us. Some treat their domestic help with kindness and understanding whereas some ill-treat them. In a thought-provoking and highly imaginative poem of 64 lines, the great Tamil patriot-poet Bharathiyar, points out the importance of a servant in a household. After describing the troubles, he faced with many an insincere servant, the poet makes Lord Krishna his dutiful and diligent servant in the poem – '*Kannan En Sevakan*' (Krishna, My Servant). I was delightfully reminded of the poem when a woman became our domestic help in an incredible manner on the very first day of our Madras life in 1983. This chapter on maids was 'born' because of my urge to write about her. A few other maids and some analogous thoughts have their presence here.

In western countries, maids are a rarity. People there manage their chores with a variety of appliances. In India, to a career lady in a nuclear family, a maid is indispensable. The following was found in a humour column: A woman was accused of pampering her maid too much by her husband and son. The lady clarified that otherwise, she might quit. The father-son duo argued that they could engage another. The lady was livid with anger, *"You can say so. Who will do all the work till we get the new one? Moreover, the new maid should be trained to suit our need. Will you both do that? It is a different matter that your training would be useless! Better the known devil than the unknown. I can easily sail through for many days in your absence. But I cannot imagine a day without her."* Though exaggerated, there is a grain of truth in it. Since my marriage in 1972, we had engaged many maids in our 13 houses in five cities. My life story will be incomplete if I do not write about some of them.

Generally, servants are submissive to people who shout at them and work quietly though inwardly they may be seething. The same type would take advantage of people who are mild and patient. Some work sincerely and respectfully irrespective of the kind of masters they have. In Jan 1972, the first domestic help we had from Kerala was a middle-aged woman. She stayed with us doing all the work and we paid her well. One day she murmured within my earshot, *"A woman is a woman even if she goes out to earn like a man. She should do some chores at home."* It was the third term in the college and my hands were full. The maid did not realize that I did a lot more work of a different kind. When her mumblings increased, we decided to end her service. But we could take her back to Kerala only during summer vacation. I have already mentioned, in an earlier chapter, my bitter experience with another full-time maid when Jaimon was a toddler.

Of the many who worked for us in Mettur during our five-year stint there, Vellaiammal alone continued for a year. She was about Amma's age (60). Even though she did not understand Malayalam, she could make out that she was often criticized by Amma. On such occasions, she would look fixedly at Amma for a while and silently go back to her work. That 'stare' would irritate Amma who would shout in Malayalam, *"Why is this oldie staring at me?"* Vellaiammal would not understand it and I would smile peacefully. Due to ill-health when she stopped the work, she said, *"Only for your sake, I worked here for so long. At your age, (I was 33) you are very patient. You surely won't have another hell!"* My patience was indeed rewarded. Amma gave me two 'testimonials' before she passed away!

There is some background to be shared before introducing the 'heroine' of this chapter. Amma was in Kerala when our shifting to Madras was finalized. Despite our repeated requests she refused to come there. As 'JMJ' were quite young, her presence at home in the new place would have been a great relief to us. Mr. Sundaram, the retired teacher who was our neighbour in Mettur, came to know about Amma's stand and uttered what I would call a prophecy: *"Don't worry, child. You'll get a good maid as soon as you reach Madras."* It happened verbatim in a curious way so as to prove the saying, *'Truth is stranger than fiction'*.

At the time of fixing the house in Madras, Jose had requested the landlady to arrange a maid for us at the earliest as I would be joining the new school within two days of our arrival. Our house was the side portion of a large house where the owner lived in the main portion. We hoped to get a trustworthy servant through the owner's help. On October 30th, Jose travelled by the lorry loaded with our things. (The kids and I would be going by train the next day.) He reached Madras at dawn on 31st October. It was drizzling and the two men who had gone along started unloading hurriedly. A woman from the opposite side of the road came in and started to keep the things in different rooms under the guidance of Jose who assumed her to be the maid arranged by the landlady. At the same time, he was surprised that she had 'joined duty' in that twilight hour when it was raining. After the lorry left, she enquired about the rest of the family. When Jose said that we would be reaching home late that night, she left saying she would come the next morning with milk sachet.

Later in the morning, Jose went to thank the landlady for the prompt arrangement of a maid. She then dropped a bombshell, *"I've told my maid to look out but haven't got one yet. I thought the woman helping you out came from Mettur."* Jose was puzzled. How could a woman come at dawn and help without being asked! She even mentioned about the 'rest of the family'. Perhaps she guessed from the lorry-load of things. The fact more surprising was that she never asked him any money for the work done!

True to her word, the next morning the mystery woman came with milk sachet. She smiled at me and said, *"You can prepare coffee for all. When did you arrive last night? There's a lot of work to do; let me arrange the things."* Without waiting for my reply, she went to do her (our!) work. The very first words that strange woman uttered were like she knew me earlier. I was terrified thinking of the tales of cheats in Madras. But I was not ready to send her away as I was in desperate need of a domestic help. I decided to be cautious till I got one with the help of the landlady. When I wanted to know her name, just a word was the reply – 'Saroja'.

A week passed without the sign of another maid. Meanwhile, the landlady warned me, *"We have been living here for many years and never once did we see this woman in this area. Since you are new to Madras, be careful!"* Despite that warning, I continued with Saroja's services for two reasons: I was quite busy in the new school as I was handling X & XII students who would appear for public exams. With three children to look after, I could not imagine doing all the work at home including washing the clothes (washing machines in middle-class families were unheard of then!) Secondly, Saroja's work was neat and she seemed to be sincere.

Ignorant of the turmoil in my mind, Saroja came twice daily and did all the work except cooking. At times, she would talk to herself and laugh out loud while doing her work. I thought her to be mildly insane and prayerfully carried on with my duties. By the time we left for school, Saroja would have finished the work inside the house. Keeping the clothes to be washed in the backyard, I would lock the house and leave for school with the three kids in tow. Saroja came in the evening too; at times even before we returned and waited for us in front of the locked house. She was the only one who worked for us without being 'trained'. Again, she was the only maid who came to us of her own accord without being introduced or recommended by a known person.

Even after ten days, another maid was a mirage. On the eleventh day, I could not go to school because Jaimon was feverish. I sent the leave application through Saroja who took Maimol and Babu to school. Even after one hour when she did not return, I became anxious. Normally, the to-and-fro walk to school would take less than 30 minutes. I cursed myself for sending the kids with a relatively unknown woman who seemed to be a bit touched. I shuddered at the thought that she might have kidnapped my children and I rushed to the landlady seeking the nearest public telephone booth. She guided me to a friend's house nearby. The school office confirmed that my leave application had been delivered. I requested the office staff to personally verify whether Mary & Joseph were present in classes 3 & 2 respectively. It was such a relief that they were! Still there was no sign of Saroja and the landlady warned me again. After another half an hour, she came laughing and talking to herself!

Though angry, with immense patience (kids were safe!), I asked her the reason for her delay. *"You see Amma, that Muniamma* (God knows who!) *started talking to me on my way back home. Don't worry; I'll finish all the work in no time."* – so saying she went inside with a broad smile. It totally disarmed me. By evening, Jaimon was better. I requested the landlady to be with him for a little while and went to bring Maimol & Babu from school. As soon as they saw me, they chorused.. *"Hereafter, please don't send us to school with Saroja Akka. Even when a car or bus was far away, she did not let us cross the road. We were late to school because of that."* I felt guilty and sorry. Didn't I suspect her to be a kidnapper? But circumstances beguiled me. I thought of the affectionate wish of Mr. Sundaram in Mettur that I would get a 'good maid' in Madras.

Saroja was in her late 30s like me (both of us 1946-born). She was just skin and bones and looked like a patient. Since she had the habit of talking to herself, she had no time to talk to me much. Her main work in the first few days was drying out many articles which were wet due to the drizzle on the day of arrival. There was no need for me to instruct her. Mr. Sundaram's prophecy of my getting a maid as soon as I reached Madras was outdone by Saroja joining duty many hours before my arrival! Initially, I used respectful verb endings (used in Indian languages for elders and strangers) while talking to Saroja who never did that. Jose mocked me pointing to that. I clarified, *"Mine is Coimbatore Tamil, which is very respectful whereas she speaks Madras Tamil, which mostly does away with niceties; it's nothing but dialectal difference. Her actions show that she respects me."* I used to give her our breakfast (Kerala style rice porridge) daily and within a couple of months, she put on some weight. Since lunch boxes had to be ready for five of us, I cooked full meals in the morning itself. Tiffin for breakfast used to be only on Sundays and other holidays.

Saroja's presence both in the mornings and evenings made her a member of the family. She told me about her drunkard husband who came home on and off. She had a 14-year-old daughter. Both mother and daughter studied only up to seventh class. Soon it was Pongal time and Saroja wanted some advance from her wages. Jose managed money matters and was never in the habit of giving advance to servants for obvious reasons. But she was 'determined' to get it and waited for 'Sir' to come home. As soon as Jose entered the house, she presented her case with certitude, *"Sir, I need some advance to celebrate Pongal. Amma said you never gave advance to servants. Where else can I ask? You have to give me some money and can deduct it from my wages."* Jose became speechless as our maids rarely talked to him. He never expected a 'direct attack' from one who had been with us only for two months. When he turned to me with a baffled look, I nodded my head controlling my laughter.

On Pongal day, I was surprised to see her coming as I had granted her leave. She had brought some sweet Pongal for 'JMJ'. It was evident by the smell of smoke that she had prepared it by burning paper. Jose and children were put off by its offensive smell and did not eat it. Saroja's guileless simplicity and love made me have a little. Two years later, when I had surgery on my neck, she took up cooking for a week and her preparations were very good.

Though I mentioned 'two years later', I did not mean that she worked for us till then. After a few months suddenly she stopped coming. I waited for three days and got another maid. Two months later she appeared with a valid reason for her absence, "*Amma, my husband took us to our native place all of a sudden. I did not have time to come here and inform you. Now we have come back for good. I'll do the work today onwards.*" On knowing about the new maid, she declared emphatically that only she should work in our house and asked me to 'dismiss' the other maid. She left assuring me that she would come the next day. I was in a dilemma and consulted our landlady who had arranged for the other maid. To my utter surprise, she advised me to take back Saroja and said that she would explain the matter to the new maid.

Later I came to know the reason behind the landlady's change of opinion about Saroja. Since the backyard of the house was common for both the families, she used to watch with admiration the way Saroja would check every item of clothing for any stubborn stain in any corner. She took more than forty minutes for washing, which would be done by other maids in 10-15 minutes. That 'certificate' just corroborated my opinion about Saroja's expertise in washing clothes. Seven-year-old Babu's white uniform shirt would be mud-coloured when he came back from school. The same shirt would sparkle with whiteness after her wash. I always thanked God for sending Saroja as if from nowhere! Once a family friend sincerely cautioned us, "*It's dangerous to keep an eccentric one as maid. She might poison your food without her own knowledge.*" How could he know Saroja's child-like nature!

In her second 'innings', Saroja worked for us for one and a half years. Twice when she fell ill, she sent her daughter to do the work. Again, she vanished and that was the time we shifted to the house in front of the ESI Hospital in the same area. After some months, Saroja came to see us, "*Amma, I went to the old house and the landlady gave me your new address. How is Sir? Where are the children?*" She asked me whether I had a maid but did not assert her 'right' to work in our house as she had done earlier. I had an impulse to take her back but checked myself. I could not cope with her 'disappearing' suddenly. Soon we shifted to Madipakkam, quite far from where we were staying. That put an end to our contact with Saroja. While writing this, I seem to hear her voice!

It is time to bid farewell to Saroja with a poignantly humourous piece. Once when my younger sister Jessie was with us, I warned her about Saroja's harmless self-talking habit and left for school. That day, Saroja was unusually garrulous:

Saroja: *Amma, I was very pretty in my younger days. Now, with these sunken cheeks, I look older than I am.*

Jessie: *What happened, Saroja? Any illness?*

Saroja: *Wait, Amma, I'll show you a photo taken soon after my marriage. Only then you will believe me.*

Jessie (shocked at seeing the photo): *Do you say it is your photo?*

Saroja: *Yes, Amma, nobody believes me when I say so. There's a lot of change in me.*

Jessie: *Saroja, please go now and come after my sister returns from school.*

Despite Saroja pleading with her to allow her to complete the work, Jessie sent her away and bolted the door. Thoroughly shaken, she later shared her experience with us and named the people in the snap – Rajinikanth and Sridevi – the leading pair of Tamil movies in those days. We burst out laughing and Jessie got angry, *"Yes, you laugh now. Had I said the fact, she might have hit me. Can't you get a sane servant?"* Soon Saroja came for evening session and complained, *"Amma, I would have finished all the work, but your sister drove me away."* Jessie nudged me and I asked Saroja for the photo. It was a small black and white photo from some movie. Telling Saroja to keep it safe in her purse, I advised her not to show it to anyone. People might say they were Rajinikanth and Sridevi. She sighed, *"Yes, Amma, everyone says so, no one believes me."* I knew it to be her sincere belief and felt sorry for her. I consider Saroja an 'angel' sent by God when I was in dire need of a maid. It is a rarity to find such sincere servants.

In Madipakkam, after many years we had another full-time maid who was from Mettur. Rajathi (name changed) was a robust woman in her late 40's. Childless and deserted by her husband, she had been living with her brother. *'A new broom sweeps clean'* – indeed, the very first morning, Rajathi started cooking at 4 am! It disturbed our sleep, but she declared it was her habit in Mettur. She was asked to change that habit to 5.30 am. Soon, she showed her true colours. She did work at express speed, especially in the evenings and was ready for T.V. programmes. At times, she politely asked for some serials which we never watched. Supper would be ready by 6pm for the sake of TV. When instructed to prepare it later to have it hot, she audaciously said that she never liked cooking 'late' in the night. The traditional grinding stone expertly used by Saroja and the other maids had to be replaced by the tilting wet grinder for her sake. To top it all, for silly reasons she often quarrelled with Maimol and Babu who were in their early teens (Jaimon was in BITS). She was the one who had differentiated between cleaning one's own house and a rented one! In short, Rajathi was the polar opposite of Saroja!

As days went by, I could not tolerate her impudence. Since Jose was silent about such matters, Rajathi showed respect to him. It was exasperating to see her indifference to me and children shown in a subtle manner. Being the principal of a higher secondary school then, I needed peace of mind to concentrate on my work. One evening when I returned from school the usual war of words was going on. I sternly told Rajathi to avoid quarrelling with the children. With a frown, she left the room at once. As usual, early supper was ready. She informed me about her severe headache and that she wanted some rest. She did not need supper and never came to watch TV.

When Jose came, I narrated the day's incident. As usual, an indifferent nod was his response. After family prayer, I went to warm up the uppuma made for supper. The very sight of it revealed the reason for her 'fasting'. Hunger made us peck at it. Later she came to clean the table and exclaimed, "*Whatever I had made is wasted now!*" Then she started cleaning the table in such a hurry that the tonic bottle in the corner shook but luckily did not fall. Looking at it,

I literally trembled. Had that big bottle fallen, it would have smashed into smithereens wasting the costly tonic which Maimol had just started taking. I thanked God for preventing the untoward.

That night Jose told me Rajathi would be dismissed the next morning. Surprised, I requested him to give her some more time to adjust. He commented that I would never be worldly-wise. *"Do you expect her to change at this age? Actually speaking, today's happening is a warning to us. Her earlier disappointments and bitter experiences coupled with her present angry mood might induce her to jump into the well in our backyard. She might even poison us!"* Earlier when something similar was said about Saroja, I just laughed that away, but not now.

The next morning, Jose made it clear to Rajathi that neither she nor we were happy about her work at our home. He asked her to get her things ready as he wanted to take her to the house of her relative in Madras. It was that man who had brought her to our house three months earlier. Rajathi was shocked but managed to not show it. She requested Jose to get her a ticket straight to Mettur. Jose refused to send her alone for obvious reasons. She glared at me, and I understood its meaning – Jose had never found fault with her and so the idea of dismissal must have been mine. In fact, I made him give her some extra amount on account of the sudden dismissal. While going, she just walked out without even a glance towards me. I vowed to myself never to engage a full-time servant again!

Three years later in Little Mount house, 'Saroja-like' Rajeswari worked for us. She was a bright-eyed, ever cheerful puny young woman and mother of three little children. When I knew she was an illiterate, I taught her to read and write Tamil. Later when I was at Holy Flower School, Salem, Rajeswari sent me a letter after obtaining my address from Maimol. Her loving letter albeit with spelling mistakes made me happy and I sent her an immediate reply congratulating her on her maiden attempt.

Rajeswari was quite nimble and hard working. Though sincere and obedient, she was slow to understand things. In those days, huge cylindrical concrete structures were kept for waste disposal in every street. When I noticed Rajeswari banging our plastic waste-bin on the rim of the concrete structure to get all the rubbish out, I told her such banging would break it soon. After some days, when the banging sound was heard again, it was a bin from another house where she had started working. I told her that theirs was also breakable. She seemed embarrassed and said, *"Sorry, Amma, how wooden-headed I am! (rapping her head twice). It did not strike me to do it because they did not tell me. Hereafter, I'll take care of theirs too."* Her innocent reply touched my heart. When she came to know that we would soon bid farewell to Madras to settle in Salem, she was in tears. She invited me to her house which was nearby. Before leaving Madras, Maimol and I visited her one-roomed tenement with sweets and biscuits for her children. She happily gave us cool drinks and snacks. When I appreciated the neatness of her dwelling, she shed a shy smile.

When we settled in Bangalore, in Jeevan Griha, I did not engage a domestic help whereas in Jacob Sadhan, the maid who worked for the previous owner continued for us. Mother of three children, young Lakshmi was also illiterate. When I offered to teach her Tamil, her mother tongue, she requested me to teach her son (6th std) Tamil because he learnt Kannada in school. The boy picked up the language quickly as they spoke Tamil at home. After Lakshmi left, I have had only Kannada-speaking maids and with that my spoken Kannada improved!

A few months after we settled in Arakere, I got acquainted with a vegetable vendor by name Mehroonissa (from Tamil Nadu) and she brought me maids whenever I needed one. She has been in Bangalore for many years. She could not send her little daughter to school due to financial constraints coupled with their community's lack of interest in educating girls. We had just then started a charitable trust in Jaimon's name – *Jacob Foundation*. We gave educational aid to that little girl, Nasreen till she passed B.Com. Later, while taking tuitions, she completed MBA privately. Mehroonissa shared her gratitude gladly, *"Amma, only because of you we sent Nasreen to school, otherwise she would have become a vegetable vendor like me. Now she knows many things. She says even if we die, our organs can be given to needy people to save them. She wants to educate somebody when she earns a better salary."* I thanked God for the chain reaction. Safia, Mehroonissa's elder daughter (has two school-going children) was engaged as our cook for two years when I underwent surgery for carpel tunnel syndrome and for the problems of varicose veins.

Now a slight deviation. An elderly woman, owner of four houses in a plot opposite Jacob Sadhan was once mistaken to be a maid! Raniamma, who resided in one house and received rent for three, had a cleanliness mania. She swept her compound and the street in front of her house many times a day. A new tenant to our house asked Raniamma to be her domestic help. On knowing Raniamma's identity, the shocked lady immediately apologised to her. Our tenant shared her experience with me and admired Raniamma's patient smile at her imprudence. Yes, it is rare to see such understanding souls.

Towards the end of Raniamma's life, when she suffered a lot, she sought my help to convert to Christianity. I made her understand that God is ONE whom we call by different names and asked her to pray to Jesus, without converting to Christianity. Satisfied with my answer, she asked for a picture of Jesus and kept it along with those of Hindu gods and goddesses. Later, when Maimol and children (Raniamma was very fond of them) came from Mumbai during Diwali holidays in 2012, they visited her, but she could not recognize them. By then she had lost her voice too. In a few days she passed away peacefully.

We are not only children of God, but also servants. The time allotted to us on this earth is for finishing our duties in the best way possible, seeking Divine Guidance at every step. But many live as if they have no such agenda in their lives. Bharathiyar who makes Lord Krishna his servant in one poem, has also written some more poems in which Krishna gets different roles. In the poem 'Kannan, En Arasan' (Krishna, My King) he sings about the glories of the deity to whom all are subjects.

Forever will I sing

Fame of Kannan, our King.

The above are two lines from that enchanting poem of 56 lines.

A faithful and good servant is a real godsend;

But truly 'tis a rare bird in the land.

– Martin Luther

16

Peace-Making for Weal

Even as a teenager, I started praying for world peace and later I firmly believed that such a prayer was sown in my spirit by God Almighty. Over the years I have been praying for World Peace and Happiness daily along with my regular prayers thrice a day.

Blessed are the peacemakers;

For they shall be called children of God.

– Jesus Christ

There was a strong reason for my girlhood wish to become a peacemaker. In the 1950s some families living in our lane in Coimbatore often quarrelled using unprintable words. Sometimes, it escalated to kicks and blows – husbands beating wives, parents raining blows upon their children, etc. Once, I shuddered with horror and sadness when a man kicked his aged mother.

As I grew up, my desire to be a peacemaker waned because of my fearful and tearful nature. Though above average in studies, I was neither good at sports nor had any oratorical or histrionic abilities. Naturally, my self-esteem was very low. I became courageous only at the age of 30 after becoming mother of two children. At 51, I enrolled myself for a week's counselling course in Bangalore. The Course Director appreciated my participation in interactive sessions. Later she said that it was rare to find people with such high self-esteem like me! My heart overflowed with gratitude to God who brought about the transformation in me through sufferings. *'Sweet are the uses of adversity'* – how true Shakespeare's words are!

Appachan was a peacemaker and I am fortunate to inherit that quality which blossomed once I became morally courageous. Generally, people try to avoid feuds in families of friends and relatives. The dove of peace that I have always been, helping people solve their problems became my passion. With love and humility when I say, they pay heed to my counsel. It is said to be unwise to interfere between husband and wife. Yet, if one of them asks me earnestly, I do intervene. Witnessing my own life, I could bring about change in the attitude of couples. Of course, only after earnest prayers I take up such ventures. Talking in person or over the phone; writing letters, gifting suitable books, etc. are my strategies in peace-making. Spending time and money for such efforts gives me spiritual satisfaction.

In the name of peace-making, some mischief-mongers add fuel to the flames. They convey what one party said about the other or their own version and finally request them to settle the matter amicably. Such people derive cheap thrill when the quarrel continues with passions flared up. Speaking truth is the ultimate virtue; but everyone need not be told all the truth. Concealing certain facts for the sake of peace and happiness is truly noble. But the one who hides the truth should not have any selfish motive, including the feeling of pride in doing so. The saying, *'Men see actions; God sees intentions'* makes it clear. Selfless people with wisdom, truthfulness and humility are the best peacemakers.

Once, during the marriage of a relative's daughter, another relative quarrelled with his wife and wanted to leave the place before partaking of the wedding feast. His father-in-law blamed him for the quarrel. Both the parties were right on certain points of arguments. So, I requested the younger man to calm down and asked for forgiveness on behalf of his wife's family. He retorted that those who humiliated him should do that and not I. He was made to understand that it was hard for many to utter the word 'sorry' with sincerity at the appropriate time. I requested him (who was much younger to me) to respect my age (46) and pay heed to my words. Finally, he decided to stay back, thereby avoiding further deterioration of the situation. *'You need great love to forgive but greater humility to ask for forgiveness',* says Mother Teresa.

Another time, a relative told me that her husband had threatened to go somewhere leaving her and their three teenaged children and sought my intervention. I was not quite well at that time, yet I went to meet that elderly man. We started with a prayer together. I then pointed out the adverse consequences, if his decision was carried out. He had his own valid reasons and so the arguments went on for nearly an hour. In the end, he condescended to stay on for the time being. By God's grace, today they are together and enjoy the company of their grandchildren.

My peace-making efforts also extended to neighbours and strangers. My maiden attempt at peace-making was at the age of 32. That was the time I had resigned from Home Science College after many problems at home. A childless couple and the man's widowed mother were our neighbours then. They had adopted the man's elder brother's daughter. The girl was in her early teens when the incident occurred. One evening I heard the muffled sobbing of the girl and the shouting of her parents. When lashing sounds were heard, I was shocked and decided to intervene. I knelt and prayed first and with palpitating heart started climbing the stairs to their house. How could I face them with my peace-making mission if they questioned me about the quarrels in our home? Besides that, both of them were older than me. Anyway, I entered the house with mixed feelings.

My unannounced visit at an unwelcome time shocked them. The old lady was silently weeping in a corner of the drawing room. The young girl ran into another room as soon as she saw me. I apologized for my sudden intrusion and pleaded with them, *"Please stop beating her. Whatever wrong she has done, this won't be the solution."* Fortunately, they never asked me any embarrassing questions. The lady poured out: *"A youth has been following her for the past one month and she never told us about it. When a friend informed us, we felt humiliated. If something had happened, won't her parents blame us for not bringing up their daughter properly?"* It was justifiable anger and so I said, *"What you say is absolutely right. I know your child to be a quiet and obedient girl. Fear and inexperience might have prevented her from sharing it with you. Please tell her calmly about the seriousness of the matter."* Once again saying sorry for my interference, I came down quickly.

While living in 'Shobana' house, one night we heard the loud crying of a woman at 11o'clock. We were new to the area and thought it could be a sick person. Later we knew that the woman, grandmother of two, had been beaten up by her husband and it happened there occasionally. It is unpardonable even if a reckless youth beats his 'better half'. How cruel of an elderly man to beat his aged wife to the extent of making her scream around midnight! As the principal of St. Thomas School, I used to be greeted by people around, including that 'gentleman' who was a retired official.

After some days, at about 10.30pm, we heard her sobbing again, somewhat nearby. Their house was diagonally opposite to ours. We came out and saw her sitting on the gravel near their gate. Her husband was yelling at her. I requested Jose to come with me to pacify them. He reasoned with me, *"Don't be senseless. He might ask us to mind our own business. Nobody, including their married daughter* (a practising doctor) *living nearby seemed to have interfered so far."* We thought of retiring as silence prevailed for a while. When I knelt down for bedtime prayer, I heard her sobs again. I went outside to check and saw her still at the gate. Her daughter was going towards her; but the man came running from the house with a stick in his hand and shouted, *"Go back"* and the girl swiftly went back to her house. She was helpless as the aggressor was her father.

Since Jose was unwilling to come with me, I decided to go alone. He warned me, *"That man might be drunk and in his inebriated state he may not recognize you. If he beats you with that stick, what a shame it would be!"* But I was determined and went inside to pray once more on bended knees. I have always derived immense courage and strength of spirit after praying for a specific action which involves risk. Maimol and Babu (Jaimon was at BITS) looked at me anxiously. When I started moving towards their gate, 14-year-old Babu came along unasked to 'protect' his 45-year-old mother! I told the lady to go inside as it was almost midnight. She wept and murmured, *"He won't let me in and will beat me again."* Suddenly, he appeared from the darkness and said sarcastically, *"What do you want, Madam? Perhaps you want to give her refuge in your home. I have no objection. Take her."* He then gave a tap on the gate with the 'stick'. I shuddered at the sound and realized it was a metal rod! No wonder the woman wailed pitiably. Anger surged within me and I prayed for patience. In a calm voice, I said, *"Why should I take her to our home? She is your wife. Whatever be her mistake, this is not the way to treat her!"* Fortunately, he calmed down and said, *"Madam, she is a lazy goose. When grandchildren come home, she groans to make some special items for them."* So, that was the 'crime' done by the old lady. *'Faults are thick when love is thin'.*

I reasoned with him, *"Mr. D____, you are an educated man. I need not say much about this situation. It is almost midnight and it is dangerous to leave her here* (at the gate) *alone. Please allow her to go inside. I request you to not beat her anymore."* For a few seconds he was silent and uttered just one word to his wife – *"Go"*. She at once got up, but almost fell. When I asked him to help her, he sneered, *"She's acting; you don't know her, Madam"* and went home quickly. She thanked me and moved with unsteady steps towards their house about 15 feet away from the gate. I couldn't help her as their gate was locked. In the following days, we heard her cries two or three times. After that, no crying was heard in the next one year that we lived there. When we prayerfully and sincerely act, desired results do happen sooner or later.

Peace-making was done once for a 'homeless' family. There were some roadside dwellers at Little Mount in Madras, near our apartment complex. Sky was their common roof One evening, as I was getting ready to go to church opposite our flat, I heard the heart-rending cry of a woman. A man was beating her with a large piece of firewood. The other dwellers there watched the scene in helplessness. The cruelty meted out to women, be it in a bungalow or a shack, is the same. When I said I would intervene, Jose was shocked, *"Are you mad? He is fully drunk. If he beats you with the firewood, no one will blame him. Everyone would say it was foolish on your part to advise a boorish drunkard!"* On my way to church, I found him sitting quietly, but the woman was still lying there and crying. Perhaps the man was in a state of 'exhaustion' after wielding the firewood. In the church, I prayed for them and prayed for myself to have courage to do something about it.

While returning home, I saw him beating her again. I said loudly in Tamil, *"Stop it. How long has this been going on! Just because she is a woman, can you beat her like this?"* Shuffling his feet, he toddled towards me saying, *"Amma, my……"* Instinctively, I stepped back and told him sternly, *"Stop where you are and speak. I can hear you very well."* By God's Grace, he stood there and continued, *"My wife has gone astray. If not I, who will correct her? Don't you think it's my responsibility?"* Yes, marriage had given him that 'license'. Patience, as usual, befriended me and I told the 'responsible' boor, *"Look here, in every family, there are problems. Beating is not the solution. If you beat her like this, she would get seriously injured and you'll have to take her to hospital."* Some menfolk from the community came forward and advised him to pay heed to 'Madam's words'. They took the firewood from him and threw it away. They could not be blamed for not doing it earlier as he would have quarrelled with them too. An outsider's words had some effect.

When I reached home, Jose, who had been watching everything from the balcony of our first-floor flat, said, *"Minutes after you walked away, he started beating her again. What is the use of your advice?"* My repartee, *"A male chauvinist will not listen to advice that easily from a woman. But I'm confident he would change gradually."* Peace reigned there for some days. As fate would have it, the man met with an accident and his leg was fractured. His wife on whom he had rained blows took care of him. How enigmatic life is! Confined to a 'corner' in the street, the man would have a chance to repent, I thought.

My peace mission once worked for Amma and Jose! When I resigned from Home Science College (1976), both were so angry that they rarely spoke to me. But they had long chats in the evenings. Once, Amma said something humiliating about Jose in the presence of his friends. After the guests had left, the unusual happened – Jose shouted at Amma! He had never before raised his voice against her. Then the next wonder – Amma was silent for the first time! It was evident that she realized the gravity of her thoughtless words and her son's justifiable anger. Anyway, they never talked to each other for three days. There was deafening silence at home except for the lisping of Jaimon and Maimol. I had already been out of the list of 'speakers'. Since Jose went to office, Amma's silence did not affect him much. But it was pathetic to see Amma always brooding over the happenings with a vacant stare. I said to Jose, *"Don't be so stubborn. For Amma's nature, she would never start conversing with you. It is not right to make her feel so lonely in her old age."* He walked away without replying. After some time, I saw them talking. Feeling contented, I thanked God.

It was a good example to prove that what we imbibe when young and the consequent mind-set would stay with us till the end. My compassionate nature did not exclude Amma though she had always been hurting me with her attitude and words. All of a sudden, a lightning thought struck me. If an ordinary woman could have such a forgiving heart, what about God – the Ocean of Mercy? Can God allow anyone to suffer eternal damnation? There is only heaven in the after-life, I concluded. Hell was invented by ancient teachers to scare people away from evil.

Some years later, I happened to read something similar at the end of the great epic Mahabharata in the English prose version written by Sri Rajagopalachary. After Krishna's death, all the younger Pandavas and Draupadi passed away. Finally, Yudhishtra was on his journey to heaven. On reaching, he was shocked to see Duryodhana, the Kuru Prince, seated on a beautiful throne with the goddess of heroism standing in attendance beside him. With hatred and anger, Yudhishtra turned his head to look for his brothers. Sage Narada present there told him to get rid of his negative feelings and stay there with his cousin. He then burst out, *"O sage, Duryodhana was a man of greed and envy. He heaped untold sufferings upon good people. Yet, if he has attained this heaven, where is the region of greater glory which must be the abode of my good and brave brothers? I want to be there; not here."* He was then taken to a dark place where worms were wriggling with insufferable stench in the air. He also saw other more weird and revolting scenes. He quickly started moving away from that deplorable place when he heard his brothers and Draupadi crying out to him, *"O Dharmaputra, please don't go away. Your presence has given us momentary relief from all these tortures."* Yudhishtra was horrified. He could neither believe his eyes nor ears. He wondered whether he was dreaming or had gone insane. Yet, he was only too willing to stay in that horrible hell to be with his beloved brothers. At once, Indra and Yama appeared before him. Darkness and horrid sights vanished and the place became bright and beautiful. Yama, the god of Dharma said, *"My son, it was an illusion created by us to test your righteous nature."* In a flash, Yudhishtra's mortal frame was gone and with that all traces of anger and hatred also disappeared. When he saw all – brothers and cousins – in great happiness and peace, he realized that everyone had attained the state of gods after the death on earth.

'Neither the expectation of heaven, nor the fear of hell would induce me to be good. I do good for goodness' sake'. If we follow this great idea of the unknown writer, we would certainly attain world peace and happiness. Shakespeare says:

All the world's a stage;

And all the men and women merely players.

It indicates that we act the part given to us. We are mere puppets in the 'hands' of the Supreme Spirit. Once our part is completed, we leave the 'stage'. If we are aware of this Divine Design, we would not harbour feelings of hatred, anger and jealousy towards anyone. The ultimate outcome would be harmonious coexistence.

Evil never befalls them that scan

Own faults as they do those of others.

– Thiruvalluvar

17

Miraculous Escapes

When young, I had been saved from near-death incidents thrice (details in Chapter 3). Quite a few miraculous escapes happened later for me and others in the family, though my first-born met with a fatal accident in the prime of his youth. But BIRTH and DEATH are immutably predestined.

Once in Madras (1984) our scooter screeched to a halt in the middle of the road. The rim of the front wheel had broken. Neither did Jose and I fall on the road nor was there much traffic in that usually busy road. We were fortunate that nothing untoward happened. I had been pillion rider with Jose safely for 44 years. I decided to stop it on my 70th birthday in 2016. But when Karnataka Government made helmet mandatory for pillion riders from 11th January that year, I quit it after riding for the last time on 10th January. I decided not to travel with a 'crown' on my head! The curious coincidence in this is that, 44 years earlier on 11th January, I started pillion riding after my wedding on 10th January, 1972!

Again, in Madras, while taking young 'JMJ' on scooter, Jose had to apply sudden brake when a youth on a bicycle crossed his path. All four fell on the road with the scooter and the youth with his cycle, to boot. Everyone escaped without a scratch as both were riding at slow speed. During accidents generally over-speed is the culprit. Once Jaimon was riding our scooter with a friend on the pillion, the fork of the front wheel broke and both fell but were not injured. Sometimes a trip over a small stone can cause a fracture. *Que Sera Sera*!

I had been a busy bee assiduously doing my duties both at home and outside (part-time teaching in Bangalore) even as I was nearing 58. In September 2003, while returning from the seminary, I fell on the road and sustained two hair-line cracks on my right instep. With that, my 'fast-walking' came to an end. When I fell, my right foot's instep and sole partially reversed their positions and 66 kilos (my weight then) got deposited on it! The doctor was surprised that there was no fracture despite the kind of fall I had at that age. When he knew about my job, he attributed it to my active life instead of a sedentary one. While sending me home with a plaster cast for six weeks, he advised me not to get it wet or soiled. Ten days later my daughter's engagement took place in Christa Prabhalaya Church at Jayanagar. When relatives came, the hostess became 'guest'. My sisters and sisters-in-law (4+4, quite a number!) managed everything in the kitchen while I took 'rest'.

Since there was no fracture, I was able to attend to my personal needs on my own. For bathing, I sat on a stool and kept my right foot on another and Maimol wound a long cloth on the bandage. She covered my leg with a plastic bag and secured it with a ribbon. Afterwards I would need her help to remove all the 'paraphernalia' and lead me to bed. Six weeks later, while removing the cast, the doctor congratulated me on its 'spick and span' state. Most of the patients went back to him, he said, with dirtied and at times stinking bandages. I was happy to say that, for decades I had made my students obey me for their studies. Now it was my turn to obey the doctor for my cure. When I said the credit also went to my daughter who helped me a lot to keep it clean, the doctor smiled at Maimol who was beside me!

Another blessing in those days was that Babu could do his work from home using the computer and mobile phone. In case he had to go out on an urgent business, he would lock the house from outside so that no one would disturb me. His study of catering technology came in handy to prove his culinary skills. Soon Maimol's wedding took place and within four months, Babu's too. I resumed my part-time teaching, therefore, after one year. I taught the novitiates in Carmel Nivas Convent in J P Nagar for three years. Of the many nuns, including the Superior, Sr. Lourdes Nadal (a Spanish nun), who became friends there, today we have contact with only one, Sr. Marykutty – a loving and caring soul. Later I taught at Nirmalaram Seminary in Arakere for some months. I also taught in two nursing institutions – some months in T. John Nursing College in Gottikere and two years in Santhome Nursing College in Hulimavu. Sr. Celine, the warden of the latter is now in Kerala and still in touch with me. Herself a nurse, that kind-hearted nun had been a great support to me during those two years that I served there. Thus, I had part-time teaching career of about ten years in Bangalore till the age of 62.

When I was 59, I fell slipping on water in the kitchen and had the 'blessing' of experiencing MRI scan for a suspected ligament tear on the knee. The third time I fell when I was 64. After having dinner for Sam's (our tenant's son) first birthday celebration, while getting up from the chair, I felt unsteady and sat again. But the chair had inadvertently been pushed by me while standing up and I sat straight on the floor. A fainting sensation overpowered me; yet I managed to smile. Sam's parents had to 'struggle' to raise me from the floor. My spinal column could have become shaky! By Divine Grace, I was not hurt in any manner. In the span of next 10 years, I had 3 more falls – twice at home and once near our gate. Thanks to God's abundant mercy, every time with no injury.

I had been saved twice from falling in the nick of time. At 63, I used to limp due to severe knee pain. Once the outlet hose of the washing machine got disconnected at the joint and there was plenty of water around the machine. Coming from the backyard's bright sunlight, I did not see the water and stepped into the 'pool'. Because of the limp, my walk was very slow which prevented my falling flat. Had I been seriously injured or fainted, Jose would have had to break open the door to get inside the house. In a few days my limp disappeared and I knew why I had limped till then!

I was about to fall one early morning when again a 'pool' appeared in our dining room. Water had overflowed from 'Pure-it' (water purifier) the previous night. Coming from the bedroom I was shocked to see plenty of water glimmering in the dim light of the night lamp. Daily I used to walk straight towards Pure-it but on that day; 'unusually' I took the other side around the dining table. If I had come the usual way, I would not have seen the water in that twilight hour. No doubt, my Guardian Angel changed the direction of walking. The falling and near-falling experiences plus assorted ailments, knees downward have made me walk like a nonagenarian these days. Years ago, my students in Home Science College used to jokingly say, *'Miss, you don't know how to walk; you go running from class to class!'*

During a night train journey, mine was a side lower berth. Stretching my legs to the opposite seat, I started reading a book. It was 9 p.m. and many, including Jose were fast asleep. Intuitively (understood the meaning later), I lowered my legs and continued reading. Within minutes the upright berth from the loosened clamp came crashing down with a thunderous sound. Jose and others were startled out of their sleep. They heaved a sigh of relief after knowing the old lady (I was 64) was not hurt. It was a narrow escape for my legs which would have been smashed into pulp. Again, had I sat in a reclining position, both my knees would have had multiple fracture. My eyes welled up with gratitude to the Almighty. The very next day, through a letter to the editor of a newspaper I requested the railways to have periodical checking more often and advised passengers to check berths and shutters for their own safety.

The most remarkable escape happened when I led the lonely life in Salem. In order to get me back to family life, my siblings 'conspired' with Jose and decided to take me to CMC, Vellore for psychiatric consultation! Marykutty told me that a meeting with a renowned priest had been arranged in Vellore to discuss my plans for social service. (My beloved sister later apologized to me for the well-meant lie.) Accordingly, Marykutty, her husband, Jose and I went to Vellore. Not aware of their 'plot', I was happy to see Akkal and her husband there. Actually, Akkal had come to stay with me in the hospital where I might have to be admitted. When we entered the famous CMC Hospital, I got an inkling of the matter. But they allayed my doubt saying that the priest had been staying there for a while. On reaching the destination, the words – Psychiatry Department – revealed the truth. Livid with rage I exclaimed, *"You've cheated me. I'm going back to Salem alone. Anyway, my life's journey is going to be alone hereafter!"* I quickly started walking back. Suddenly two male nurses took hold of me and started walking towards the consultation room. I pushed them with all the strength I could muster at the age of 50 and shouted, *"Please leave me. I have no psychiatric problem."* That, of course, 'confirmed' to the people around that I was a nervous wreck. A doctor gave me an injection and I was taken to a room which had already been booked by my folks. Except Jose and Akkal, the others went back.

The next morning, I was taken to a room where I met three doctors. Without wasting a moment, I implored them, *"Good morning doctors. Please listen to me. I have no psychiatric problem. My thinking is quite different from a normal person's. That doesn't mean I have lost my mental balance. Kindly don't give me any medicine which might impair my memory and wisdom. Will you please tell me the nature of injection given to me yesterday?"* One of them smilingly assured me, *"Don't worry; we will not come to a conclusion without hearing what you have to say. The injection was just a tranquillizer to calm you."* The main points of my narration then were about my long (30 years) teaching career and how I had decided to serve the society in a more meaningful way for the rest of my life. My interest in the unity of religions following Gandhian principles was shared with them. After intently listening to me they discussed among themselves in a low voice. Then one doctor said, *"You may not need any medicine right now. Yet you have to stay here for a few days for our observation."* With great relief and happiness, I returned to the room with Akkal and Jose who were waiting outside. I thanked God and joyfully remembered two lines from a poem by Bharathiar:

Oh Power Divine, you have created me with flaming wisdom;

Won't you give me the strength to do good to the world?

We stayed there in a large room with a backyard. The daily routine was quite interesting! After bathing and washing our clothes, we went to the canteen for breakfast. Then we took a walk in the vast campus full of trees. Back in the room we read the newspaper and the books I had brought. I carry one or two books wherever I go. Taking lunch in the canteen we came back to room for a nap. In the evening after tea with snacks we had another 'health walk'. At 6.30 pm I visited the doctors for the observation session. Then, supper, reading and sleep followed; in that order! On the day of 'discharge', we went for a Tamil movie in a nearby theatre and returned to Salem.

Later, what Akkal said would give an accurate picture of my 'treatment' in CMC, "*Alice, doctors have confirmed that you have no mental illness. I came here wondering how I would make you take medicines at the appointed hours.* (I was quite rebellious then!) *Now I feel I had been on vacation and thoroughly enjoyed the stay with you. Please get rid of the idea of social service from your mind till your children settle in life.*" I must be the only 'patient' who stayed in CMC for some days without taking any medicine for the 'cure'. While bidding farewell Dr Suja Kurian said, "*You have no psychiatric problem; yet please come after two months for a review. It would help you get convinced about staying with your family. Moreover, I am interested to know more about your ideas regarding unity of religions.*" With tears of joy, I thanked her but we did not go there again. I was overwhelmed with gratitude to God Almighty for the bittersweet experience.

Varicose veins had been on my legs from my late 40s. I did not bother about them much as they were painless. When I was 62, one morning (19th Nov 2007) after bathing, I was baffled to see a pool of blood around me in the bathroom. It was a mystery as there was no wound on my body at that time. When I saw blood spurting from my right ankle I bent and pressed the spot to stop the bleeding. But it continued and I prayed for my 'invisible wound'. The bleeding then stopped within a few seconds. I wondered why I never had any pain all the while. Curiously on the same date next month – 19th Dec – blood spurted from the same spot while walking. The first-time technique did not work and I applied ice cubes and the bleeding stopped. Later I knew from the vascular surgeon that my handling of a bleeding vein was dangerously wrong. Bending and pressing would give more pressure to the vein resulting in more bleeding. As first-aid I should sit immediately and keep my affected leg in a raised position and bandage the spurting vein. In case the condition worsens, I should be admitted to hospital immediately. Merciful God condoned my ignorance twice!

Since blood spurted twice on 19th, both in November and December, 19th January 2008 became ominous. After breakfast on that day, while cleaning the dining table, I felt the right foot getting wet. Blood had already spurted from the same spot to a half circle on the floor. Sitting on a chair, I raised my leg to another chair. Jose bandaged the vein but by then my right foot was completely covered with blood, though the spurting had stopped. If I had walked then, there would have been Alice Paada like Krishna Paada on Krishna Jayanthi! So, Jose did 'paada seva' (cleaned my foot with wet cotton) before letting me walk. When he urged me to go to hospital, I joked that nothing would happen till 19th February. But the real reason was that my sister-in-law Celine was very serious with cancer and was in a state of counting her days. In case surgery was the only option for me, I did not want to have it at that crucial time.

Coincidentally, a long-lost friend contacted me over the phone and enquired after my health. She advised me to try homeopathy for my varicose veins. I immediately acted upon her suggestion. Whenever I took those mustard-seed-like homeopathic white pills, my little grandsons – Aryan and Arush – used to pester me for those tiny candies, which I 'relished' for nearly a year! Meanwhile we visited the ailing Celine in North Parur and within a month, she passed away.

During the next five years I had been unusually travelling a great deal including a pilgrimage to the Holy Land in 2012 and my varicose veins had been very 'friendly'. But in 2013, when the spurting recurred, I underwent Endo-venous Radio Frequency Ablation Surgery for both the legs at St. John's Medical College Hospital in Bangalore. My husband's cousin Sr. Mary Mercy, belonging to 'Daughters of Mercy' order was working there then. Her prayerful care for me whenever she was free, became a great blessing for which I am forever thankful to her.

Actually, two years before this surgery, I had a miraculous escape in Babu's newly bought flat. One evening, when all had gone out, only Rayan (aged 3) and the maid were with me. The child was sleeping on the sofa and the maid was preparing supper. To look at a photo closely, I opened the glass door of the show case – 4' length 1' breadth fixed at 3' above the floor – and it fell down with an ear-splitting sound to break into smithereens. Rayan woke up with a start and the maid came running from the kitchen. The scene in the living room made her request me to move to a safe distance till she cleaned the place. On recollecting the sequence of the event later, I was amazed at the various ways we were saved on that day. First, all in the family except the kid (asleep!) were out. Secondly if the heavy glass door had fallen in front of me, the blood from my varicose-veins-ridden feet would have made the hall look like battlefield after a war! Fortunately, it opened fully and fell just behind me causing no injury, not even a small glass piece pierced me! Lastly, the maid came very late that day. It took nearly an hour for her to clean the place as there were many glass pieces on the carpet too. I would have been in the soup if she had finished the work and gone home at the usual time. I never had a mobile then and Babu did not have land line connection. Yes, the maid had to be 'late' on that day. Moreover, to my great relief Rayan did not make an additional scene by crying. My heart sent up countless thanks to God Almighty.

But it did not end there. The same night when Babu opened the dining room cupboard, the glass door came off the clamp. The incident just narrated by me instinctively made him hold it before it fell down. Five-year old Aryan was standing near him! The next day Babu got all the glass doors replaced with fibre-glass doors. Careless work of the carpenter was certainly the cause. But little Rayan told everyone the 'truth' as he knew it, "*It was Ammachi who broke that door*".

Amma had a few close shaves while she had been with us. When she was 63, in Mettur a big he-goat pushed her and she fell on the road but was not hurt. (10 years later, when she was in Kerala, tripping over a stone she fell and had three hair-line cracks on her toes.) In Madras, she was saved thrice from dangerous situations. One evening, after making some snacks as she turned, her hand tilted the cooking bowl with hot oil. Had it fallen to her side, she would have been very badly scalded. The second incident happened while we were living near Little Mount Church. After attending evening Mass, Amma was coming down the steps holding her son's hand. Tripping on a small stone she lost her grip from Jose's hand and swayed and abruptly sat on the previous step. The church on the hillock had many more steps and she, at 72 was rather obese. Had she fallen?! I shuddered at the very thought of it. The third incident escape was while struggling to get up from the commode, she held on to the nearby wash basin. The pressure exerted by her was so much that it came crashing down. Neither did it fall on her feet nor did any sharp piece pierce her.

On 24th May 2006, Amma died due to cardiac arrest at late night at North Parur in Kerala. In order to reach for the funeral the next day, we decided to take a flight from Bangalore; but tickets were not available to Kochi. Babu who was based in Chennai then, sent us e-ticket to reach Chennai where he would join us, as three air tickets were available from there to Kochi. We reached Chennai airport in time and unfortunately heard the announcement of our onward flight's 2½ hours' delay. Babu blurted out, "*If your flight from Bangalore were delayed, I was pondering over my plight of having three tickets with one to travel. I never expected this!*" Later with one more delay of 1½ hours Jose exclaimed, "*If they announce delay again, I might get heart attack!*" We earnestly prayed for God's merciful intervention. Finally, we reached the cemetery at 7.30 p.m. instead of reaching home much earlier. It was drizzling and we came to know there had been heavy rain throughout the day. After our prayers for the departed soul, the body was interred as all the rituals had already been over. A friend said that our delay had set tongues wagging. It seems one remarked, "*Maimol's husband and his mother reached from far away Mumbai much earlier. It took such a long time for her only son and family to come from close-by Bangalore.*" Maimol could not come because doctor had advised bed rest during that period of her first pregnancy. There were a few more caustic comments which hurt me deeply. However, with God's blessing we could reach before the burial.

About the critical moments faced by my children, Jaimon's measles when he was 3 and his narrow escape had already been written. When Maimol was nine, she had high fever for a week and her mouth became askew leaving her unable to speak. As usual I tearfully vowed to do an act of self-denial. With prayers and medicines, she had complete cure after a few days. A mother can bear her illness but not when her children suffer.

At the age of 7, Babu was severely affected by dysentery and was on liquid diet. One day he started vomiting whatever he had, including medicine. The anxious thought of dehydration terrified me. Jose was at office which was far away. Near the Secretariat Colony area in Kilpauk, autos were rare to sight (1984). Taking Babu on my shoulder I almost ran to the clinic more than half-a-kilometre away. On reaching the clinic upstairs, sorrow and gasping prevented me from speaking coherently. Dr Paulo, the Malayali doctor who had been treating 'JMJ' since the time we had settled in Madras gave Babu an injection and wrote for different medicines. When the doctor came to know that I had gone there walking, carrying Babu, he called his driver to drop us home. I thanked him for his thoughtfulness. Babu has always been on the fatter side but to make my 'task' lighter he was somewhat lean then!

Now, some dangers faced by our things. In 1994 Maimol went to Delhi to attend an NCC camp. At the end of it she left for Madras on 9th October which happened to be her 19th birthday. On 8th midnight her camp mates sang birthday song and gave her birthday bumps. Merriment continued on 9th as it was also the last day of the camp. The same night they boarded the train and on 10th morning she could not find her suitcase. All started searching thinking it to be a prank by one of her friends. Then they knew it to be a sure case of theft. She submitted a complaint to the Railway Police within the train and tearfully prayed for it. The suitcase contained all her things including the prizes and the certificates she had received at the camp. It also had the beautiful silk sari given to all the cadets representing Tamil Nadu. Happily going from Madras and returning empty-handed from Delhi was too much for her to bear.

Early next morning, just before the train chugged into Madras Central, she was woken up by her friend and asked to verify if a particular suitcase was hers. Hoping against hope she looked at the place pointed. And lo, it was very much there! The mystery of the missing suitcase unfolded when she checked it. There was evidence of someone having tampered with it. The lock was thoroughly damaged but it had not budged. All sides had markings made by a sharp tool. In short, it was in a pathetic condition; yet truly a 'V.I.P.'! Risking his 'career', the good and just thief brought it back to the same place. Later Jose sent a letter of appreciation to the V.I.P. company.

Here is another 'just' thief with common sense. In 1990, we were in Coimbatore as usual for summer vacation. 14-year-old Babu lost his purse in the local bus there. He laughed at the pickpocket's disappointment in getting less than ten rupees from his purse. But he was upset about losing his school identity card, a list of telephone numbers and birth dates of his friends (non-mobile era!). After two weeks, the purse lost in Coimbatore was returned to him at his school in Madras! How did the magic happen? The 'good thief' was satisfied with the meagre amount he got and deposited the purse in a post box. What presence of mind! A schoolboy's identity card must have moved his heart. On receiving the purse, the Madras post office sent it to the Principal of Don Bosco School at Egmore, where Babu was studying. Can we expect such good service from today's post offices? Experiences of encountering such 'ethical' thieves can be shared through dailies, weeklies and WhatsApp!

Next is the theft of our new motorbike – the gift by Jaimon to his brother on his 21st birthday (Dec 1997). Babu had been working in Madras then. He was immensely happy to receive a brand-new Hero Honda Splendor from his loving brother. Within six months Jaimon passed away and Babu resigned his job and came to Bangalore. He joined Oxford College of Hotel Management at J P Nagar as a Lecturer. In a month's time he got Karnataka registration for his bike and it vanished the very next day! Babu had been riding it to many places before he changed the registration and it was 'safe'. The shrewd thief must have had an eye on it as it was stolen when parked near the college where Babu had been working.

After submitting a written complaint at the police station, Babu went there now and then to enquire. Three months later he claimed the insurance amount and bought another Hero Honda Splendor of the same colour. We considered it as Jaimon's gift. Subsequently, we shifted to Jacob Sadhan at Arakere about 5 km away. Two months later, a policeman from J P Nagar brought the good news of the recovery of our motor bike. At once, Jose and Babu went and found it to be ours, but in a very bad shape with some parts missing. If we claimed it, the insurance amount would have to be returned and so we sadly let it go. The police department equalled the postal department in providing excellent service!

In 1986 danger threatened our precious books. There had been incessant rain for a week in Madras. When water level rose to one's knees on the roads, schools, colleges and offices were closed. The side portion of the house where we lived then had three moderately high steps to enter the house. But the landlord warned that water might come in, if rains continued as it had happened once earlier. We kept things which could be damaged on the sofa, tables and chairs. But I was worried about the large number of books kept in two trunks and a few cardboard boxes and pushed under the cots. Due to rusting the trunks had small holes underneath. Unless the rain stopped, there was no way for water to recede. I had recourse to prayer. The first two steps were covered with water by then. 'JMJ' were asked to join me in praying for our books. I told them that children's prayer would be more powerful. Within minutes the third step also 'disappeared' and water waited menacingly at the threshold. Had it rained a little longer water would have entered the house. To my great relief and joy, the rain stopped for good. It was a 'mini tsunami' which would have swallowed our books! We thanked God for the immense blessing.

Ten years later in 1996 there was another threat to our books. Now we had nearly a thousand books. Like me, my children are also book lovers. We presented books to each other on birthdays. When we arrived at our apartment in Bangalore, we pushed sack loads of books under the cot as usual. I smiled complacently thinking of Madras 'flood' because our flat here was on the first floor. But my happiness was short lived. We happened to see a big rat inside the house the very first night! Though the security man drove it away I could not get rid of the fear of rat from my mind. What if the same rat or some others came and nibbled at the sacks and the books? Constant prayers for books began again. The three years we lived there; dust was pulled out from under the cot with vacuum cleaner but never the sacks. Yet, when we went to Jacob Sadhan, the books were just as we had bundled them. No rats or insects had dared to damage them! I consider it as a miracle in answer to my earnest prayers.

My 'woman Friday', Saroja once marched towards danger in 1984! In the Secretariat Colony house in Madras, when a cobra was found in the landlady's portion of the house, she and her daughter ran out of the house shouting, 'snake, snake'. We came out from the side portion. Menfolk were not present in both the families. Saroja boldly went straight into the room where the snake was with its hood up. She reverently said it was 'Nagaraja' (king cobra) which would do no harm and piously knelt down to worship it. I begged her to come away as there was hardly 10 feet between the woman and the reptile! Finally, I had to pull her out lest she should touch its hood and pray. By then, the men from the neighbourhood came with sticks and rods and chased it out. When they were killing it, Saroja was crying, "*O God, this is sinful. It is nalla paampu (good snake).*"

In 1999, a worker was engaged to fix curtain rods for Jacob Sadhan's first floor portion. He leant the rod on the compound wall and went upstairs to pull it up. Jose warned him about the two overhead tension wires (high and low) in front of the house. He assured us that he would be careful. Soon we heard a thudding sound and a scream. We both ran upstairs. The man was lying on the balcony and the iron rod had fallen on the other side. He slowly raised himself and sat up when he saw us. He looked dazed and admitted the mistake he had made. Concentrating on one wire, he failed to notice the other for a moment and the rod touched it. Fortunately, the current tripped but he got the shock and fell away from the rod. Thus, a greater danger got averted. Jose offered to take him to a clinic nearby, but he refused. I made him a cup of coffee and we told him to do the work the next day. Since he felt much better, he insisted doing it the same day. We gave him extra amount for his neat work with 'enthusiasm' despite getting a shock! Actually, Maimol was in the balcony where the rod fell and had left the place to come down, seconds ago. I tearfully thanked God for saving the young worker and all of us too. The impact on the balcony grill was such that it had to be welded the next day.

Dog lovers might get angry when I say man's 'best friend' is a dangerous animal. I do love dogs as I love all beings. But I do not like their proximity. Right from girlhood I had the fear of dogs because of a bitter experience of seeing a little girl of my age dying due to the bite of a rabid dog. Jose was bitten by such a dog when he was about 10 and had been given 14 injections on the belly around the navel as it was in vogue those days. In fact, his fear of dogs is more than mine. Today the increasing number of street dogs in our country has become a serious threat to people especially children.

Neither a mad dog nor a stray one, but a pet dog posed danger to Jose and me. One of our friends staying nearby had a fierce-looking, ferocious dog which had bitten even the family members twice. Only after locking the main gate, they would let it out from the kennel. Once when we visited them, the gate was not locked and we climbed the stairs to their house on the 1st floor. Our friend was shocked to see us and said that their dog had been let out, just then. We 'ran' into the house asking her to close the grill door immediately. The minute she did that, our 'friend' came galloping with deafening barks. She excused herself and took it down.

Coming up, she apologised for the inconvenience (read danger!) caused. The dog had been barking for some time and her son, while going out let it free after informing her. As she was about to come down to lock the gate, we 'appeared' before her. Her explanation was convincing but the danger involved was too real to be ignored. With a pale face, Jose made an apology for smile. My 'teacher way' was different. She was made to understand the gravity of the incident. If the dog had come while we were climbing the stairs we would have been doubly injured – the dog bite and the fall from the steps out of fear. She regretted the happening and said she would be more careful in future. Anyway, I decided not to go to that house as long as they had that dog. In those days, informing earlier about the visit was ruled out as most of the houses had no phone connection. What surprised me most was that dogs are endowed with a sharp sense of smell and keen sense of hearing and yet it was amazing that our friend's dog did not come up till we reached the house. It was God's boundless mercy indeed!

With such an ingrained fear of dog, it was surprising that I became friendly with a huge dog during my room-alone life in Salem. On the third day of my lonely stay, I heard a knock on the door in the late evening. On opening the door, I saw Jose with a big dog beside him. That nearness indicated that the dog need not be feared. Nevertheless, I wondered about its presence there as the landlord living in the ground floor had no dogs. My perplexed look brought answer from Jose: *"This is the landlord's dog. It was with their elder son in a different city. Now it is going to be here. Since their son had been using this room earlier, it would be mostly in this balcony. They said Bency is a very friendly dog. I came to inform you about it."* I thanked him and he went back.

I did not close the door immediately. For the first time in my life without fear I looked at a dog (a golden retriever) standing close by with great interest. Believe it or not, Bency also looked at me lovingly! At once we became friends; but I kept my distance. Clever Bency could understand it and never came near me nor entered the room. I shared my meals (bread, biscuits, buns, etc) with him often. Sometimes he would scratch the door to get his share. The presence of Bency outside my room most of the time was a solace to me. Even today it is hard to believe about my companionship (only in the mind!) with an animal which was dangerous in my opinion. Bency must have had 'divine training' in anticipation of my lonely life in that single room.

Let dangers deflect; may miracles march on!

God moves in a mysterious way;

His wonders to perform.

He plants his footsteps in the sea,

And rides upon the storm.

– William Cowper

18

Charm of Books and Gandhiji

The rationale behind combining books and Gandhiji is that my love of the former led me to discover the wonderful personality of the latter. My zealous admiration for the Mahatma is a surprise to many. Some have asked me whether anyone in our family had participated in Dandi March or stayed with him in his ashram. 'No' has always been my reply. Sunday moral science class children wanted to know whether I had talked to Gandhiji. To their young minds, an elderly woman like me was fit to have had such a talk. They became saucer eyed when I said I was just a 2-year-old kid when he died at the age of 78. All this has earned me some sobriquets like Gandhi Teacher, Gandhi Aunty, Gandhi Baktha and Woman Gandhi!

Gandhiji was a rare human being. His all-embracing love excluded none. In my opinion, the world would be a paradise if many were like him. Albert Einstein says: '*Gandhi, the greatest political genius of our time, indicated the path to be taken. He gave proof of what sacrifice man is capable, once he has discovered the right path..........Generations to come will scarce believe that such a one as this ever in flesh and blood walked upon the earth*'. World leaders and great men from all walks of life have eulogized the Mahatma. I have many books on him and by him. The more I read about him, the greater is my admiration.

Now, let me turn to books - my first love! Many women would have an urge to buy a sari or dress or an ornament when they see it. The same kind of urge pushes me to buy books. Jose would ask me whether I had read all the books at home. Of course, I have not read many of our books but that would not deter me from buying new ones. Before marriage I had much time to read. But after marriage 24 hours were not enough to juggle with various duties as a mother-cum-teacher. Jaimon, at 18 months would run to Jose if he got the newspaper shouting in Malayalam, *"It's Daddy's"* and come to me if it was a book, *"Mummy's, Mummy's"*. How well the child had observed paper in his Daddy's hands and books in mine. But the books my child had seen in my hands in those days were either textbooks for preparation or notebooks for correction.

After graduation in 1965, I started earning at the age of 19 as a primary school teacher. I joined a scheme by which paying ten rupees per month for 10 months I could buy books worth 120 rupees. Unlike these days, books were quite inexpensive then. At times I had bought good second-hand books for even less than one rupee! In 1976 a monthly spiritual journal, 'Prem Marg', was subscribed for the annual rate of one rupee fifty paise! In 8 pages it had inspiring articles on true incidents. When we shifted to Mettur in 1978, I failed to renew the subscription. I totally forgot about it later due to pressure of work both at home and in school. In 2009, while arranging my books, I found some copies of Prem Marg. At once I wrote to the editor in Pune asking for the subscription rate and received a prompt reply. The editor had thanked me for my letter of appreciation after a gap of 33 years. He considered it as great recognition for their little newsletter. The annual subscription was Rs.24. I subscribed at once but unfortunately, they stopped printing it after 4 years in 2013.

I encourage reading habit in others and so I do not mind lending books to kith and kin. But my 'generosity' ends there. To get back the books I would remind them more than once, if necessary. The following sayings prove that books lent, are mostly never returned:

He who lends a book is an idiot; he who returns the book is more of an idiot. - Arab proverb

I never lend books. From personal experience I know books are never returned. Look at my large collection; most of them, borrowed. - Anon

During adolescence and early adulthood, I read a lot of fiction both in Tamil and English. They were either borrowed or from libraries. The books I prefer buying are on spirituality, philosophy, biographies, autobiographies, better-yourself books, etc. Reading my own books would be of secondary importance as I would read the borrowed ones first so as to return them quickly. Jesus says, *'Do unto others what you would like others do unto you.'*!

I like gifting books for celebrations like weddings, birthdays, First Holy Communion and housewarming ceremonies. How keen and determined I have been in this regard can be understood by some examples. Once I was the fountainhead behind presenting a huge encyclopaedia to a new-born baby! Dr Balakrishnan, the Founder of Holy Flower School in Salem had his first grandchild when I was the principal there. The vice-principal and the teachers decided to present a first-rate cradle for the baby and sought my opinion. I said, *"The baby's parents might have already bought a cradle. If not, let them buy it. We can get an encyclopaedia for the amount."* The staff looked at me in bewilderment. One of the senior teachers (I was newly appointed) stammered out, *"Madam, what's the use of a book to a new-born?"* I explained, *"The baby grows up and reads it later. Till then all in the family can read and get benefited"*. The principal's strong opinion could not be opposed! A different notion from the usual is always viewed eccentric.

In Bangalore, ten ladies including me had learned *'Soundarya Lahari'* by Adi Shankara from an elderly lady who used to conduct free shloka classes. At the end of our session after a year, everyone decided to gift her a silk sari. My suggestion to present her a book did not go well with the elderly women. I, being a 'student' (aged 52) could not enforce my will! However, I requested them to relieve me from the group to enable me to buy a book for my share of the amount. They might have thought it befitted my 'sanyasini' dress. I bought a children's encyclopaedia and recorded in the first blank page my gratitude for having learned *'Soundarya Lahari'* from her. I also wished her an enjoyable time reading the book to her 2 little grandchildren. Later she appreciated my selection and said that her grandchildren were very happy to listen to her reading. After a few years, she shared the glad news that those children had started reading it on their own.

Another time, while selecting a book for Kaushik, grandson of my friend Mrs. Saroja, a thought suddenly struck me. The boy's twin sister, Kavya, would never have such a function as it was the occasion of wearing the sacred thread by Brahmin boys. I therefore presented two books suitable for the boy and the girl. Jayanthi, their mother, later called, *"Aunty, once my children opened your gift packet, their interest in unwrapping the other ones waned. They began reading the books at once."* If we become slaves of reading habit when young, we would grow up with wings of freedom!

Work both at home and outside left me practically with no time to read especially when my kids were young. But some books are 'to be chewed and digested'. I decided to read one or two chapters from such books daily before going to bed and started with the Bible in Tamil. Till then I read the Bible in English daily but in a different way. I prayed for the verses needed for the day's problem and opened the Bible at random. Amazingly I would get relevant passages which brought peace to my mind. I was happy to know later that Gandhiji had done the same with the Bhagavat Gita.

Appachan used to read the Bible in Malayalam daily. Some months before his demise in 1962 he decided to read it from the beginning to the end but could not complete it. The Old Testament with 1095 pages had been completed and the mark which he noted to indicate the finished chapter stopped in the 288th page of the New Testament which had 334 pages. I felt sad about it many times in those days. That was also the reason to start with the Bible in my new way of reading. It took 10 months for me to finish reading it in 1976 (OT 1107 and NT 355 pages). With humility and pride, I would like to say that I read the Bible two more times in Tamil; twice in English and NT alone once in Malayalam. This does not mean that I know the Holy Bible thoroughly. But reading it many times helped me elevate my mind and spirit. I read some more books in a similar way. *'Profiles of Gandhi'*, a big-sized book of 236 pages was read in three months. *'Gita Pravachan'* by Vinobhaji (Tamil translation) – 356 pages – was completed in three months.

Such books cannot be read like fiction. The full benefit is obtained only when we read part by part and meditate.

I received a copy of '*Sathiya Sothanai*' (Tamil title of Gandhiji's autobiography) from Shri. R. Venkataraman, the former President of India, on 17th July 1995, when I was the Principal of Holy Flower School in Salem. I had earlier read the abridged version in English. The unabridged Tamil version (605 pages) was completed in seven months in 1995. It is impossible to retain in memory all that we read. But the more we read good books, the wiser and the humbler we become.

Whenever a book is bought, I sign it with date. Today I am surprised to see the prices of many books I bought long ago. Here are a few details of some books of mine:

Name of the book	Date of purchase	Pages	Price (Rs.)
Thirukkural by Thiruvalluvar	03.03.1961	438	2.00
Poems of Bharathiyar	05.07.1968	364	2.00
Gita Pravachan by Vinobha Bhave	07.08.1969	356	3.00
Great Short Stories of the World	27.11.1969	1078	15.00
The Penguin Dictionary of Quotations	29.11.1969	664	3.15
Roget's Thesaurus	30.01.1971	405	10.00
Vivekananda – a Biography	28.12.1973	350	3.50
Ida S. Scudder of Vellore	06.09.1985	226	2.00
Parent's WHEN-NOT-TO-WORRY Book	06.09.1995	262	10.00
Random House Webster's Dictionary	13.12.2001	2230	1000.00

My love of reading 'prevented' me from becoming computer-literate. When we bought a P.C. in 1999, Maimol and Babu vied with each other to teach me the basics of computing. I felt by learning it my reading time would be reduced. Moreover, I had stopped teaching then and thought that computer knowledge was not quite necessary for me. Anyway, Maimol created an email-id for me (alicekjose@ rediffmail.com) and what I wrote for publication in dailies and monthlies would be typed and sent by her. After her marriage, Jose has been doing it for me. Even if I had learned to operate computer, while typing I would have proceeded at snail's pace! But as Abraham Lincoln says, '*I am a slow walker; but I never walk back*'!

Two excellent quotations conclude the part regarding charm of books:

'Reading is to the mind what exercise is to the body.'

– *Sir Richard Steele*

'As water gushes forth when we dig deeper;

With more reading intellect becomes keener.'

– *Thiruvalluvar*

I do not remember hearing much about Gandhiji from my parents. Yet, the very act of Appachan keeping the Mahatma's picture in the first leaf of our family album is more than a thousand words. Of course, I knew about Gandhiji through history classes in school. But much of my knowledge about him is from books by and on him. Above all, with my love of truth, the affinity got cemented. Gandhiji's love of truth made him transform the saying '*God is Truth*' into '*Truth is God*'. I respected all religions but believed Christianity to be the greatest of all. Gandhiji's ideas influenced me to realize that TRUTH is the basis of every religion and therefore all religions are great. Without converting to Christianity, the Mahatma followed the teachings of Jesus Christ to the letter and in spirit.

Jesus said, '*To him who strikes you on one cheek, offer the other also*'. Gandhiji followed it faithfully in his life. Again, it is said in the Bible, '*He who has two coats, let him share with him who has none*'. The Mahatma went a step further and stopped wearing shirts when he saw millions in his motherland having no shirt. Martin Luther King, the great Afro-American leader states with conviction: *'From my background, I gained my regulating Christian ideals. From Gandhi, I learned my operational technique.......... Christ showed us the way and Gandhi showed us it could work.'*

Great people all over the world have admitted Gandhiji's irresistible influence in their lives. His biography is written by many from different countries and Louis Fischer's 'The Life of Mahatma Gandhi' is the most famous one. Fischer writes: *'I have met Lenin, Churchill, Franklin Roosevelt, Willkie, Stalin, Litvinov, Attlee, Einstein, Lloyd George, Eleanor Roosevelt and many other famous people. I have never met a more remarkable person than Gandhi. He did not preach about God or religion; he was a living sermon.............. Gandhi was a strong individual and his strength lay in the richness of his personality, not in the multitude of his possessions. His goal was TO BE; not TO HAVE.'*

In this connection, I am reminded of Robert Browning's famous lines:

'How very hard it is, /To be a Christian.'

Though not a Christian, Gandhiji took the hard way to follow the Christian principles. How 'hard' life is for the majority of the Christians who superficially follow the Christ! Many consider themselves to be good if they attend Holy Mass on Sundays. To lead a true Christian life is indeed very hard. For that matter, to be a true Hindu or a true Muslim is also equally difficult. After all, religions are man-made. The Supreme Universal Spirit is ONE. Swami Vivekananda avers, *'To be good and to do good; that is the whole of religion'.* Sri Narayana Guru, the great reformer of Kerala affirms, *'Whatever be the religion, man must be good.'*

My reverence for Gandhiji perplexes many Christians. One Christian asked, "Do you *consider Gandhi to be greater than Jesus?"* My clarification: "*You have thoroughly misunderstood me. As a true Christian I feel Jesus' presence in me. I have often meditated on the sufferings and humiliation undergone by Jesus and shed tears. Years later Gandhiji came into my life. He stood first in my list of the true followers of the Christ. In our country of many religions, as long as we preach uttering the names of Rama or Jesus or Allah, we sow the seeds of division and harvest problems ending in violence. If we follow our religion faithfully and spread Gandhian ideals, we can have peaceful co-existence. Gandhiji himself admitted that his ideas and ideals were taken from ancient wisdom, 'I have nothing to teach the world; Truth and Non-violence are as old as hills'. Gandhiji's greatness lies in the fact that he practised what he preached."* The questioner seemed to be gratified.

My long teaching career in many institutions helped me spread Gandhian ideals among students. I hit upon a novel idea to spread Gandhian message at the time of Babu's marriage. On 7th March 2004, we distributed booklets by Gandhiji on different topics during the wedding reception in Chennai. Prior to that, Babu and I went to Gandhi Bhavan in Bangalore to buy the books. We chose many booklets priced Rs.5 each. A helper in the Bhavan said one prized Rs.3 had very good messages. Another came with a seven-rupee booklet saying it had more pages. I said, *"Every book by the Mahatma would be of immense value. Since these are for distribution in a function, I want them to be of the same price. Generally, people would be eager to look for the title and the price of the neighbour's book; reading it happens later. Let all of the books be of the same price to avoid displeasure".* Eventually, we got 350 booklets for Rs.5/- each.

I would like to record here the names of some of the booklets: My God, Key to Health, Nature Cure, Character and Nation Building, Gandhiji's Life – In His Own Words, Unto This Last, etc. The last mentioned was paraphrased by Gandhiji from the original with the same title written by the famous English writer John Ruskin (1819-1900).

It is my proud privilege to record in my autobiography the encomiums showered upon the Father of the Nation by many famous Americans. I gratefully acknowledge for some passages taken from the book – *'Profiles of Gandhi - America remembers a World Leader'.* It was edited by Norman Cousins and about 60 Americans from all walks of life including 6 American Presidents have eulogised the Mahatma in it. The writers include church leaders, politicians, authors, philosophers, scientists, journalists and social activists. The book was first published by India Book Company – Delhi in the Birth Centenary Year (1969) of Gandhiji. In 1971, I bought the 1970 edition for Rs.6.50. What a treasure for such a low price! It would be an eye-opener for many, especially today's politicians and bureaucrats, if they read this book. It should be made available as low-priced edition now, for wide reading by common people too.

Here are a few lines from Norman Cousins' introduction: *'Ultimately the greatness of a man must be measured not by the amount of adulation accorded him but by the impact of his life on others……. Gandhi had a profound impact on Americans, as the life story of Martin Luther King has dramatized. The writings in this book represent a genuine reflection of Gandhi's hold on the moral imagination of the American people'.*

Lyndon B. Johnson – 36th US President

'All mankind is richer for the life and legacy of Mohandas K. Gandhi………20 years after his death, with the world still beset by divisiveness and anger, the need for the Gandhian message is greater than ever……. The light of Mohandas K. Gandhi burns brightly still as a beacon for Indians, for Americans and for all the world.'

Will Durant – American historian and philosopher, famous for the book – Story of Civilization

'Gandhi is in all probability, the most important and beyond all doubt the most interesting figure in the world today…………..Not since St. Francis of Assisi has any life known to history been so marked by gentleness, disinterestedness, and simplicity of soul and forgiveness of enemies………..We have the astonishing phenomenon of a revolution led by a saint!'

Pearl S. Buck – The first American woman to win Nobel Prize in Literature

'The world longs for goodness. The people search for righteousness. There is no weapon, no bomb so powerful as the force of a great good spirit………. Gandhi did what he told others to do. When people saw that

this was true, they believed in him…………...We long for the peacemakers. No war brings peace, for violence only brings more violence. Oh India, dare to be worthy of your Gandhi!'

Dr E. Stanley Jones – A Methodist Missionary who wrote, 'Mahatma Gandhi – An Interpretation'

'He (Godse) sought to stop the Mahatma and his ideas. Stop him? He only succeeded in freeing the ideas and the Spirit of the Mahatma from his frail body and making them the possession of the human race. For, an astonishing thing took place. Gandhi marched into the soul of humanity in the most triumphal march any man ever made since the death and resurrection of the Son of Man'.

Dr John Haynes Holmes – Minister of the Community Church of New York

Dr Holmes met Gandhiji for the first time on 12th September, 1931 in London. But 10 years prior to that, what he had said about Gandhi in his Church in New York is amazing:

'………. I climbed tremulously into my pulpit on Sunday morning, April 10, 1922 to preach to my people on the subject, 'Who is the greatest man in the world?' and to answer my own question, M. K. Gandhi of India. The audacity of this declaration in the light of what was known and not known, at that time about Gandhi, here in our western world, seems now incredible!…………When I think of Gandhi, I think of Jesus Christ. He lives His life, he speaks His words, he suffers, strives and will someday nobly die for His Kingdom upon earth'.

John Gunther – Political Journalist and Foreign Correspondent

'…………...Mr. Gandhi is the greatest Indian since Buddha. He is a unique kind of dictator, one who rules by love. The record of Mr. Gandhi's positive qualities is a long one. His unbelievable simplicity, his quick and shrewd intelligence, his uncommon intuition, his consideration for others, his tremendous knowledge of India, his great source of power, i.e., people

cannot lie to him...........His own sincerity, his own love of truth is so great that he brings out truth in others.'

Mrs. Mary Bethune – Afro-American Leader

'..............A great warm light has been extinguished with the death of Gandhi. He dies as he lived, seeking through understanding, compassion and love to absolve the ignorant, bigoted and self-seeking.............. Mahatma Gandhi cannot die, his spirit is free to stir men's souls in every corner of the earth. As we, mothers of the earth, stand in awesome fear of the roar of jet planes, the crash of atom bombs and the unknown horrors of germ warfare, we must turn our eyes in hope to the East where the sun of the Mahatma blazes.'

Dr Henry Grady – First US Ambassador to India

'..............The spirit of Mahatma Gandhi will live and grow and his influence will increase with the years. A great human spirit lives on though his body has returned to dust.......... The world is a better world for his having lived, but the greatness of this extraordinary man will not die with him.'

Norman Thomas – Statesman of American Socialism

'...............In this century of monstrous violence, it was and is our extraordinary good fortune that Gandhi lived............If ever men achieve a world peace, to no single man will it owe a greater debt than to Mohandas K. Gandhi.

Eleanor Roosevelt – Wife of President Franklin D. Roosevelt and an independent activist

'............... Gandhi gave up his considerable income as a lawyer and everything he had and chose instead the simple and austere life of an ashram. The people loved him for his sacrifice and renunciation and it was, largely, the secret of his enormous influence with them and was what made it possible for him to become a national leader.'

Erik H. Erikson – A leading figure in the field of psychoanalysis

'................Gandhi describes himself as having despaired of the possibility of combining of the business of salvation with his intense kind of intimacy, he concluded that, 'He who would be friends with God must remain alone or make the whole world his friend'. Thus, bettering the mother of a joint family, he adopted all of humanity and made himself meticulously responsible for India and the empire.'

Margaret Bourke-White – Well-known journalist and photographer

'..............I arrived in 1946 when India stood shining and full of hope on the threshold of independence............I had a historical drama to photograph, with a full cast of characters, including villains and one of the saintliest men who ever lived. And when the saint was martyred, I was near.'

Her impression on seeing Gandhiji for the first time: *'.......There sat the Mahatma, cross-legged, a spidery figure with long, wiry legs, a bald head and spectacles. Could this be the man who was leading his people to freedom – the little old man in a loin cloth who had kindled the imagination of the world?'*

Multitudes of Gandhiji's contemporaries in India had great love and admiration for him. Luminaries like Nehruji, Patelji, Vinobhaji, Rajaji and countless other freedom fighters adored the Mahatma. Needless to say, that he was a god to the public of his times. Here are the words of three famous Indians:

Rabindranath Tagore says, *'Gandhi stopped at the thresholds of the huts of the thousands of dispossessed, dressed like one of their own. He spoke to them in their own language. Here was living truth at last and not only quotations from books. For this reason, the 'Mahatma', the name given to him by the people of India, is his real name. Who else has felt like him that all Indians are his own flesh and blood?'*

The erudite, silver-tongued V S Srinivasa Sastri shared his birth year (1869) with Gandhiji and passed away in 1946. His scholarly speeches in English had earned him high praise from King George of England and the then Prime Minister Winston Churchill. Such a versatile genius had great admiration for Gandhiji, though he criticised the Mahatma at times. He had written Gandhiji's character traits in detail under five headings: Gandhiji's Piety, His Forgiveness, His Utter Selflessness, His Moral Courage and His Self-examination. It is my earnest request to all readers to search the internet and enjoy reading the details. Gandhiji once told his friend Sastri, '*Your criticism soothes; your silence makes me feel nervous*'!

The great modern Tamil poet Bharathiyar had composed beautiful poems in praise of Gandhiji. He hails the Mahatma as the redeemer of Mother India who had lost her pristine glory and precious freedom. Gandhiji's selfless service to attain independence and to uplift the downtrodden of our country played upon Bharathiyar's heart strings. One of his poems on the Mahatma ends with the words:

By attaining lasting glory

You are the greatest in the world.

It is interesting to note Gandhiji's self-assessment: '*Some call me a saint. Others call me a rogue. I am neither the one nor the other. All that I aspire to be – and I hope in some measure succeeded in being – is an honest, god-fearing man.*' His writings are voluminous and about him volumes have been written by people of different nationalities. Everything makes for good reading and inspires one to be a better human being. His sincere and humble statement, '*My Life is my message*' says it all.

The man who doesn't read good books

has no advantage over the man who can't read them.

– Mark Twain

19

Fasting and Self-Denial

The denomination known as Jacobite Syrian Christian in which I was born and brought up, gives great importance to prayer, fasting and abstinence. The followers recite lengthy prayers seven times daily – dawn, forenoon, noon, afternoon, evening, dusk and night. They avoid fish and meat five times in a year for periods of different lengths – 3, 13, 15, 25 and 50 days. Appachan's sisters in Kunnamkulam turned vegans and even avoided the vessels used for cooking non-veg items during those abstinence periods. They observed the prayer times so conscientiously so much so that, as a little girl I thought they were praying throughout day and night. In Coimbatore, we prayed thrice a day. Morning and bedtime prayers were short and individual. Family prayer at 8 pm used to be for more than half-an-hour with Bible reading, readings from prayer books, devotional songs and ended with silent prayer.

I was very much influenced by the prayerful life of my parents and aunts. After I lost Appachan at the age of 16, fasting and abstinence became an integral part of my life. I observed the two long-period abstinence – Advent (24 days before Christmas) and Lent (7 weeks before Easter) regularly. During those periods I became a vegetarian, and in some years, I turned a vegan, too. A few years saw me giving up all kinds of sweets including ice cream during the abstinence. Since we faced many a problem after Appachan's sudden death, my intentions were for our meritorious success in the examinations and later to get good jobs. Above all, I prayed for Divine protection to prevent us from going astray.

Appachan insisted that we should pray with piety and solemnity. Once during the family prayer, Marykutty and I (aged 7 and 8) started giggling for some silly reason. Appachan signalled us to stop. The more we tried to suppress the laughter, the louder it came out. He twisted our ears (mildly!) and sent us out of the room. Since he rarely punished us, our giggling stopped instantly. We begged his pardon and joined the prayer with gravity.

I thought of becoming a vegetarian even before my marriage because of my admiration for Gandhiji. But I found it hard to give up mutton and chicken - my favourites. I never ate beef and pork and did not like fish much. Anyway, a precursory incident occurred four years after my marriage resulting in a firm decision regarding the issue. On Easter Sunday in 1976, Amma killed a cock and left for me to pluck it. After attending to the needs of my little ones (Jaimon and six-month-old Maimol), I could go for cleaning the fowl only after about 30 minutes. As soon as I touched the bird it started writhing and convulsing in silence. On seeing it I began to weep uncontrollably. It affected me so much that I made a vow there and then not to eat meat anymore.

Aged 30, I had been breast feeding Maimol and so for health reasons I continued eating fish. Once, Amma mockingly pointed out that fish also would writhe while dying. Discerning the truth behind her remark I stopped eating fish also. Two years later how I started taking fish on the advice of the doctor and at the loving command of my spiritual guide, Mother Mary Leo, has already been shared. At the age of 52 (1998) again I became a vegetarian after Jaimon's passing away. Finally, I gave up vegetarianism when I turned 70 (2016) for no particular reason! My brother Joy teased me, *"People generally eat well in youth and give up such items in old age for religious or health reasons. You have admirably reversed it!"*

When Sri Lal Bahadur Shastri was our Prime Minister, India faced acute food scarcity. He appealed to the nation to fast one night every week. I ignored it as I had been observing religious fasts now and then. Soon, the P.M. passed away most unexpectedly in Tashkent on 11th January 1966. I felt guilty about my indifference to his appeal.

Thereafter I fasted every Monday night, for 37 years starting at the age of 20. In between I discontinued fasting during pregnancy and breast-feeding periods at Mummy's behest.

For ten years from 1994 to 2003, I never took any medicines; not even a pill nor used any kind of balm. Prayer was the only way of getting cured. Actually, I used to criticise people who refused to take medicines and prayed for healing. My argument was that medical science being God-given knowledge, it was meaningless to shun it. But it was my turn to be 'senseless' in due course! While staying in Holy Flower School hostel once I had an attack of flu. I had fever and shivering every evening for four days. Following the adage, *'starve away fever',* I forwent supper at night. I prayed fervently for health to do my duties as Principal. It was rather mysterious that I felt completely well in the morning. After taking a refreshing bath and breakfast I would go to school. The helpers in the hostel were worried and requested me to consult a doctor. But on the fifth day 'the adamant evening fever' bade farewell to me.

Mummy was the inspiration behind my full fasting every Friday for the same ten-year period. She started it at the age of 60 and for 6 years she drank only water every Friday. Her intention for the vow was to live in her own house as she had always lived in rented ones in Coimbatore since her marriage in 1942. Appachan was planning to buy a house when he suddenly passed away. By God's grace her only son (Joy) constructed a house later and she lived there contentedly for eight years before her death in 2004 at the age of 80.

The intention for my Friday fasting was 'WORLD PEACE & HAPPINESS'. As usual Jose mocked me, *"Do you think your starving one day a week would usher in peace and happiness in the world? Sheer madness!"* My reasoning: *"What I do is fasting; not starving. The only similarity in these two is that one forgoes food. There is a world of difference otherwise. One fasts to fulfil vows taken for religious or personal reasons. Starving is the fate of the poor or is done by people who vent their anger on food. One who fasts does not feel hungry. But the starving ones would experience pangs of hunger. Among millions of people in the world, at least a million must be fasting or doing some acts of self-denial for world peace. We have no way to know it. For that matter, only close relatives and some friends know about my fasting."*

Even earlier I used to observe full day fasting during crises and sought Divine Guidance for solutions. The day chosen would mostly be 1st March, Appachan's memory day. While on foreign tours Jose did not allow me to fast. Though I was confident, he had his own misgivings. After the trip, it was compensated by my fasting two days (Tuesday and Friday) in a week. Once I wanted to test whether I could fast for three consecutive days and completed two days without any problem. On the third day fasting was given up due to hunger and exhaustion. Later I understood that if the fasting had been for a noble cause, I might have fasted even for more days. A 'test' on fasting failed me!

Of the basic necessities of life, food takes the primary place. When we voluntarily avoid such a compelling necessity, our mind becomes fertile soil for noble thoughts. We can also feel the sufferings of the starving people but not in the same degree. First and foremost, fasting people generally do not feel hungry. Secondly, after fasting they can eat whatever they want. But the staving poor may not know when they would get something to eat. Feeling deeply for the pathetic plight of millions of people in India, Gandhiji exhorted everyone, *"The rich must live more simply so that the poor may simply live."*

In 1994, when I started full fasting on Fridays I asked 'JMJ' to fast every Friday night and they willingly began doing it. Jaimon continued it even after going to Dubai. He wrote in a letter to Maimol, *"……. today's friday and i stop eating and drinking by 6 pm according to mummy's wishes…."* (08/03/1996). I was happy to know that he (aged 25) fasted the whole day on Good Friday in 1998. Maimol and Babu were surprised and asked him over the phone how he achieved the feat. His reply, *"Being a holiday I slept for a long time. After returning from church, I spent time in reading and listening to music. I did not know how time passed nor did I feel hungry."* After two months he was no more.

Maimol had observed Friday night fasting for nearly two decades. Twice during pregnancies and while nursing her babies I advised her to discontinue fasting. If having dinner on Friday night occasionally became imperative, she used to fast on another night instead. *'Like mother; like daughter'* continues! Babu fasted on Friday nights initially for four years. Since then, he has been a vegetarian every other year. The starting and ending of this is on 28th October – Jaimon's date of birth. For the past 10 years he has not been having any sweets also during the 'vegetarian year'. Since 2011 he has been observing full fasting on every Good Friday. Becoming a good role model works wonders in bringing up children. More than words, our deeds influence our children.

Almost all religions give utmost importance to fasting. Prayerful fasting takes us nearer to God. Here are a few quotes from Gandhiji, the 'authority' on fasting:

'A complete fast is a complete and literal denial of self. It is the truest prayer.'

'What the eyes are for the outer world; fasts are for the inner.'

'A genuine fast, cleanses the body, mind and soul. It crucifies the flesh and to that extent sets the soul free.'

When I first read about the Mahatma's 'mouna vratha' on Mondays, I was enchanted by the idea. But with three little kids to take care of and being in the teaching field, I could not even dream of such a vow. The mirage became reality many years later when Maimol and Babu with families settled in different places. I started the vow of silence on a Friday, the Martyrs' Day (30th January) in 2009 and continued it on every Friday for six years. Some pre-arrangements were necessary for it. I requested Jose, our tenants, neighbours and the maid not to talk to me on Fridays. Sign language and written messages (if urgent) came in handy. I inflicted 'house-arrest' on myself on Fridays to aid the vow. Yet, the exception was Good Friday every year. So, I took a small card to the church with the following message on it:

May God Bless Us All

Fridays are my days of silence. Have a good day!

I showed it to friends who came to speak to me after the prayers and rituals. Needless to say, they smilingly avoided me!

As Jose and I were leading a retired life by then, it was easy for me to observe the vow. Even when someone visited us on Fridays, Jose entertained them with talks and I offered them tea and snacks. Smiling and silently listening would be my contribution to the conversation! Of course, there was no hard and fast rule in that. In his absence if anyone came home, I would talk to them. Vow of silence bows before hospitality. Jesus says:

'The Sabbath was made for man and not man for the Sabbath.'

Our telephone had a day of 'rest' on Fridays as kith and kin contacted Jose on his mobile. I did not have a mobile for a long time; I was quite content with the land line! In case the telephone rang in his absence, I would not lift the receiver. When my brother knew it, he warned me that I might miss some important message. I reminded him of the 'ubiquitous' mobile. Now, I would like to share with the readers some of the comments made by friends regarding my vow. A naughty youngster with a twinkle in his eye remarked in my presence, *"Uncle, isn't Friday your favourite day?"* I welcomed it with a hearty laugh. A newly married one told his wife, *"Aunty doesn't need such a vow. How happy I'd be if you take a day off from talk."* The 'seriousness' of his suggestion could be easily gauged from the happy way the young lady herself shared it with me. Another woman felt sorry for Uncle for his pathetic condition at home on Fridays. She overlooked the fact that it was a pre-arranged plan due to my vow and only for a day in a week. Moreover, she was told that uncle could tell me when he wanted something to be done and I would silently carry out his 'order'!

Some expressed their wish to observe the vow of silence 'inspired' by me but found it very hard. I could successfully do it for two reasons. First, my long-time wish to observe such a vow. Secondly only two of us were at home. When Maimol and Babu came with families for vacation, I let my vow take 'vacation' too. Even after giving up the vow, I keep silence now and then, though not on a regular basis. The painful thought about the dumb hits me hard after observing such a vow. *Speech is silvern; but silence is golden* – the proverb gained deeper meaning.

Generally, I avoid vows like pilgrimages or donating money and things to churches famous for their power to fulfil our wishes because of the time and money involved. When I faced troubles or felt sad and anxious especially when our children fell ill, I would have recourse to tearful prayers and self-denials. As I had a sweet tooth, I gave up all kinds of sweet things one by one. It came to the point of my avoiding sweets for some years. Jose once confronted me, *"Do you think the child got well because you stopped eating a particular sweet?"* My belief was that along with prayers and medicines the vow also worked in making my children get well. Also, I told him that the peace I experienced through such acts of self-denial was inexplicable.

Another vow taken for seven years was not to participate in wedding celebrations. Again, I avoided travelling unless it was imperative. As if to compensate that God made me travel many times after that both in India and abroad. In 2010 alone I went totally ten times (a record-happening!) to Coimbatore, Chennai, Salem, Thrissur and Kochi for various reasons. Some years later, I gave up ice cream for four years for no particular reason. Perhaps, force of habit!

To experience sufferings of the poor in a little way, I avoided using a blanket while sleeping at night. At the age of 48 I started the vow in Salem where even winter will not be very cold. But our arrival in Bangalore when I was nearing 51, coincided with the coldest winter for decades. (Courtesy: Newspaper reports in 1996). Night after night I shivered and slept curling up like a foetus in the womb. During illness Maimol would cover me with the blanket after I slept but I would remove it as soon as I knew it. I kept the vow for eight years and finally the hair-line cracks on my instep tolled the knell for the practice. I got used to it so much so that even now, I rarely use a blanket.

On similar lines, I avoided hot water for bathing. It was splendid in Salem. But in Bangalore, the very sight of water in that coldest winter sent cold shivers down my back. I prayed to God earnestly to give me the strength to withstand the coldness at the age of 51. After a few days, bathing was done once in 48 hours! Years ago, when I read that in the cold regions of western countries people never bathed for days together, I wondered how one could be without taking bath daily. It is not a big deal when there is no 'problem of sweat'. Bangalore's chill weather became an eye-opener! The next year (1997) dawned with no abatement in coldness. I begged God's forgiveness and bathed daily in warm water. Every vow of mine is a covenant with God. When I give up the vow within a few days I seek God's pardon.

When Mummy came to stay with us in Bangalore during Christmas in 1996, she insisted that I start eating non-veg items and I felt no qualms about eating meat which I had avoided for 20 years then. When Jose and I went to Dubai in April 1998, Jaimon was pleased to get me some exotic non-veg food items. Six weeks after our return, he passed away and I became a vegetarian again. (I felt Mummy's compulsion helped me fulfil my son's wishes for me.)

Today fasting and self-denials continue to the extent my health permits. I am indeed fortunate that my B.P. and sugar levels have always been normal. After the surgery for varicose veins in 2013 in St. John's hospital, I had to undergo surgery on my left palm for ganglion, trigger finger, carpel tunnel syndrome, etc. in 2017. It was done in Christian Medical College (C.M.C) Hospital in Vellore. Jose and I had to stay there for two more weeks for my daily physiotherapy sessions. Once again, I had to have surgery for varicose veins in 2019 at Manipal Hospital in Bangalore. Thus, I have had operations on five different parts of my body. It started with a 'four-stitch surgery' on my chin as a little girl. Then came the one on the neck; followed by: on abdomen, legs and hand. Hope and pray there would be no more surgeries!

Over the past some years, I have been occasionally experiencing acute chest pain for a few minutes. When it recurred for the third time we went to a cardiologist. After the tests he certified that it is 'non-cardiac chest pain' and advised me to drink warm water slowly and take rest if it occurred again. It was a coincidence that it happened for the first time on March 1st, 2008, on Appachan's 46th memory day. As he had passed away due to heart problems, I had certain misgivings. On that day, Babu was leaving for Chennai after two months to be with his family. If I revealed my painful condition, he would cancel his trip since I would be all alone at home. Jose was in Kochi at that time. I tearfully prayed to God to make me well and at once was blessed by God! To my great happiness, the pain vanished. With no knowledge of my pain and the instant relief through my earnest prayer, Babu left for Chennai. I thanked God countless times from the bottom of my heart.

I have absolutely no fear to die; but have immense wish to live in good health for some more time to see the New Heaven and New Earth. God alone knows what is written in the 'book' of my life!

Very few live austerely; many are indulgent.

That's the reason millions are poor on earth.

– Thiruvalluvar

20

Peerless Pearl Now Shining Star

'The worth of life is not in its length but is in its quality.' The truth of this statement is revealed through the life of my first-born Jacob who passed away four months before his 26th birthday. It was never my habit to praise my children to others. However, I never failed to congratulate them on their achievements and encourage them to shine better. At times, I advise them with healthy criticism and thank God for giving me good and intelligent children. This truthful account of my son who is no more is given here with good intentions. His exemplary life would certainly be a model to many.

When Jaimon lost his life in Dubai due to a tragic road accident on 19th June 1998, System Construct (the company where he was the Senior Marketing Engineer) took the onus of sending his body to India. After the legal formalities in Dubai, six days later, a huge rectangular box labelled *'The mortal remains of Jacob Kalapparambath Jose'* arrived at our apartment in Bangalore on 25th June. Mr. Fadi Chehabeddine, the M.D. of System Construct had thoughtfully sent a file through an employee who accompanied his colleague's body. The file had copies of 23 condolence letters received by him during the week. They condoled Jacob's untimely and unexpected death with deep sorrow. I had to wipe my tears many a time while reading through them and was reminded of Thiruvalluvar's famous couplet:

Happy is a mother at the birth of her baby;

Greater is her joy when he is called worthy.

I would like to record here a few lines from those letters:

".... In the short time that we interacted with Jacob, he proved himself to be such an honest, likeable thorough gentleman. Such was his personality that we felt at ease during all our business transactions...."

– C. S. Balakrishnan, Sr. Manager,
Bhawan Technical Contracting Co. (L.L.C.)

".... We have found Mr. Jacob to be an extraordinary person who could promote the services of your company very effectively. His departure is indeed a great loss to all, including us at Tomaco. He will be greatly missed..."

– Tom Johns, Chairman, Tomaco Pvt. Ltd. (L.L.C.).

".... Mr. Jacob was not only a very efficient and capable executive but also was an excellent person. During our association with him, I, in particular, had struck a good personal rapport with him...."

– Harinder Garga, Dy. General Manager, Thakral, Gulf FZE.

".... It is impossible to come out of this news and mind is not ready to accept the truth. He was gem of a person, always cheerful, very cordial, talented and having all the possible qualities required by sales engineers. I am sure that the loss to System, society and the family are irreparable. Only time can heal the loss...."

– N. S. Thakker, sent by the Award-Winning Cheyenne Bitware

Often, friends and relatives used to praise Jaimon for his intelligence and personality. Once I told him that praises should be taken to the heart and he should thank God, parents, teachers and all others who had helped him succeed in life. But criticism should be taken to the head and analysed. If there were truth in it, he should correct himself, otherwise ignore it. I specifically mentioned, *"Never allow praises to go to head and criticism to heart as the consequences would be disastrous".* He nodded with a smile.

As a child, Jaimon was very talkative. Though we were in Coimbatore he could speak only Malayalam till he went to school. At 3+ he was admitted to the nursery school attached to the Child Development Department of Home Science College where I had been a lecturer then. The school provided balanced diet to all the kids taking the payment along with the school fees. After some time, I asked his teacher whether he had learned to speak in Tamil and English. She expressed her happiness in learning some Malayalam from '*Jacob's non-stop storytelling*'!

The nursery school was also the study centre for the college students of the Child Development Discipline. Children were promoted to higher levels according to their learning ability and other development skills. Jaimon completed the three levels of nursery classes in 15 months. His first nursery report was a forerunner of his later achievements in many fields. Three months after he joined school, the nursery teacher Ms. R. Amritha Gowri, sent us the first report and here are a few lines from it (he was 3½ then):

Jacob is interested in all kinds of activities. Likes to listen and repeat stories; sings English songs; repeats Tamil songs. Very keenly observes things and answers the questions asked and raises questions also.... eats by himself without spilling; likes everything...

General remarks: Very Good, Smart, Intelligent.

Jaimon was admitted to Lisieux Matriculation School in Sai Baba Colony, Coimbatore, in first standard. Since he was only 4½ years' old, the Principal made us foreknow that he might not be able to appear for tenth public examination due to underage. Fortunately, he later studied in a CBSE (Central Board of Secondary Education) school where age limit was not an issue at that time. At the age of 14 years and 6 months he completed 10th standard securing centum in Maths and 97% in science.

Many are my memories of Jaimon's early years and I would like to mention a few. A priest once asked him (aged 3) whether he would become a priest when he grew up. Amma said, *"How can a naughty child like him become a priest?"* The priest smiled and patting Jaimon on the cheek said, *"Little children are at times naughty. That doesn't matter. Jaimon, you should study well and always speak truth."* After some days when Amma scolded him for being troublesome, he reminded her of the priest's words verbatim! All, including Amma, burst out laughing. Later in his high school days, an incident happened that proved his integrity. I will come to it presently.

When Jaimon was 9 years old (1981), he handed over his savings of Rs.30 to an NGO for the refugee camp. Amma and Jose chided him for doing it without taking permission from the elders. What they said was correct; but I was happy about his thoughtful action at that tender age. His readiness to give the amount (all new one-rupee coins eagerly collected) for a good cause foretold what was to happen later in his short life. He had a compassionate heart and would always help others in need, both physically and financially.

His concentration, while studying was remarkable. He had steady study habits and spent time in exercise and playing too. On the days of public examination, he freed himself from studying. His routine including physical exercises was meticulously followed even on the exam days. When he got ready to go to the exam centre, I advised him to take a book for last minute reference. His reply surprised me, *"No, Mummy, I have prepared well. I want to be tension-free on exam days"*. Generally, all students (including me in my school and college days) would be glancing through books till they step into the exam hall.

On the first day of his 10th public exam, he touched my feet to take blessings. Malayali Christians usually take blessings from parents or elders by bowing their heads with joined palms. Sensing my surprise, Jaimon said, *"My maths teacher (Mrs. Chandra at Sindhi School) asked me to do it while taking your blessings all the days of exams."* Later when Maimol and Babu followed their Chettan's example, I called Jose to my side and together we blessed them.

Jaimon had Hindi as his second language up to 10th standard. For the +2 course he opted for German in which he scored 181 out of 200 for the public examination. Meanwhile, he had appeared for NTSE (National Talent Search Examination) and passed the first 2 levels. However, he did not clear the final level. Yet, he received the S. J. Jindal Trust Scholarship awarded to meritorious students for the +2 course. Scoring 91.5% for it in 1989, he continued to get this scholarship for the B.E.(Hons) course at BITS (Birla Institute of Technology and Science), Pilani, in Rajasthan.

Jaimon had always been a good big brother (almost a father figure from his late teens) to Maimol and Babu - both just adored him. What I told him when he was a young boy was grasped by him in letter and spirit, *"You are the first child of the family and your sister and brother would always try to imitate you. If you are well behaved and study well, they will also do the same"*. He helped them in studies in higher classes and as a career woman I found solace in that. Once, 10-year-old Babu requested Jaimon for his bicycle to have a ride. Despite Babu's repeated requests Jaimon (aged 14) never allowed him to ride it. Some of his later actions revealed the truth. It was due to the concern for his little brother who might fall and hurt himself. Eleven years later, while working in Dubai, Jaimon wanted to buy a motorbike for Babu's 21st birthday. He deemed it proper to get Daddy's permission for that and spoke to Jose over the phone in vain. In his next letter to me he sought my help. *"dearest mummy,.......last week when i spoke to daddy i had asked his permission to buy babu a bike. you know daddy, he never says ok right away; he doesn't even say, 'i'll think about it'. he, as usual immediately said no. kindly show him the 'right way' no, no, i'm sorry. pls advise me what to do...."*. This is part of a long letter written on 20th November 1997. (Jaimon was adept at writing lengthy interesting letters.) Eventually with our blessings, he gifted Babu a new bike on his 21st birthday.

He was good at both studies and sports (volleyball and basketball} and participated in many competitions like oratorical, essay-writing, quiz, drama and dance. He had won many prizes and certificates. He learnt guitar and taught Maimol to play it too. After +2, he started his graduation (B.Sc. Physics) in Loyola College in Madras. Subsequently when he got admission in BITS, he left for Rajasthan. Tamil Nadu Government's results for professional courses came much later and he got selection for BE, MBBS and BDS. Yet he wished to continue in BITS.

I was sad and worried to send 16-year-old Jaimon to far-away Pilani. During night-time family prayers I used to cry silently. Seeing this day after day, Jaimon requested me not to come to the railway station. It was to avoid an emotional scene there. However, two days before his journey, while praying I felt the Inaudible Voice saying, '*I AM there; don't worry*', and peace pervaded my mind. At the station when I bade adieu, my eyes were just clouded. Many of his friends, both from Sindhi and Don Bosco schools, had come to the station. They made it a joyous occasion by garlanding him, followed by clapping and singing. Finally, they carried him to the compartment to bid goodbye. (Nine years later, when tragedy struck, many of them came home and never felt shy to shed tears. The MOTHER in me consoled them.)

My sister Jessie and her husband had been in Dubai for many years during that period. They sent copies of Jaimon's biodata to some companies and arranged for his visiting visa. He had by then gained work experience in a company called A. A. Consultants in Madras for some time. He joined System Construct in Dubai and his progress there was quick and remarkable. After his premature death some felt it to be due to evil eye. But my faith in Divine Eye was my consolation. Some others doubted whether a jealous rival conspired to eliminate him through a contrived accident. However, the details given by the Dubai Court ruled out such a plot. The accident was caused 'unknowingly' by a middle-aged man who was under the influence of alcohol. He was very rich and was in a high position in Dubai. On arrest, he was reported to have said, "*I don't know what happened; I slept at the wheel.*"

The accident occurred when Jaimon and his friend Manoj Krishnan were returning home after watching the 1998 World Cup Football Match on a huge T.V. screen installed in a 5 star hotel. Here are a few lines from the judgement given from the Dubai Court:

"......, UAE national, working as Bank Manager (Dubai National Bank). According to the case records, on 19-06-1998 at 3 a.m. the accused was driving his private car (BMW No.60 - Private) and along with him inside the car were........,............,............, and he was travelling from Jabal Ali to Dubai with extreme speed (120 kmph) and he was under the influence of alcohol. The accused while passing near ALDICCA Bridge collided with a motorcycle (his car front collided with the rear of motorcycle) which was driven by Jacob Kalapparambath Jose and Krishnan Manoj as pillion rider. The accident led to the death of both the victims on the spot......."
(Jaimon and Manoj used their cars to go to office and for all other purposes. As fate would have it, they rode a hired bike to go see the match at the hotel.)

The judgement had other details such as the kind of fatal injuries the young men had; the punishment awarded to the accused; the compensation amount. I have omitted the names of the Bank Manager & his 3 friends in the above quote. Though 120 kmph is not considered high speed in Dubai, the bridge on which the accident happened had low speed limit, hence the words 'extreme speed'. The judgement was in Arabic and Jose got it translated to English in Bangalore. I could not bring myself to read it then. When later I read, tears streamed down my face. To write my autobiography in Tamil when I read it again in 2012, there was only heaviness in the heart, no tears. How true the adage - *Time heals all wounds.* Similarly, the saying, *Time wounds all heels* is true to the core. None can escape it.

Like me, my children also valued friendship very much. Our hearts bled when Jaimon was taken back by God with his dear friend, Manoj Krishnan. They had studied together only for 2 years in the higher secondary classes at Don Bosco School, Madras. Manoj had done his B.E. in Bangalore. Later they met in Dubai working in different companies. In a letter dated 12-3-1997, Jaimon wrote, *"in school we were just hi-bye friends... now manoj has become my very good pal."* During his yearly visit from Dubai, my son never missed going to Madras to meet his friends. In 1997 (last visit), when he returned from Madras, Manoj was with him to celebrate Christmas with us in Bangalore. That was the first time we met him though we had heard a great deal about him from Jaimon. For the two days that Manoj stayed with us, we were charmed by his smile and sociable nature. He was the son of P. K. Nair and Lalitha, a Malayali couple settled in Madras. His parents and his only sister Swapna and her family became our friends after our great loss.

Jaimon's close friend, Gopal Rangachary (his senior by two years in BITS) created a website for him some months after his demise. Personal websites were not popular then. Gopal's introduction, (given in the Appendix) states that it is in celebration of Jacob's life. Many of Jaimon's classmates and friends have shared their thoughts and feelings in it. Gopal insisted that the family must also write in it. It took some months for us (Jose, Maimol, Babu and I) to add our thoughts to it. They can be viewed at https://sites.google.com/view/jacobkjose. The words of some of his friends are quoted here:

"………an extremely friendly, personable and charming guy. I have always seen him smiling……."

– Atreya Changanty, BITS

"………. amazing guy, great guy, wonderful guy………...superlatives run out when you describe Jacob…...."

– ABC (Arjun Balachandran, friend at Don Bosco and BITS)

"……….one of the most hardcore guys I came across and also one of the most modest. Chaps like this make you remember college and all things worthwhile…...'

– Loki (Alok Gupta, BITS)

"…………. that's Jacob, ever-smiling, lovable person with a charming personality……"

– Kozhi (Ramesh S. Soundappan) friend, senior @ Sindhi School and BITS

"……..though I can no longer spend time chatting with him, I am sure of one thing – knowing him made me a better person…...."

– Gerry (Gerry George, BITS)

"……the best thing about Jacob was that he had time for everybody and made everybody feel special……..."

– Shruthi (Japee, friend)

"……. Jacob was a real smart guy who used to excel both in study as well as sports……"

– Jagu (Jagadish), Classmate at Sindhi School

"It is often with good things that their value is realised only when they are gone. But, thankfully in Jacob's case we all realized that he was someone special the moment that we met him……. One of my seniors and close friends, Dhruva came to me and said: 'There's this great junior of mine who's joined – I've told him to be Mess Sec. next year.' That was in my third year and the moment I met him I realized why he would be someone who would make a mark in BITS…...."

– Woody (Gopal Rangachary) Senior at BITS

*"………...he was a lot of a motivator and a very trustworthy guy……
…a genius according to me…...."*

– Raja (Mark Manual), friend

"………. when he greets us with his sincere smile, we leave our troubles behind for a while. His astounding intelligence in all his endeavours always inspired us in ours……when we all complete our life's journey, I am sure we'll meet him at a bright alley. He will greet us with his sweet smile as usual………"

– Scynthia Jasper, Classmate at Malco Vidyalaya.

"..........it totally amazed me then and it amazes me now..........to think of all the different people who knew him.......and who felt close to him........."

– Vazhi / Ramki (Ram), friend both at Sindhi School and BITS

"...........Jacob's presence is always felt within me; his voice lingers in my ears. Thoughts of him will never be wiped away. Jacob's sweet memories will always be remembered......"

– Ajju (Ajay Tolani), colleague, System construct.

"Sometimes I wish Ram never mentioned to me about this page. I could have carried on with my life just knowing that Jacob is somewhere out there............When a little girl was asked if she knew what those letters 'R.I.P.' (Rest in Peace} on graves meant, her answer was 'Return if possible?'.........I prefer her answer.

– Shaky (Rajasekharan) BITS

We came to know about a particular incident written by Kranti, Jaimon's classmate in Sindhi School only through this site. It had happened more than a decade earlier when Jaimon was in 10th Std. (aged 14):

"........The physics class was getting boring and the kids started getting unruly and noisy. One of the boys, Vijay, a last bencher, threw a piece of chalk at the teacher. She turned around in rage and demanded to know who had done it.......... No one said a word though everyone knew who had done it. So, she started picking people.......... You have to realize that we were in an age when you don't pull the rug under your classmates or you'll be ostracized for ever and at the same time you want to be in the good books of 'Miss'. Anyway, I stood up when my turn came and said, 'I don't know Miss. I think it came from behind somewhere.' So next she picked Jacob who stood up and said something that stunned everybody – 'I know who did it; I won't lie to you. But I can't tell you who did it'. That completely caught Miss unawares. She threatened to punish him and Jacob said OK. Of course, by this time, all this was getting too

much for Vijay so he confessed. But Jacob demonstrated integrity par his age and I'll always admire him for that."

What other reward do I need for bringing up children in the path of truth?

While working in Dubai Jaimon came thrice to India during Christmas time. The first was to Salem in 1995 when I was leading the lonely life. We went to Mother Teresa's organisation with cakes, biscuits and usable old clothes. He donated a good amount there as Christmas gift. The visit in 1996 was to Bangalore when he brought many things for all four of us and a few more for friends and relatives. They included video cassettes of my favourite films – Gandhi, Ben Hur, Sound of Music and Gone with the Wind. All the things he selected and bought in Bangalore were very useful items - 6-inch-high orthopaedic double bed (for aging parents!), a huge Godrej bookcase with glass doors; VCR, washing machine, vacuum cleaner and a big carpet. When he asked me what I needed in the kitchen, my quick response was, 'nothing'. Nevertheless, he exchanged the old pressure cooker and mixer for new ones. How fortunate are the parents who have such caring and responsible children!

Third and the last time when he came to Bangalore in 1997 as usual, we visited Mother Teresa's 'Shishu Bhavan' with gifts and donations. There we saw an infant with a huge head and became sad. Jaimon's eyes welled up. I thanked God for his compassionate heart. 'JMJ' were made to be aware from childhood the sufferings of many due to poverty and diseases and asked to be generous always. They were also told to thank God for the countless blessings they enjoy in life.

Before leaving for Dubai, Jaimon gave me a huge book on 5th January 1998. I became speechless with joy on seeing the title - 'Mother Teresa 1910 – 1997' (A Pictorial Biography by Joanna Hurley). I had read an amazing review about that book and desisted from buying it because of the high price – Rs.800. Jose blamed me for making him buy such an expensive book. Jaimon said, *"Mummy never knew about it, Daddy. It's my surprise gift to her for the New Year. I selected it as she* admires Mother Teresa very much". Jose exclaimed: "*If Mother were alive today* (the noble soul passed away exactly 4 months earlier on 5th September 1997) *she would have had a cardiac arrest looking at the price of a book on her!*" I put a period to the controversy by saying that the lion's share of the profit made by the sale of the book might go to Mother's organization – Missionaries of Charity.

When Mother Teresa breathed her last, Jaimon sent me a condolence letter from Dubai. In my reply I wrote that though sad at the news, I was contented she went to her Eternal Home at the right time appointed by God. It was a befitting end for her selfless life with loving service till the age of 87. If others were to take care of her in her old age, it would have been both physical and mental agony for Mother. A few months later, my loving son passed away and my words, '*right time appointed by God*' echoed in my mind.

'JMJ' fought a lot in their preteen age period. At times I used to feel helpless to control them as I did not like beating or shouting at them. Once, disobeying me, when they started fighting in karate style, I knelt and tearfully prayed, with hands out-stretched like Jesus on the cross. Twelve-year old Jaimon at once stopped fighting and told the younger ones to be calm. He came to me to beg my pardon. After some days when they quarrelled again (quite natural!), I prayed in the same manner. Immediately Jaimon left the room taking his siblings along. He might have thought it to be a kind of emotional blackmail. After that I prayed in such a manner when alone, begging God for patience and wisdom in my dealings with them.

As a teenager and while working in Madras, Jaimon used to argue with me a great deal. I would feel desperate at times unable to convince him my viewpoint. Once, an argument went to the extent of making me cry. He abruptly stopped arguing and went out. When he came back, he gave me a book with a smile. Some days earlier I had asked him to get me the English translation of the Holy Quran and the book so thoughtfully bought was titled '*The Meaning of the Glorious Koran*'. On seeing what he had written in its first page, I became teary-eyed:

to my dear mummy, in repentance, Jaimon 08.03.94

Jaimon used to write many letters to us and to close relatives and friends. Reading his letters had always been gratifying. Over time, he abandoned using capital letters. There is a touch of love and care in all his letters and a few lines from some are quoted here:

03.10.94 – to me - '...... *although i'm not reading the bible every day, i don't fail to pray every day at wake-up and sleep time....*'

24.10.94 – to me - '.........*i'm looking out for a library to join (there aren't many in dubai). people here are too busy making money to read anything!....*'

17.02.95 – to me - '.........*my m.d. has given 2500 dirhams (=22,000 rupees) to buy suits, jackets, trousers and ties for projecting a good company image (same amount every 6 months). i thought of your khadi sari; it made me feel guilty for some time, then i decided that everything is happening as it should and that there is a purpose for all.*'

(I replied to him immediately:'....... *you need not feel guilty at all as I started wearing khadi only at the age of 48. Anyway, your thoughts are in the right direction. Carry on and leave the rest to God.......*')

17.02.95 – to babu – '....... *keep tripping and having fun, but don't forget your roots, i.e., our home; keep in touch with daddy and mummy......*'

09.09.95 – to Maimol – '....... *you don't worry about anything. Que sera sera, what will be, will be! Whatever happened, nothing will be too bad (mummy's prayers will take care of that) ......*' (This was to console Maimol regarding my lonely life in Salem).

31.09.95 – to me – '......*and mummy whatever happened don't take any medication from the so-called psychiatrist. i have full faith, belief in you......*'

11.02.96 – to me – '........ *i want you to be happy and peaceful, to attain that please do whatever you have to; i'm fully with you and i am sure, so will be maimol and babu....*'

27.07.96 – to me – *'............how's your health? although you are very very strong in spirit and mind, please take care of your health....'*

06.09.96 – to me – *'...........pl take care of your health mummy. you don't know how much you mean to me; all i'm today and will ever be because of you and daddy.......'*

04.09.97 - to Maimol - *'......a very big congratulations! wow, what a job!! can't believe my kiddo sister is actually in the man's world (I beg ya pardon) in the women's world!.......'* (This was on Maimol's first job as Software Engineer in Churchill Software in Bangalore.)

25.04.97 – to me - *'.......... how is daddy's business? tell him to take it easy and not tax himself too much and that goes for you also, my dear mummy.........it is the time of the golden dusk of your life, please live it to the utmost without any kind of worries and anxiety......'*

Generally, letters to Jose would be more business-like regarding his work and money matters. At the end of the letters, he always wrote *'yours lovingly'* or *'with love'* and *'jaimon'* to us and *'chettan'* to Maimol and Babu. But in his last letter to me, he had written, *'with lots of love (more than you can imagine), jaimon'.* It was my son's final farewell to me.

Every Friday, Jaimon used to talk from Dubai so regularly that we were wondering why he did not call us 'that Friday'. Once he said, *'What I write reaches you after a week and your reply requires another week to reach me. We would have spoken over the phone twice by then. Of course, all that we share through letters cannot be conveyed over the phone'.*

After self-realization in 1994, many religious and philosophical ideas passed through my mind. A particular thought came often during the weeks before Jaimon's death. It was that the full story of a person's life is 'written' at the time of the baby's conception in the womb. Many believe in this, but I felt it in the innermost recesses of my heart. I even thought that someone close to me would depart suddenly and I should console the bereaved family with this idea. When I realized the message was for me, initially I was thoroughly shaken but soon recovered. I seemed to 'hear' the 'Inaudible Voice' within me: '*Everyone thinks you lost your son suddenly in a fatal accident. When I sent him as your first-born everything had already been decided. Don't get depressed and waste your life. Take heart and carry on with your duties.*' I had read somewhere that a mother feels like losing a part of self when she loses her child – of any age. I am fortunate to know that God is there to fill that void.

During his last visit in December 1997, the usual one-month vacation was reduced to two weeks due to some urgent work in Dubai. Mr. Fadi, the M.D. had allowed him to take two weeks in June (1998) instead. Every time when he came, he travelled to Coimbatore, Salem, Chennai, Thrissur and Parur to meet kith and kin. Due to lack of time, he could not go to Kerala during that visit. He promised over the phone that he would visit them in June. Ruby (youngest sister of Jose) in her disappointment chided him for not going over there. Before leaving for Dubai what he said became prophetic, "*Mummy, every time I come, I visit everybody and I am tired of it. Now Ruby aunty is cross with me. In June let all of them come to Bangalore to see me; we'll arrange a feast for them*". In June, his body came; all came to see and had meal after the funeral. Was it a 'coincidence' that he passed away in June?

When he was to come to India in June, 'suddenly' he wanted both of us to stay with him for a few days in April during the famous Dubai Shopping Festival at that time. Generally, most sons and daughters who have moved to foreign countries, take their parents there only when a necessity arises; but he was different in every way. Since I had taken a vow during that period not to travel unless it was imperative, I declined to go. Moreover, Maimol would be alone as Babu had been working in Chennai then. Jaimon had a solution for every problem. He pointed out my friendship with many nuns and asked me to leave Maimol as paying guest in one of the convents. Jose had a different kind of 'problem'. He said, "*I won't take you to Dubai in khadi pyjama and kurta. Only if you wear sari and ornaments you can come with me*". I told Jose to proceed without me. When Jaimon knew about that controversy from Maimol, he called from Dubai, "*Daddy, are you taking mummy to a village in Kerala for people to stare at her? In Dubai nobody is bothered about such things."* Then he spoke to me, *"I'd be happy only if both of you come together. Daddy need not come alone. I beg you mummy, please come and stay with me for some days".* Immediately I said 'yes' and gave the receiver to Maimol before Jaimon heard my sob. How adamant had I been to make my grown-up son beg me for something he wished to do for my happiness!

Some happenings of the time pointed to the fact that Jaimon and Manoj would make their 'trip to Heaven' together. In April we were there for 12 days. Some days earlier Manoj's parents had visited their son for a week. Manoj who was a year older than Jaimon had been engaged then. His would-be and her mother went there after we returned to India. A few days after their return, the fatal accident happened. No doubt, the All-Knowing One 'arranged' the three trips.

When Jaimon took us for sight-seeing, Manoj was mostly with us like another son. Mother- tongue played a great role in bonding. One day Manoj said in Malayalam, *"Aunty, you have come to stay with your son for the first time. Why are you returning so quickly?"* I teased him because his parents stayed only for a week. His response to that revealed him to be a thoughtful youth: *"Neither my parents nor I spent for their trip. (His father was retired G.M., Finance in Indian Airlines). Their stay could be only for a week. But think of the huge amount spent by Jacob for your air fare and for that sake you must stay for more days".* Actually, Jaimon had asked me to stay for a month at least as Jose had to return to his job. I had convinced Jaimon about the necessity of my presence at home as Maimol's final exams for M.C.A. were fast approaching. When I told Manoj about it, he had an understanding smile.

One day in Dubai, Jaimon took us to a big book shop and asked me to select the books I liked to buy. Jose protested saying that hundreds of books at home were 'waiting' to be read. Jaimon's reasonable reply silenced him, *"What can I buy for Mummy? She doesn't need sari, jewels or cosmetics. I can gift her only books. For my happiness, let her buy books Daddy".* He then left us there to meet someone nearby. Jose was shocked when he saw a book priced 120 dirhams in my hands and questioned me, *"What do you mean by selecting a book for 1200 rupees?"* (1 dirham = Rs.10 then). I told him that my selection had already been over and I was just scanning that book. Our 'hushed tone' brought Jaimon back. On knowing the reason, he said, *"Don't bother about the price Mummy. If you like that book you can have it".* (In a flash I remembered Appachan's similar words years ago, when I hesitated to ask for a rather expensive skirt material). Jaimon then said in an amused tone, *"Daddy, please don't calculate everything according to Indian currency. Dirham must be seen as dirham. By God's Grace I have a good pay packet now. Whatever I earn is for all of us."* The 'trophy' I got after the war of words is a treasure-trove of wisdom:

'Towards A Meaningful Life'

The Wisdom of the Rebbe Menachem Mendel Schneerson

– Adapted by Simon Jacobson.

Towards the end of our stay, he told me, *"Mummy, I earned a lot and could usefully spend a lot. I feel as if I have lived a full life".* Rarely does a person realize the fullness of life at the prime of his/her youth. A day later he drew my attention to a particular song for its fine tune and meaningful words. Listening to it, I became happy about his growth in wisdom. Only after his demise did I realize how 'deeply meaningful' the lyrics were! It starts with the words,

I close my eyes only for a moment and the moment's gone…

…All your money wouldn't another minute buy.

The refrain is:

All we are is dust in the wind,

Everything is just dust in the wind.

Jaimon had many cassettes of English songs. Who really made me listen to that particular song from among more than a thousand ones - my son or God?

On 29th April 1998, Jose and I were getting ready to return to India. Jaimon was busy packing things for us - pants and shirts for Daddy and

Babu, dresses and ornaments for Maimol; books and some kitchen utensils for me. He had also kept a huge album for 300 photos and wanted me to keep all the snaps of Dubai trip in it as he had clicked many. At the time of saying goodbye, I blessed him and was about to kiss his forehead. He asked me to wait for a second to wipe his sweaty forehead. That was my last kiss to my beloved son. When his body arrived in a white shroud a week after his death, we could see only a tiny portion of his face. I was not even allowed to touch him. It was my fate to keep all the snaps of his funeral in that huge album. We had not been in a condition to even think of taking photos then, but an over-anxious relative took many for the funeral on 25th June.

While waiting for our return flight at Dubai airport, Jose said, "*I think it's time for Jaimon to get married. He is earning well and has now taken a flat for himself.*" My sister, her husband and Manoj had come to the airport to see us off. Before any of us could make a comment, Jaimon said, "*After marriage, next in line would be raising a family. I don't think I know much about bringing up children. Let me learn about parenting first.*" His thoughtful words made me happy. I wanted him to marry only at 28 and he was not even 26. Jose said that he was eager to have a grandchild. Without any hesitation what Jaimon said made everyone laugh, "*Why don't you adopt a little one from an orphanage for your present eagerness?*" From his expression I could make out that he meant it in all earnestness.

Later an incident happened to confirm my thoughts. Jaimon had sponsored a 15-year-old boy by name Hari (physically and mentally challenged) from the Spastic Society of India, Madras, committing Rs.15,000/- per year. We came to know about it only when the Director of the Society contacted us over the phone after his death. She got our Bangalore number from the obituary column of The Hindu and wanted to confirm whether it was Hari's sponsor who had met with the fatal accident in Dubai. Jaimon had already paid the half-yearly amount of Rs.7,500. From the Director's talk, I could sense that she had a doubt whether or not the sponsorship would continue. I assured her of our decision to continue and paid Rs.15,000/- every year for four more years.

Above all, his reflective writing in his diary at the age of 16, about a real incident came to light only 10 years later when he was no more. While studying in +2 at Don Bosco, Egmore, he happened to travel with a dead body in an electric train. The writing under the title 'My Reflections' (given in the appendix) is overwhelmingly philosophical. It ends with the question – *'Which will be my day?'* Why should there be such a thought in the mind of a 16-year-old boy with bright prospects in life?

On 10th June, 1998, I signed up for body donation inspired by an article written by a body donor. He quoted a line displayed in the Anatomy Department of St. John's Medical College, Bangalore - *'Here the dead teach the living'.* I was thrilled to think that I would be teaching even after my death! I became a teacher for the first time at the age of 19, exactly 33 years earlier on the same date (10th June 1965). As Jose was against this idea, he refused to sign the agreement form. Since Jaimon was in Dubai, I made Maimol and Babu sign it. My registration No. is 87. On the 9th day after that, Jaimon passed away leaving me with the ever-living beautiful memories. After all, what is in a body which would perish one day or the other?

During the one week that we waited for the arrival of his lifeless frame, hundreds of thoughts bombarded me. Right from his birth, scenes flashed before me. My face and eyes became swollen due to much crying. Yet, not once did I question God for giving me such a terrible blow. I convinced myself that there must be some strong reason behind it and it would be revealed later. This is the thirst of a grieving soul for the light of Truth. After the initial shock, I constantly prayed repeating the same words in Malayalam, *"Deivame, shakti thaa, shanti thaa; Karthaave, shakti thaa, shanti thaa".* My prayer was answered in full measure. God gave me incredible strength of spirit and immense peace of mind.

Though my son lost his life in the early hours of Friday (weekly holiday in Dubai), I knew the truth only on the third day i.e., Sunday 21st June. My sister Jessie in Dubai got the news on Saturday and called me to inform that Jaimon was in ICU due to an accident. She could not reveal the truth to me then. Minutes later Jose received a call from System Construct; but he hid the terrible fact from Maimol and me as he feared for our reaction. Without my knowledge, he phoned Babu in Madras and my brother Joy in Coimbatore. Only after their arrival on Sunday morning did Jose inform us about our great loss. Till then Maimol and I had been praying for Jaimon's life. Perhaps those prayers helped me to receive the undeniable fact courageously. I could even thank God for taking my loving son on a Friday – my full fasting day. It may sound unbelievable, but that is the Truth.

The funeral mass was on Thursday, 25th June at Christa Prabhalaya Church in Jayanagar, Bangalore. His body was interred at St. Patrick's Christian Cemetery on Hosur Road. After a week, during night-time family prayer when I opened the Bible at random, amazingly I got the following verses:

'For his soul pleased God, therefore He hastened to bring him out of the midst of iniquities;

But the people see this and understand not, nor lay up such things in their hearts.

That the grace of God and His mercy is with His saints, and that He hath respect to His Chosen.'

– The Book of Wisdom ch.4:14,15.

I felt the words quite meaningful in connection with Jaimon's life and death and those verses were printed on his memory card for the Requiem Mass.

We received more than a hundred letters and messages to condole his death. After one month I replied to all of them thanking for their prayers and consoling words. Out of the 23 condolence letters received by System Construct in Dubai and sent to us by the company's MD, 13 companies had conveyed their condolences to 'Jacob's family' also. To all those 13, I replied with heartfelt thanks. It was Divine Grace that I did not lose my attitude of gratitude even at the hour of my deepest sorrow.

For Jaimon's first Death Anniversary, we sent his commemorative card to all friends and relations requesting their presence for the

Requiem Mass followed by lunch. We were thankful when most of them honoured it. We had also sent one card to System Construct where Jaimon had worked for three and half years. We were moved to tears when the company responded to it in a special way. Their thoughtful message was followed by the signatures of 47 members of the office staff led by the signature of Mr. Fadi, the M.D. of the Company. (Given in the appendix)

'Jacob Foundation' continued to do its charity work in a humble way for almost two decades. I pray to God that Jaimon's worthy life should be an inspiration to many. I gratefully remember my prayer in youth to have children who would better the society with their life. Through his short life, Jaimon did exactly that. One can clearly understand what I say when one reads the write-ups on his web site. The great Tamil poet Thiruvalluvar's couplet may be aptly quoted here:

Better-learned progeny is a joy to parents;

And sure enough, a blessing to humanity.

In conclusion, let me write the engraving on Jaimon's tomb. I contemplated prayerfully on his life and got those words:

Beloved Jaimon,

On earth you were a rare gem.

Now you are a shining star.

Mummy & Daddy

Dearest Chetta,

In every way you were simply great.

In spirit you are ever with us.

Maimol & Babu

The chapter-ending quote is by Indira Gandhi (the Iron Lady of India) when she had her first baby, Rajiv. The sentiments expressed therein are an echo of my thoughts when I gave birth to my first baby, *Jacob.*

To a woman, motherhood is the highest fulfilment. To bring a new being into this world; to see its tiny perfection and to dream of its future greatness is most of all experiences and it fills one with wonder and joy.'

– Indira Gandhi

21

I Am a Chosen One

Though I began the story of my life by raising a query, 'Am I a Chosen One?', in this concluding chapter, I unequivocally say that I am a Chosen One. There are some valid reasons for my unusual presumption. This thought had been with me since 1994 and got confirmed in 1998 with the great sorrow I experienced at Jaimon's tragic end in the prime of his youth.

My way of thinking, right from the beginning, has always been different from that of my siblings and I realised it much later in life. When we were young, Mummy used to read the Bible during night family prayer. One particular verse in the Old Testament puzzled me. God says, *'Israelites are my people'*. As a little girl I sadly thought why God did not say Indians were also his children. That agitating thought faded gradually from my memory.

In my early 20s, what I read in a magazine brought back my girlhood thought with a revelation. In a Tamil weekly, a Hindu writer had questioned, *'Why is our country still in a poor state even though Mahavishnu, the Protector, is said to have taken all his incarnations in India?'* I recognised a similarity in the two ideas: *'Israelites are God's children'* and *'Vishnu's all avatars are in India'*. The former was said by an Israelite and the latter by an Indian. Judaism and Hinduism are two of the oldest religions. It was a time when people were not much aware of the existence of others far away and about their gods. In every community some chosen ones uttered God-inspired truths and the rest followed them faithfully. In my opinion, the chosen ones would feel that truth in the innermost recess of their hearts. Of course, all this is relative truth. God alone is ABSOLUTE TRUTH. No one can fully understand that Supreme Being. Anyway, that realisation hit me forcefully.

It is a well-known fact that Chosen Ones would be tested severely. In a book titled 'Church Humour', the following was found:

People of Israel: *Oh God, are we Your chosen people?*

God: *Of course, my dear children.*

People of Israel: *We have been the chosen ones for a long time. It's high time you chose the people of some other nation.*

There is a limit to endure suffering – a 'hint' to God from Israelites! However, the Holy Bible says: '*I have chosen thee in the furnace of affliction*'.

A few years ago, a Hindu friend confronted me: "*Our gods did not suffer like your god when they came as incarnations. Why did Jesus undergo sufferings and humiliations? It is unimaginable that the Son of God should die on the cross like a criminal!*" During that period, I had been engrossed in thoughts about the unity of religions and my convincing reply to her: "*First and foremost, please don't differentiate between gods. God is ONE who is Omnipresent, Omnipotent and Omniscient. All over the world, people have given beautiful names and imaginative forms to that NAMELESS and FORMLESS ONE. It is the same God who has been sending seers and sages to different parts of the world at different times. All of them taught about love, compassion, truth, honesty, justice, etc. Coming to the question of sufferings and humiliations, Rama, the heir to the throne was humiliated when he was asked to go to the forest for 14 years. Didn't he have sufferings during that long sojourn in the jungle? Wasn't he followed by misfortune even after returning to Ayodhya? Prince Siddharth renounced everything at the age of 29; mortified the flesh and attained enlightenment at the age of 35. Becoming the Buddha, he led the hard life of a mendicant till the age of 80. Even Prophet Mohammed met with sufferings and humiliations when he tried to reform the people of his time. Mahatma Gandhi, the modern-day apostle of peace also suffered a great deal during his non-violent struggle both in South Africa and India.*" My friend agreed that she had not thought of the matter from such an angle.

The above conversation took place rather recently. But when I was 22, what a Hindu family friend said about Jesus astonished me: "*While talking to some of my Christian friends, they said that it would have been easy for Jesus as Son of God to bear all the sufferings. But I admire Jesus as a man of virtues and wonder how a 33-year-old youth could pray for forgiveness to his tormentors.*" Then the realisation painfully dawned on me that I was also one of 'those' Christians. Thereafter, meditations on the life of Jesus the man, made me shed copious tears.

It naturally led me to ponder over Mother Mary's life and more tears rolled down my cheeks. Angel Gabriel announced to Mary that she would conceive by the power of the Holy Spirit and bear a Son. Though perturbed initially, young Mary gladly sang for finding favour with God: '......... *behold, henceforth all generations will call me blessed............* 'True, world over, many venerate her as Blessed Virgin Mary. But the price she had to pay for it during her life time, right from conceiving Jesus till his ignominious death on cross, is unimaginable. Many in Jewish Community of the times might not have believed her conception to be divine. Bearing that humiliation would have been heart-breaking for her but for the love and protection of St. Joseph, her divinely-selected spouse. Finally, she had to see her only Son being mercilessly whipped, crowned with thorns, ridiculed, nailed to the cross and left to die.

At first, my sincere thought was that our family – Appachan, Mummy and their seven children – were the chosen ones. The sixth child passed away soon after his birth. Of the remaining six, religious and philosophical thoughts were aplenty in my mind. It made me conclude that I was chosen first and through me, the rest would be. In that case, why was I chosen first? It was my firm belief that the queries were God-given for me to seek the answers. All of a sudden, a passage from the Old Testament came to my mind:

Can a woman forget her suckling child, that she should not have compassion on the baby of her womb? Yea, they may forget, yet will I not forget thee.

Behold, I have graven thee upon the palms of my hands…

– Isaiah 49: 15, 16

A strange thought struck me suddenly. Did Mummy 'forget' me at any point of time in my life? I had never doubted Mummy's love for me. In fact, I did doubt Appachan's love due to my foolishness (narrated in an earlier chapter). Such worrisome thoughts often dogged me in late 1993. As if to aid in my pursuit, another forgotten incident most unexpectedly flashed through my mind. It happened in 1963, a year after Appachan's death. One of our relatives (a young bachelor) was playfully throwing my youngest sister Jolly (aged 2) up in the air and catching her with precision. At the age of 17, I felt it to be a risky play and pleaded with him to stop. His immediate response in an amused tone shocked me, *"Why worry if one of the five girls 'goes'?"* If Appachan had been alive or if it were a boy, he might not have commented in such a casual manner and that made the 'cut' deeper. For some time after the incident, the feeling that my little sister might come to some harm frightened me. He could not be blamed for his thoughtless remark. It is a well-known Indian mentality to pity the family with many daughters. His sympathy for the five fatherless girls might have induced him to say it.

As years rolled by, I forgot about it and my mind recalled it on two occasions. The first occasion was due to the same relative who soon got married and became the father of 7 children. Curiously, they were also like us – 5 girls and 2 boys – the only difference being the youngest were sons. Surely, I did not think that he was 'punished' for his playful words. It was a case of *'coming events cast their shadows before them'.* Another coincidence was that, like Appachan, he also passed away unexpectedly in his early 50s. By God's grace, all his children are well-placed today and care for their mother.

The second occasion was due to my unending thoughts and emanated from the first occasion. When I almost died of dysentery at 18 months, someone might have consoled Mummy, *"Now that you have three daughters, don't worry about losing this one"*. Again at 8 years, when chickenpox choked me to the point of death, yet another 'compassionate' relative might have said, *"You have four daughters now. It doesn't matter even if she fails to recover!"* For the second time when Mummy heard such words, she might have thought the viewpoint to be correct. My idea is not to find fault with Mummy. People in those days were obsessed with the burden of many girls in families. Finally, when we were five daughters, it was I who heard the trivial comment on a girl child's death.

All these reflections led me to the time of my first encounter with death when I was six months old. Mummy had prayerfully cried out then, *'Deivaputhrane rakshikka'* (Please save God's son). Decades later, at the age of 47, I realized that the words referred to me. To keep it hidden at that time, she was not made to say, *'Deivaputhriye'* (God's daughter). Some might think my explanation to be a far-fetched fancy. Yet others could question, *"How can you call yourself deivaputhri?"* Aren't we all children of God? The crux of the matter is that one should REALIZE this and not merely know it.

To cut a long story short, it was God who made Mummy first pray for my life fervently and later 'forsake' me helplessly. Everything happened to prove the biblical verse *'Can a woman forget her baby? Even if she does, I won't'*. We are mere puppets in the hands of God. Leo Tolstoy's wise words:

There is a minimum of free choice for people. But unless they imagine that they have free will, people cannot live.

Despite such high philosophical thoughts, I was thoroughly shaken when my youthful son passed away due to a road accident some years later. Yet I recovered quickly as I convinced myself that God of Justice did not spare me 'the furnace of affliction'. Placing full trust in God, I sought solace from different sources. Aunt Achayi (Appachan's elder sister) who lost her young husband and three little kids to cholera within the span of two months came to my mind to meditate upon. I also thought about another tragic death. Thangamma, the first child of Aunt Rosy (Mummy's younger sister) was born and bred in

Trichur. As the only daughter in their family, she became very close to us. After marriage she came to live in Coimbatore and it took her to the seventh heaven. Three months later, she conceived and after three more months, she took eternal rest at the age of 25. The 'culprit' was jaundice for which the symptoms were the same as pregnancy – giddiness and vomiting. There was no yellowness in her eyes or urine and that belied her condition. Jaundice had affected her blood stream straightaway and she had a sudden death due to the late diagnosis of the disease. My aunt was inconsolable. Eagerly awaiting her first grandchild's arrival, Aunt Rosy was destined to lose her daughter. I could strengthen my mind and spirit by deeply thinking about these two aunts who had borne deep sorrow. Adam Lindsay Gordon says:

Life is mostly froth and bubble,

Two things stand like stone.

Kindness in another's trouble;

Courage in your own.

My earnest thoughts and sincere prayers have always been for world peace and happiness. Needless to say, everything ultimately depends upon peace in the minds of individuals and in families. Children brought up by wise parents do not deviate from the right path and would have fraternal feelings. In many families love dries up especially after the marriages of siblings. They start comparing their material prosperity and other achievements and get stressed. In the end, the prosperous ones are proud and the others, jealous. At times, those who come from the same womb, fight for wealth earned by the parents and go to the extent of killing each other. In modern days, there is a mushroom growth of old age homes. Children as they grow up tend to lose their love and respect for their parents. Of the Ten Commandments in the Bible, the fourth one is to be specially noted here: *Honour your father and your mother.* Many love their parents and some do so for selfish reasons. But honouring one's parents is rarely done.

When my mind was flooded with such thoughts, I received The Holy Quran from Jaimon in 1994. As is my wont, I prayed for a while before reading that Sacred Book for the first time and opened it at random. I was awestruck by the verses I first saw in it:

Thy Lord hath decreed, that ye worship none save Him, and that ye show kindness to parents. If one of them or both of them to attain old age with thee, say not 'Fie' unto them, nor repulse them, but speak unto them a gracious word.

And lower unto them the wing of submission through mercy, and say: My Lord! Have mercy on them both, as they did care for me when I was little.

– Surah XVII, verses 23,24

Moreover, I read about an incident in the life of Prophet Mohammed as narrated by Abu Hurairah: A man came to the Prophet with a question: *"Who is to be close to my friendship?"* The Prophet answered, *"Your mother, your mother, your mother, then your father, then the one close to your kinship and the one after."* Islam which gives much importance to prayer, fasting, alms-giving and fraternal love, is one of the wide-spread religions in the world. Some extremists spoil the name of Islam. The very name 'Islam' means 'peace' and also 'submission to the will of God'.

Instead of fighting in the name of religions, we can follow the good principles from all the religions. This broad-mindedness would certainly lead to peaceful coexistence. Rig Veda says: *'Let noble thoughts come to us from every direction.'* How many Hindus pay heed to this exhortation from their sacred scripture! There is a Tamil saying, *'Yaadhum oore; yaavarum, kelir'* (I belong to every nation; all are my relations) which echoes the idea of *'Vasudhaiva Kudumbakam'*.

As a self-realized soul, I felt it was my duty to correct relatives and friends when they went astray. Some gratefully appreciated my frank and sincere efforts for their good. But some ignored my advice subtly. When I lost my son, the latter's indifference wrung my heart. Their attitude seemed to be: *'She came to correct us as if she is God's representative. Now, God taught her a lesson'.* My belief is in a LOVING

GOD; not in a punishing one. A good person is made to suffer or sacrificed at the altar of TRUTH. It is part of Divine Plan for people to repent.

The tradition of honouring the marriage vows at any cost is gradually giving way to divorces. As an educated and employed woman, I almost took that path. But by God's grace, I was saved by the timely guidance of two good souls. I decided to sacrifice many things so that my little ones would have their father's love and care. Today, many among our kith and kin, consider our life as an ideal one to be emulated. Praise the Lord!

At the time of our wedding (1972) many hailed us as a made-for-each-other couple. I thought ours was a wonderful match for a curious reason. His first employment in MALCO was on Jan 27th which is my birthday. Of course, he had joined duty 10 years prior to our wedding. My appointment as a Lecturer in Home Science College was on 4th August which is his birthday and this was nearly 3 years before our marriage. When Jose knew that all my records have 29th Jan as my date of birth (an inadvertent error), he came up with another interesting coincidence. Though 27th was the date for him to join duty, he actually started working there only from 29th! An elderly man in MALCO office advised Jose to do so because it would be inauspicious to begin the work, especially when it is a first-time job, on a day immediately followed by a holiday. In 1962, 28th January was a Sunday! With that old man's blessings, Jose worked there for 33 years.

I was overwhelmed with happiness thinking that God had gone into such 'minute details' in uniting us! But within four years, eyes ever clouded with tears, I questioned God: "*I did not fall in love with the person of my choice. It is You who guided my elders to arrange this marriage. O God, didn't I deserve a person of my nature and ideas?*" My better understanding later made it clear that any marriage (arranged or love) is the plan of God. No wonder the saying arose, '*Marriages are made in heaven*'.

It is a pity that today marriages are mostly marred on earth. Let me come to my experiences which taught me to see things in the right perspective. Despite my age (26); education (M.A.) and a responsible job (lecturer), I lacked worldly wisdom at the time of my marriage. Every individual is unique and everyone knows it. But to experience the truth of it in one's life is rather difficult. If Jose had a nature like mine, perhaps our life would not have been a success as it is today. When Jaimon was 24 years old, he estimated us in a wonderful way: *"We have one of the best of parents; Daddy makes us worldly wise; Mummy guides us spiritually."*

If Jose had been equally spiritual, we might have led an austere life in an ashram. There is nothing wrong in such a life. But God's plan for us happened to be different. Jose was responsible for money matters and having no worry about such dealings I could carry on in 'my way'. My domain consisted of looking after 'JMJ'; cooking & maintenance of home; reading, writing and most importantly teaching. Above all, I could find peace in spiritual thoughts. Unless there is LIGHT within me, I cannot shine for others.

The thought of separation in the initial years of my married life was due to some strong reasons. Whenever problems arose at home, Jose would be either silent or take his mother's side. As a young wife, I felt terribly let down in those days. Contentment possessed my soul through bringing up my children and with my teaching career. Today I am happy about the way everything has happened. Since Jose 'forsook' me, I could go closer to God. Secondly, from personal experience, I realized later that when adult children talk back or argue, it is unbearable for a mother. So, the support Jose gave his widowed mother absolved him from that guilt, though I had to bear the brunt of it! More than anything else my own nature was my 'enemy'. Instead of bearing everything patiently and shedding tears, if I had fought back (with words!) for my right, my mother-in-law might have treated me better. As Jose is her only son, she would have been more cautious in dealing with a 'quarrelsome' daughter-in-law. There was a passing thought once, *'Why shouldn't I act like a cruel daughter-in-law as in the movies?'* That idea was in vain as Alice and acting have always been poles apart!

His short temper was another cause of my sorrow. He used to be cross with me often. Here again, patience and tears were my 'foes'.

If I had shouted back, he might have calmed down. Now Jose has changed a lot. More than ten years ago, looking at an old photo of his, a teenaged girl blurted out, *"Uncle, you look more handsome now!"* All burst out laughing as he was 70 then. I smiled at my own 'secret' thought – when short temper disappeared, it is no wonder he is better-looking now!

Jose was extremely economical in those days and it gave me many moments of anguish. I have always been careful in spending money. Yet after much thought when buying something was suggested, it would seem unnecessary for him. Being employed, I could have spent to my liking. But due to my principle, it was avoided. Soon after wedding, it was I who entrusted to him all the dealings of money. Going back on my word was unimaginable to me. Devoid of bad habits, he spent thriftily and had been putting away some amount for a rainy day. Needless to say, everything was for the family's welfare. Nevertheless, when small wishes of mine were thwarted, naturally arguments arose with my crying in the end.

In retrospection I never feel that I have lost much in married life. In a way, self-denials had been thrust upon me but I carried on surrendering my will to God's. Now the feeling of freedom is experienced in boundless measure with all the changes I have brought about in my personal life.

'And you shall know the truth and the truth shall make you free.' - St. John 8:32.

For my patience, I have had abundant recompense. How true Rousseau's words are: *'Patience is bitter; but its fruit is sweet.'*

Today, God is my constant companion with whom I often converse inwardly. Two words in Malayalam – *'Deivame Nanni'* (Thank You God) are dissolved in my system. Before writing anything, I use my watchword *'May God Bless Us All'*. Besides the regular prayers, I prayed for new prayers and God blessed me with a few. There may not be any new ideas in these prayers; but the way they are worded is mine. I record here some:

Morning Prayer

Oh God, let me not pray for tomorrow. Please help me to do today's duties beautifully and wisely; happily and peacefully.

Night Prayer

Oh God, thank You for all the blessings received today. Please forgive me for the sins I have committed knowingly or unknowingly; willingly or unwillingly; intentionally or unintentionally. I earnestly pray for world peace and happiness. Kindly give intelligence, knowledge, wisdom, love and patience to all parents, teachers and all the others who are involved in bringing up children. I implore You to give food for the hungry; water for the thirsty; clothes for the ones in rags; shelter for the homeless; cure for the diseased and solace for the afflicted.

Prayer for a Better World

Oh God, may this world be ruled by Your Love and not with violence;

May this world be ruled by Your Generosity and Forgiveness and not with money;

May this world find Peace and Happiness at the earliest. Thank You God.

The world sees and hears our actions and words; but God is more watchful of our thoughts. According to Christian Theology there are Seven Deadly Sins - Pride, Anger, Lust, Avarice, Gluttony, Envy and Sloth. I have coined a mnemonic, like VIBGYOR, to remember all these sins – PALAGES. When the mind is invaded by unbridled passions, remembering the sins through this mnemonic would help us nip them in the bud. I have shared this useful tip with many for their moral and spiritual well-being. Once, a friend asked me why murder, robbery, adultery etc. are not included in the list of sins. There is a difference between sins and sinful actions. The seven sins harboured in the mind induce people to do sinful deeds. A man becomes a murderer because of anger or lust or avarice or envy. He robs because of sloth or avarice. Lust or pride leads to adultery. Thus, for all sinful words and actions, the root cause is impure or cruel thoughts. Saintly people may make mistakes, but rarely do they sin as they are pure in heart. Thiruvalluvar says:

All righteousness is contained in purity of heart;

All the rest is showy display of art.

To make our world a paradise let us follow St. Jerome's words:

Good, better, best,

Never let it rest,

Until your good is better,

And your better is best.

Is there a limit for becoming better and better? There is a meaningfully-worded beautiful picture in our showcase. It has always had positive vibes. Let me quote those words and bid adieu to the readers.

I'm super good, but I'll get better.

– Zig Ziglar

Peroration

After reading my life's story, close relatives and some friends might wonder whether I had forgotten or concealed some significant happenings. There are chances of my forgetting what they remember, but I certainly avoided writing some events to protect the identity of individuals involved. Admitting my mistakes is my prerogative and is done in this book. In the same manner I cannot reveal the wrong doings of others who had hurt me deeply. A few of them are supposed to be very close to me.

Years ago, during a sermon, the priest elaborated on Jesus' precept, *'Love your enemies'*. He emphatically said, *"As an individual, your enemies are not in America or Africa; nor in Pakistan or China. They are mostly in your family circle and among your friends. When one hurts you by his/her words and deeds; shows enmity directly or indirectly you should not hate them or be indifferent. You have to forgive them and pray for their well-being. Of course, it is better said than done. But Jesus expects us to love each other with forgiveness."*

I recall the sermon when people whom I love wound my feelings unjustly. They rarely used hurtful words to me but their indifferent attitude, subtly sown, was enough to make me shed tears. Such emotional outpourings reduced considerably after self-realisation. Anyway, forgiving them from the bottom of my heart helped me improve my physical, mental and spiritual health. Writing about such controversies would make matters worse. Moreover, to some amenable ones I had a free and frank talk and they begged my pardon appreciating my openness. The more we forgive; the more will Divine Love be in us. Alexander Pope says: *'To err is human; to forgive, divine.'*

Jesus Christ asks us to *'turn the other also to the one who smites thee on one cheek'*. In our day-to-day life, we do not go about slapping each other. There is a figurative meaning also in this. Turning the other cheek is achieved by being silent. But it is very difficult to be quiet when hurtful words are hurled at us, as words cut deeper than swords. So, even if our ego induces us to use more wounding words, we must restrain ourselves. If not, silly matters would lead to gigantic problems.

All of us have heard of the exhortation, *'forgive and forget'*. If we have great love and immense patience we can easily forgive; forgetting is not that easy. As long as we have mind and memory, we may remember them. But it is important that we should never harbour bitter feelings nor contemplate on vengeance. The Holy Bible says: *'Let not the sun go down upon your wrath'*. In this connection a relevant couplet from Thiruvalluvar comes to mind:

The joy of retaliation is only for a day;

The glory of forgiveness lasts for ever.

Thomas Stephen Szasz's words sum up my thoughts on forgiving and forgetting:

The stupid neither forgive nor forget;

The naïve forgive and forget;

The wise forgive but do not forget.

My admiration for Mahatma Gandhi and Mother Teresa is well known among relatives, friends and students. I also admire many more great men and women of the world. Here are a few names from that long list: Thiruvalluvar, Swami Vivekananda, Bharathiyar, Vinoba Bhave, Socrates, St. Francis of Assisi, Father Damien, Abraham Lincoln, Albert Schweitzer, Florence Nightingale, Helen Keller and Ida S. Scudder. Needless to say, they are ever living and ever inspiring great souls.

In the original Tamil version of this life story, I wrote thus: *'Among the people living today, my great admiration is for three – Pope Francis, Nelson Mandela and Dr A P J Abdul Kalam.'* While my book was getting ready for publication, Mandela passed away in December 2012. To Dr

A P J Abdul Kalam, who was also a great scholar in Tamil, I could send a complimentary copy of my autobiography published in 2014. He sent me an e-mail within a week with his blessings. His magnanimity did not exclude 'this strange woman'! Subsequently he passed away in 2015. A copy of Dr Kalam's message is added in the Appendix.

Dr Kalam's thoughtful response was in stark contrast to the attitude of some people known to me very well. After receiving the complimentary copies, they remained silent. Even a few words of criticism would have made me glad. It is said, *Indifference hurts more than hatred*. However, I am happy to say that some who bought and read my book had words of appreciation. Perhaps, anything given for free is undervalued by some.

I had also sent copies to all the institutions where I had studied (5) and taught (20) with covering letters. Silence was the response from them except one school where I began my education in 1951 as a little girl of five! T.E.L.C. Elementary School in Coimbatore invited and honoured me with a shawl and a beautiful memento. Thank you, my first alma mater! Also, our then Parish Priest, Rev. Fr. Saji Pariyappanal of Santhome church at Hulimavu in Bangalore presented me a memento (a glass replica of our newly built church), congratulating me on publishing the story of my life. It was a pleasant surprise when he announced it on a Sunday after the Holy Mass as I was not informed about it earlier. I am indeed grateful!

In conclusion, let me humbly bow before many anonymous noble souls who do good work silently to make this world more beautiful and a better place to live in.

Whosoever it be that speaks,

Wisdom grasps the truth in it.

– Thiruvalluvar

Acknowledgments

With humility and gratitude, I bow before God for the special blessing which enabled me to write the story of my life first in Tamil and now in English.

As a septuagenarian, I have taken immense pains to edit and translate it from the Tamil version. Yet my effort alone would not have brought it to the present form. I have great joy in thanking some who helped me in this venture.

First and foremost, my thanks are due to my husband, K. C. Jose, without whose support this work would not have seen the light.

The Tamil version was edited and proof read by one Mary (my sister - Mary John) and now that onerous job was done for the English edition by another Mary (my daughter - Mary Kuriakose). From the bottom of my heart, I thank my daughter who has painstakingly done a good job not only in editing and proof reading but also turning the manuscript into the digital form.

Joseph, my son took up the responsibility of publishing it with all its financial commitments. My heart-felt thanks to him.

My acknowledgments would be incomplete if I do not make a special mention about my three children in general. Jacob, my first-born who is no more today was the one who encouraged me to write 'something' with my vast experience both in personal and career life. 'Computer illiterate' that I am, my doubts regarding quotations and some other matters were clarified by Mary and Joseph who had always obliged me by searching the net! Thanks to Google, too!!

Last but not least, I thank Notion Press for publishing this work in a fine form.

Appendices

245

Jacob's Reflections at the Age of 16

1988

MY REFLECTIONS

It was monday, the 21st of November I was returning from school and was waiting for the train. The time was 5.05 P.M. The trains are usually over-crowded at this time.

The train arrived. I stood somewhere at the middle of the platform. The compartments rushed past me one by one. I could see people hanging out through the jammed doors. Suddenly I saw one of the vendor's compartment coming almost ~~empty~~ empty I could not believe my eyes. Along with me many others too had spotted it and we all made a dash for it.

Every one of us stopped still on our tracks at the door way of the compartment. For just inside lay the dead body of a man completely covered by a tarpaulin. I could hear muttered words of disgust and anger and curiosity from the passengers next to me. Then every one of them turned and went to fight for survival at other compartments. No wonder the vendors compartment was empty!

I was at indecision whether or not to enter it. Well, I decided, there is nothing to be afraid of a dead man and entered the compartment.

The first sense was smell, a disgusting odour of blood

and salt. The rest was sight.
I saw totally 8 people in the
whole compartment — 4 boys of
about 20 years of age singing
some popular hit songs in tamil
and drumming away. They were
dressed very shabbily. There was
a very old couple, very quiet too.
Besides them there was a middle
aged man with a beard carrying
a heavy package and a fiftish
man with a parcel of what
appeared to be glass.
　　　　I sat down and turned
my attention to the body. On
second look, I discovered that
it was not fully covered as I
had imagined earlier. The legs
below the knees were visible.
One leg had its toes smashed
together with dried flesh and
blood over it. In between the
toes and the ankle, the flesh

had been torn apart and stark white bone was visible. The other leg ended at the ankle with nothing beyond it. Slowly a kind of sickness came over me and I was thankful that the rest of the ~~body~~ was covered.

By this time the next station had arrived and a group of people rushed to our compartment. The same thing happened — not one of them came ~~it~~ in.

People try to avoid death and ~~and~~ anything connected with it

[When I say people, I do not exclude myself.] They generally do not like to even look at dead bodies when each one of them is fated to end the same way. Is it because they do not want to face reality? Or is it because they do not want to spoil their temporary happiness by thinking about eternal oblivion?

The next station came and the 4 shabbily dressed young men covered the exposed legs and took it out of the train. I looked out and my eyes met the electric cremator at the nearby cemetry. Only 2 people entered the compartment at that station.

The train rolled on and left me to my sober thoughts. On arriving at the next station, a happy lot of people (because they had found an empty compartment) entered it and chatted away standing on the very spot where a very still form, who had been probably as gay as ~~them~~ them, & had lain until a few minutes earlier. I heard one of the passengers commenting to another — "What the hell! This compartment is so empty, that I can't believe it. Look out! there may be a dead body or something".

Ah! How true! How true!

As the train rolled on to my destination, one question popped up on my mind —

Which will be my day?

K

Introduction to Jacob's Website
by Gopal Rangachary

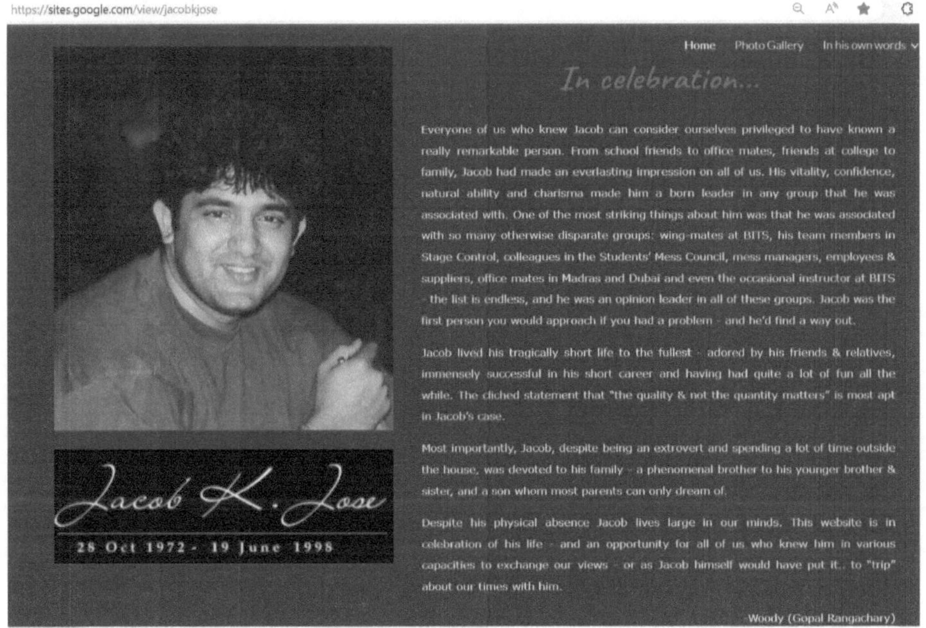

https://sites.google.com/view/jacobkjose/

A Memorable Response from System Construct

SYSTEM
CONSTRUCT

12 June 1998

Mr. & Mrs. K. C. Jose
Jeevan Griha, Flat 61, Block 7,
J.P. Nagar, 1st. Phase,
Bangalore - 560 078

Dear Mr. & Mrs. Jose,

We the Management & Staff of System Construct join hands with you and other family members as you commemorate the 1st Death anniversary of our most dear employee, colleague and friend Jacob. Our prayers go out that God Almighty alone may comfort and console each and every one of you. The Jacob we remember was a highly popular, vibrant and dynamic personality. Indeed an irreplaceable gem.

God bless you all.

With prayers,

MANAGEMENT & STAFF

P.O. Box 9325, Dubai - U.A.E., Tel: 350303 (20 Lines), Fax: 353129, E-mail: system@emirates.net.ae

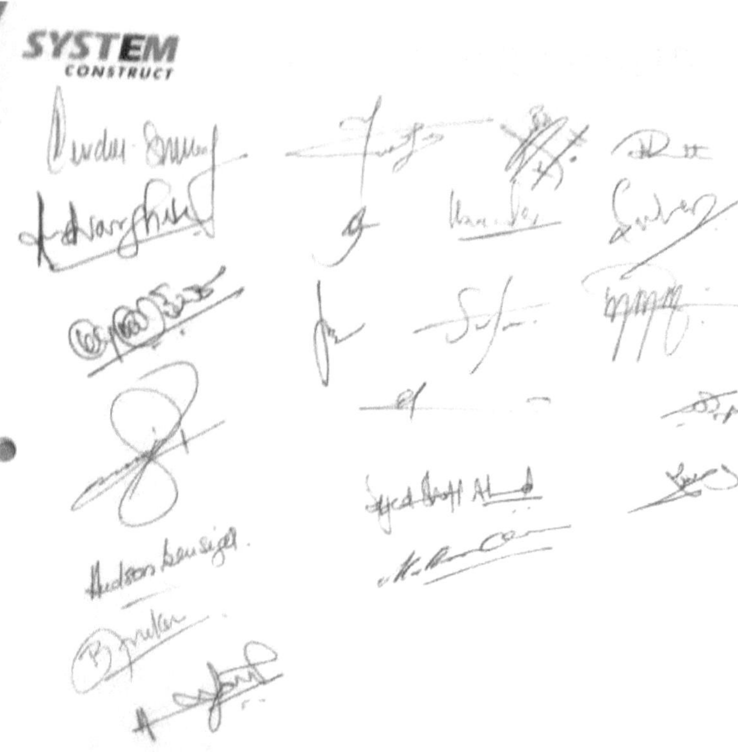

Daughter's Letter for Author's 50th Birthday

21/01/96

Dearest Mummy,

i believe you are doing well. My sincere B'day wishes. i do not have words to express my love, gratitude, etc towards you. But i attempted doing so once, no, 4 times actually in March '95. i thought nobody should know of it. i'd written it in my diary. But if you didn't know it, what's the big deal? These are my feelings towards you; were in Mar. '95, still are today when i read through what i'd written Mar 10:

Mummy, what all you have done for me! You taught me great values — cleanliness, thought of the poor, not to waste anything, to respect food & be thankful for it, not to show anger on it, to appreciate beauty in small things, in the sunset, in the night sky. you instilled in me the mystery of the stars, the universe. you showed me how to be moved at the plight of others, how to enjoy a book, how to clean vessels, how to wash clothes, how to clean oneself — physically, i've understood, spiritually, not yet. You have showed me

Love is a universal language.
Time is the Translator.

what kindness is, what giving is, what forgiving is, what patience is. How you have suffered to bring me into this world, and then each day, doing everything for me, when i could do nothing for myself, teaching me how to speak, to write, improving upon it, allowing me to be independent, treating me as an equal with your sons, bringing us up with total impartiality, teaching me what is right and what is wrong at the impressionable age, narrating to us numerous stories and making us sleep, when you were most tired. Mummy, you instilled in me patriotism, courage, admiration for great people.

These are a few of the things that i remember, though; i know there is much more, like the iceberg whose tip only is seen when its greater self is hidden beneath. How did you do it? How did you achieve so much? You have moulded me into a human being. God, make me worthy of my mother.

undated:

You gave me the little knowledge for music, you taught me how to appreciate it. You showed me how to do things with meaningfulness, how to sit during prayer time, how to say the prayers with meaning, how to sing hymns not only for their music but grasping & taking in the lyrics. You taught me how to enjoy what i do, you showed me how to listen to each person. What awes me — your utter faith in prayer.

(innumerable) Milk at night — wiping away our milk filled mouths with your wet hands; the way i played with your hair, making it up in all non-sensical ways; learning Malayalam together; each time i had leg pain — you used to apply Velankanni oil & massage the aching part — how soothing it was! You played with us, for us — cards. carrom, though you don't like it. Once you won chettan for me, when i was always losing to him & crying over it.

19/3:

You taught me honesty through your words & *Love is a universal language.*
Time is the Translator.

deeds. You showed me the art of doing the little day-to-day activities with perfection, showed me the life of simplicity. "Simple living + high thinking" — You are the living embodiment of this for me.

02/4 : You taught me how to pray — Pray earnestly for what you want + be satisfied with what you get. Take anything that comes as God-given. Pray the greatest prayer of "Your will be done"; though I still haven't got it into me to pray, i can understand the significance of that prayer + how it has affected my way of thinking. Thankyou, Mummy.

Today, i have only one thing to say to you — "You are the truest person i've known in my life".

With love,

Vaishnavi

Expressions of Love by Students

To OUR BELOVED TEACHER
        ACCORDING TO OUR VIEW,
you have Achieved your goal
you Loved and were loved by all
your life is Inspired by love
your Character is the best
Thus you have Enlightened your soul.

                        yours ever
29-10-83   Students of IX class

Received with
        thanks.

Respected teacher,
    You 'ere a mother,
    To a weeping child,
    And a guide,
    To a stranger lost his way.
    We 'ere mere letters,
    And you made us books.
    You 'ere a lamp – while
    we roamed blind in dark.
    You 'ere the string – for
    We only a guitar,
    We 'ere lonely – while
    You were a friend,
    All for us! And only for us!

    Do not you know?
    The meaning of 'anger' – for
    Ne'er had we seen,
    You go red.

    The smile you bore,
    The patience you have,

Your humble' and polite nature,
Makes us put down our heads,
For, though we tried, - we
Find it harder a task.

We 'ere un'ble to pay the de't,
For your selfless wisdom given to us
Like the earth, Shown kindness by
                                    Sun
But ne'er is to pay i's de't to him.

We part with you,
Like an eye from its lash,
'A petal from its flower,
And sweet from honey.
Thy path we'll follow,
And our love for thee,
Forgetting you is impossible
Like a mother to her child.
                    From,
            Students of Malco Vidya
            Mettur Dam 2

29-10-83

Received with thanks

To.

<u>Mrs. Alice K Jose</u>

By,

X. Standard.

Malco Vidyalaya.

Mettur Dam - 2

27.10.83

பிரியமான உங்களுக்கு
பிரியா விடையளித்து.
விடை பெறும் நாங்களும்,
வாழ்த்திடனை வழங்கிடுவோம்.

தென் தமிழ் சொல்லெடுத்து
தெவிட்டாத மொழியெடுத்து - உங்கள்
வான் புகழ் பாட வந்தோம். உங்களை
வாழ்த்திடவே கூடி வந்தோம்!
சினங்கொள்ளாத மனங்கொண்டு
சிரித்திருக்கும் முகம் கொண்டு
இதமான விழி கொண்டு, அதில்
ஈராயிரம் கான விளக்குகளை சுமந்திருந்தீர!
அன்பிற்கும் இன் பண்பிற்கும்
மாண பிற்கும் நல்ல மனத்திற்கும்,
அறத்திற்கும் செங்கரத்திற்கும்
ஆலயமே! அறிவொளியே!
மாணமுற்ற மாணிடனையும் - வைரி
மாணாக மாற்றிடுவாய்!
நாணமுற்ற மனத்தினையும் - நல்
இணைமாக தேற்றிடுவாய்!.
எங்குமிங்கல்லாம் பறறிருக்கே!
நினைவெல்லாம் மங்கிக்கது! - உள்ளம்
பஞ்சாகிப் பறக்குதே!
இன்ப மிரிவை நினைக்கையிலே.
தலை எழுத எனதுடங்க.
மை யெழுதி படிக்கையிலே
வரி ஒன்றும் கிட்டாமல் வாடி
நெஞ்சிருதே நெஞ்சமம் மா!
வரி ஒன்றும் கிட்டாமல்
வாணத்தை நோக்கினையிலே
மறிந்து விட்ட நெஞ்சமது
மறுத்திடமா யாவற்றையும்!
வானத்தை நோக்கினையில்
வரி ஒன்று கிட்டியது; ஆம்
"வானிலவின் ஒளியது போல்
படிங்கிளிர் அறிவொளியினை"

Received this Expression of Love & Respect from my students (Represented by the SPL-B G.Shivkumar and the Secret S.K. Saswathan) with heartfelt gratitude on 13th Oct 1993 when I joined duty after the medical leave for two months for a major operation. (Abdominal Hysterectomy) I'm thankful to God Almighty for this!

15/10/93

A lady who is strict
Student's freedom she does not
                restrict
She is very Kind
And has good thinking in mind
She is our respected Principal
A good teacher of good principles.
    Though we will miss her
                very much
    As she is going away
    We are saying good-bye
                with a smile
    But with sadness in the
                heart, this day.

Received with Thanks   —
Th. Alice
    30/12/95   'Holy Flower' — Salem-16

                                by
                        R. Savitha, IX A

Dr A.P.J. Abdul Kalam's Email to the Author

From: **apj** <apj@abdulkalam.com>
Date: Wed, Aug 6, 2014 at 12:50 PM
Subject: Am I a Chosen One
To: alicekjose@rediffmail.com

Dear Mrs Alice Jose,

I was happy to receive a copy of your book - "Am I a Chosen One".   Thank you for the same. I went through Chapter-18 (Books and Gandhiji) with great interest.

May God bless you and your family.

Regards,

Kalam

--

Office of Dr. APJ Abdul Kalam,
10 Rajaji Marg,
New Delhi - 110011

www.abdulkalam.com,
www.facebook.com/kalambillionbeats

<u>Tr. Alice's Writings</u>
Take the Cross and Walk

Take the cross and walk

O God, what a predicament!

A girl at the threshold of teenage

To carry the cross big enough

To crucify the infant Jesus!

(Is there a day without crucifixion?)

Bearing the cross on the shoulder

Walked I through the busy streets.

Heightened was the distress

While passing by a Boys' School!

Command was from a trainer

And who was the one?

None other than a nun,

Spiritually wedded to Our Lord.

But she and her companion

Reluctant to carry His Cross.

Trudged I with the Symbol of Salvation

Heavy on my shoulder and with tears.

Trod they behind like troopers

With 'whips' in their hearts.

The wooden cross, 'character' in a play

Transported thus sans fare

From a convent to its school.

Since then… many a cross has been borne

Big and small; heavy and light

Without demur, sans shame.

Today, how willing am I

To take such crosses to my grave.

Peace and joy rule my heart

Mysterious are Thy ways, O God!

– Written on 07-Jun-1977

India Sans Indira

Oh, cruel Death, thy merciless icy hands
Hath now embraced the Queen of Land of Lands.
India's towering glory with moral might,
Hath today fallen with no chance to fight.

Ah, beloved soul of our Motherland
Thy brave blood's shed by betraying hand.
Cowardly guard! How treacherous,
How utterly preposterous!

Now India stands sans Indira in pain
A rudderless ship on turbulent main.
Where's the Captain? Where's the beacon bright?
Whither shall we go; people without sight?

Immortal India preaches non-violence
Incorrigible Indians indulge in violence
In the name of mourning, they beat and loot
Innocent brothers and sisters, they shoot.

Friends, Indians, my beloved countrymen!

Shan't we enhance our vision and acumen?

Let's be pledged to India's Himalayan fame

Let's be true Indians, not just in name!

– Written on 04-Nov-1984

Gurukul's Diamond Jubilee Poems

வைரவிழா வாழ்த்துப்பா

அன்பின் அருளுருவே போற்றி

ஆருயிரின் ஆன்மாவே போற்றி

இணையில்லா இன்பமே போற்றி

ஈடில்லா ஈசனே போற்றி

உண்மையின் உறைவிடமே போற்றி

ஊக்கத்தின் ஊட்டமே போற்றி

எல்லையிலா கருணைக்கடலே போற்றி

ஏசுவே எம் இறைவா போற்றி

ஐயனே ஞான ஒளியே போற்றி

ஒழுக்கத்தின் இலக்கணமே போற்றி

ஓங்கார நாதமே போற்றி

ஔவியத்தின் எதிர்மறையே போற்றி

உயிரின் உயிரான உம்மை
உயிரெழுத்திலே போற்றுவமே
வைரவிழா காணும் குருகுலத்தை
வாழ்த்தியருள வேண்டுவமே

திருமதி. ஆலிஸ் K. ஜோஸ்
ஆங்கில ஆசிரியை
'குருகுலம்'

Oct. 1987

This is Our Gurukul

'Glory to God' as our goal,
Under the guidance of
Right thinking folk,
Unique way, do we tread
Knowledge, do we spread
Universal brotherhood and
Love, being our watchwords.

Lutheran, though in name
Unity, certainly, is our aim.
Towards a 'Bold Theological Vision
Honouring God through our mission
Ecumenism, foremost in mind
Rich treasures, do we find
Always moving forward
New concepts introduced.

Theology, Dalit, is for one
Human Development, also won
Eve-teasing to Women's Study gives way
Offers Communication, a bright ray
Learnt all, with a new thrust.
Onerous, some may say, yet,
Greek, Hebrew and Sanskrit
Incorporated in learning list
Curricular and co-curricular
Activities, our syllabus constitute.
Laudable, the work of Research Institute.

Commitment, team spirit,
Oneness, devotion-many a merit
Leads us to a life of meditation
Lights the lamp of dedication
English language binding us often !
Gurukul on its Diamond Jubilee in '87
Ever be blessed by God in Heaven !

by
Mrs. Alice K. Jose
Lecturer in English
Gurukul.

Oct. 1987

Xavier Absalom

XAVIER ABSALOM – his was a great life,

At ninety – eight joined he the Heavenly Choir.

Versatile, wise and inspiring was he

Independence and zeal close to his heart

Ever lived he with good words and kind deeds

Rarely found a soul so tenacious!

Asset great had he – POSITIVE THINKING

Bonhomie personified, travelled he

Spring, Summer, Autumn, Winter

An incredible journey through and through

Love and piety always ruling his life

Observer of strong precepts, lived he well.

My days with him ever will I cherish!

– Written on 10-Nov-2010

Prayer for a corona-free world

God Almighty, Ocean of Mercy,
Thy children of the Earth, do we
Beseech Thee in this hour of need
Away from corona, please lead.

Angel-like doctors and nurses
Fore'er toil to ward off curses
We pray for them with gratitude
Salute them with meek attitude.

Countless are gripped by the virus
Deaths of our dear ones shatter us
With Thy Guidance we're sure to cope
Thy Bounty is our only hope.

Loving God, we had been thoughtless
Selfishly led life meaningless
Humbly now we admit the Truth
All are equal to Mother Earth

Help us count our blessings always
Shun temptations in many ways
Great or small, all are made by Thee
Shall live in amity, pledge we.

Thank Thee God for World beautiful
Forever are we most grateful
God, in the grave crisis today
Helpless are we, show us the Way.

- By a septuagenarian who feels she is a citizen of the world.

– Published in a Magazine - Written on 28-Mar-2020

Visiting 'The Living and the Dead' – A Brief Travelogue

A Blessed Journey by an aged couple with their son

for 8 days by car from 21" to 28th Jan 2023

Travellers: Jose (79), Alice (77), Joseph (Babu - 46)

We travelled to 14 cities and villages (12 in Kerala and 2 in Tamil Nadu) and visited 50 particular places totally.

3 churches in Thrissur, Chalakudy and Kunnamkulam

4 cemeteries in Kuzhuppilly, Nedungad, Parur and Chalakudy

1 hospital in Irinjalakuda

42 Happy Homes! (Relatives - 38 & Friends - 4)

Joyfully met 143 persons (Relatives - 135 & Friends - 8)

Total distance covered - 1450 kms.

₹ 52,000 - amount worthily spent on this precious trip.

Cakes, sweets, savouries & fruits for kith & kin - ₹14,600

Diesel & toll fee - ₹10,000

Amount deservedly gifted to some relatives - ₹26,000

Miscellaneous - ₹1400 (This includes breakfast in a hotel on the first day of the journey which started at 7:00 AM on 21" and lunch & tea in hotels on the last day of the journey. We reached home at 7:00 PM on 28th Jan.)

Everywhere, all were extremely glad meeting us; some, after a long time. Many were vying with each other to invite us to breakfast, lunch and dinner. Since we had only 'one stomach each', we had to decline some of them! However, they compensated it with tea or juice and a variety of snacks. Exquisite breakfasts, sumptuous lunches and delicious dinners with pleasantries galore were a feast to all senses; needless to say, to the heart too! Babu never failed to take photos everywhere.

As this year's New Year Resolution, I had requested my family not to have cake-cutting celebration at home from my 77th birthday onwards. But God Willed it otherwise. I cut 2 cakes on 27th January 2023 - one in the morning in Thrissur and one in Coimbatore at night. Again, on that day, there was a once- in-a-lifetime occurrence too. I had breakfast in Thrissur - my mother's birthplace; lunch (with payasam!) in Kunnamkulam - my father's birthplace and dinner in Coimbatore - my birthplace. I thank God Almighty from the bottom of my heart for this Special Blessing.

Throughout our journey, we had showers of Blessings upon us. Only one late evening in Kerala, we had literal showers! This fantastic 'fast journey' has made me a 'slow walker' now because of knee problem. But as Abraham Lincoln says,

"I am a slow walker but I never walk back."

Again, as Job asks in the Bible:

"Shall we receive good at the hand of God and shall we not receive the bad?"

THANKS BE TO GOD

Alice K Jose - 14-Feb-2023

Ten Tenets

Rules for Modern Times on Gandhian Principles

1. **H**ave unwavering faith in the Supreme Universal Spirit.

2. **H**ave immense faith in prayer and fasting.

3. **H**ave a most positive approach to life.

4. **E**arn money by fair means and spend a portion of it for common good.

5. **E**arn the day's satisfaction by doing at least a few acts of selfless service.

6. **L**ove and respect all alike, meaning treat everyone with justice.

7. **L**ove to lead a simple life with high thinking.

8. **B**e true to oneself and to others.

9. **B**e non-violent even in thoughts.

10. **B**e honest, hard-working and helpful.

The acronym **'HELB'** (repetitions avoided) can be a mnemonic to remember all the ten.

Alice K Jose 10-Jun-2008

www.ingramcontent.com/pod-product-compliance
Lightning Source LLC
Chambersburg PA
CBHW021424150726

47989CB00001B/103